THE C[illegible] [illegible]RARY

PROFESSIONAL LIABILITY

THE COMMON LAW LIBRARY

JACKSON & POWELL

ON

PROFESSIONAL LIABILITY

FOURTH SUPPLEMENT TO THE SEVENTH EDITION

Up to date to October 2015

SWEET & MAXWELL THOMSON REUTERS

Published in 2015 by Thomson Reuters (Professional) UK Limited,
trading as Sweet & Maxwell, Friars House,
160 Blackfriars Road, London SE1 8EZ
(Registered in England & Wales, Company No.1679046.
Registered Office and address for service:
2nd floor, 1 Mark Square, Leonard Street, London, EC2A 4EG)

For further information on our products and services, visit:
www.sweetandmaxwell.co.uk

Typeset by Wright and Round Ltd, Gloucestershire
Printed and bound by CPI Group (UK) Ltd, Croydon CR0 4YY

Main Work 9780414047808
First Supplement 9780414026780
Second Supplement 9780414031043
Third Supplement 9780414035416
Fourth Supplement 9780414055001

No natural forests were destroyed
to make this product; only farmed
timber was used and replanted

A CIP catalogue record for this book
is available from the British Library

AMANDA SAVAGE, LLB, BCL
Of the Middle Temple, Barrister

ANNABEL SHAW, BA
Of Gray's Inn, Barrister

FIONA SINCLAIR QC, MA, LLM
Of the Inner Temple and of Lincoln's Inn

GEORGE SPALTON, MA, LLM
Of Lincoln's Inn, Barrister

DAVID TURNER QC, MA
Of Gray's Inn

CAN YEGINSU, MA, LLB, LLM
Of the Inner Temple, Barrister

HOW TO USE THIS SUPPLEMENT

The Fourth Supplement to the Seventh Edition of *Jackson & Powell on Professional Liability* is ordered according to the structure of the main volume.

At the beginning of the supplementary coverage for each chapter, the mini table of contents from the main volume has been included. Where a heading on this table of contents has been marked with the symbol ■, then there is relevant information in the supplement to which you should refer. Where a heading is marked with the symbol □, the material under that heading was added to or amended in the previous supplement but has not been updated further in this supplement.

Within each chapter, updated information is referenced to the relevant paragraph in the main volume. The instructions in the square brackets explain how the added material relates to the main volume.

TABLE OF CASES

Carillion Construction Ltd v Smith [2011] EWHC 2910 (TCC); 141 Con. L.R. 117; [2011] C.I.L.L. 3097; [2012] Bus. L.R. D61 9–373
Carpathian Resouces Ltd v Hendricks [2012] FCA 496; (2012) 290 A.L.R. 252 11–081
Catt v Association of Chief Police Officers [2012] EWHC 1471 (Admin); [2012] H.R.L.R. 23; [2012] P.N.L.R. 27; [2012] A.C.D. 91 .... 11–004, 11–049
CF Partners (UK) Ltd v Barclays Bank Plc [2014] EWHC 3049 (Ch) 2–164
CG Group Ltd v Breyer Group Plc [2013] EWHC 2722 (TCC) 9–376
Cheshire Mortgage Corp Ltd v Grandison [2012] CSIH 66; 2013 S.C. 160; [2013] P.N.L.R. 3 11–080
Chester v Afshar [2004] UKHL 41; [2005] 1 A.C. 134; [2004] 3 W.L.R. 927; [2004] 4 All E.R. 587; [2005] P.I.Q.R. P12; [2005] Lloyd's Rep. Med. 109; (2005) 81 B.M.L.R. 1; [2005] P.N.L.R. 14; (2004) 101(43) L.S.G. 34; (2004) 154 N.L.J. 1589; (2004) 148 S.J.L.B. 1215 13–059
Cheung Shui Han v Luk Ka Ling [2012] HKLRD 537, Hong Kong CA 11–138
Chief Constable of Hampshire v Southampton City Council [2014] EWCA Civ 1541; [2015] P.I.Q.R. P5 4–019
City Index Ltd (t/a FinSpreads) v Balducci [2011] EWHC 2562 (Ch); [2012] 1 B.C.L.C. 317 .... 14–055, 14–068, 14–070, 15–059, 15–066
Clack v Wrigleys Solicitors LLP [2013] EWHC 413 (Ch); (2013) 163(7557) N.L.J. 17 .... 11–217, 11–263
Clark v In Focus Asset Management & Tax Solutions Ltd [2014] EWCA Civ 118; [2014] 1 W.L.R. 2502; [2014] 3 All E.R. 313; [2014] 2 All E.R. (Comm) 159 .... 14–103, 14–113
Clay v AJ Crump & Sons Ltd [1964] 1 Q.B. 533; [1963] 3 W.L.R. 866; [1963] 3 All E.R. 687; 4 B.L.R. 80 9–074
Cleightonhills v Bembridge Marine Ltd [2012] EWHC 3449 (TCC); [2013] C.I.L.L. 3289 9–074
Clydesdale Bank Plc v Workman [2013] EWHC B38 (Ch); [2014] P.N.L.R. 18 11–352
Collins v Secretary of State for Business Innovation and Skills [2014] EWCA Civ 717; [2014] P.I.Q.R. P19 .... 5–095, 5–098
Connolly v Croydon Health Services NHS Trust [2015] EWHC 1339 (QB) 13–059
Coombs v Dorset NHS Primary Care Trust [2013] EWCA Civ 471; (2013) 16 C.C.L. Rep. 376; [2013] P.I.Q.R. P16; [2013] M.H.L.R. 194 .... 13–034, 13–043
Co-operative Group (CWS) Ltd v Pritchard; sub nom Pritchard v Co-operative Group (CWS) Ltd [2011] EWCA Civ 329; [2012] Q.B. 320; [2011] 3 W.L.R. 1272; [2012] 1 All E.R. 205 5–149
Co-operative Group Ltd v Birse Developments Ltd (In Liquidation) [2014] EWHC 530 (TCC); [2014] B.L.R. 359 .... 5–037, 5–077A
Cornwell v Newhaven Port & Properties Ltd [2005] EWHC 1469 (Ch); [2005] O.P.L.R. 277; [2005] Pens. L.R. 329 18–030
Coulthard v Neville Russell (A Firm) [1998] B.C.C. 359; [1998] 1 B.C.L.C.143; [1998] P.N.L.R. 276 CA (Civ Div) 17–033, 17–042
Cox v Bankside Members Agency Ltd [1995] 2 Lloyd's Rep. 437; [1995] C.L.C. 671 .... 8–101A
Craven v Bar Standards Board Unreported 30 January 2014 7–053
Crawford Adjusters v Sagicor General Insurance (Cayman) Ltd [2013] UKPC17; [2013] 3 W.L.R. 927; [2013] 4 All E.R. 8 2–110
Credit & Mercantile Plc v Nabarro [2014] EWHC 2819 (Ch); [2015] P.N.L.R. 14 11–262
Crestsign Ltd v National Westminstr Bank Plc [2014] EWHC 3043 (Ch) 15–022, 15–059, 15–070

TABLE OF STATUTES

TABLE OF STATUTORY INSTRUMENTS

TABLE OF PROFESSIONAL REGULATIONS

CHAPTER 2

DUTIES AND OBLIGATIONS

1. PROFESSIONAL LIABILITY

(c) *Regulation and Professional Standards*

[*Add at end of paragraph*] **2–012**

And the possibility that statutory duties may be more extensive than those required by the exercise of skill and care must always be borne in mind. So, in *Green v The Royal Bank of Scotland Plc* [2013] EWCA Civ 1197; [2014] P.N.L.R. 6 it was held that Conduct of Business Rules under the Financial Services and Markets Act 2000 imposed duties which were more extensive than the duty of care which can be owed in tort by the maker of a statement.

2. CONTRACTUAL LIABILITY

[*Add at end of paragraph*] **2–013**

Moreover, the retainer may define the scope of the services to be provided by the professional person, so that he will not be under an implied duty to go beyond what is required by his retainer unless he has in some way assumed a wider responsibility or the retainer has been varied: see, for example, *Mehjoo v Harben Barker (A Firm)* [2014] EWCA Civ 358; [2014] P.N.L.R. 24.

[*Add at end of paragraph*] **2–014**

The scope of a professional's retainer—i.e. what he is obliged to do and what advice he is required to give—will be a combination of the express and implied terms. So, for example, an accountant will not be under a duty to advise a client as to steps which could be taken to reduce the client's tax bill unless either expressly retained to do so or if there is some other basis for finding such a duty, for example a previous course of dealing: *Mehjoo v Harben Barker (A Firm)*

[2013] EWHC 1500 (QB); [2013] BTC 509 (Silber J.), where there is a helpful review of the authorities at [126]–[129].

2–017 [*Add to n.33*]

See also *Nationwide Building Society v Davisons Solicitors* [2012] EWCA Civ 1626; [2013] P.N.L.R. 12 where the Court of Appeal overturned the trial judge and held that provisions in the Council of Mortgage Lenders Handbook which required there to be a "fully enforceable first charge by way of legal mortgage" over the mortgaged property and that all existing charges "must be redeemed" involved the exercise of professional skill and reliance on the acts or omissions of the vendor's solicitors and so did not create strict obligations. Morritt C., with whom the other members of the Court of Appeal agreed, held at [57]:

> "The effect of the absolute undertaking for which counsel for Nationwide contended would be to impose on Davisons the equivalent of a guarantee that all existing charges would be redeemed and Nationwide would obtain a fully enforceable first charge by way of legal mortgage over The Property. If that was the intention of the parties almost all the rest of the CML Handbook would be redundant. In these circumstances I would hold that the obligation imposed by para.5.8 goes no further than an obligation to exercise reasonable skill and care in seeking to procure the outcome it refers to, namely the redemption of all existing charges and obtaining a fully enforceable first charge by way of legal mortgage. In my view the judge was wrong to have concluded otherwise."

3. TORTIOUS LIABILITY

(b) *Theoretical Basis for the Duty of Care*

(vii) *The Co-existence of Different Approaches*

2–057 [*Add to n.151*]

See further *Robinson v Chief Constable of West Yorkshire Police* [2014] EWCA Civ 15; [2014] P.I.Q.R. P14 where the decision in *Marc Rich & Co AG v Bishop Rock Marine* [1996] 1 A.C. 211 was followed and the three-stage test in *Caparo Industries Plc v Dickman* [1990] 2 A.C. 605 was applied to a claim against the police for damages for personal injuries by a victim of crime.

2–060 [*Add to n.167*]

However, in *Robinson v Chief Constable of West Yorkshire Police* [2014] EWCA Civ 15; [2014] P.I.Q.R. P14 Hallett L.J., with whom Sullivan L.J. agreed, held at [40] that "the *Caparo* test applies to all claims in the modern law of negligence". This is correct in the sense that all of the tests should be equally applicable to any case. But no one test applies to the exclusion of the others.

(viii) *Commonwealth Approaches to Duty of Care Issues*

New Zealand

[*Add to n.170*] **2–062**

See also *Minister of Education v Econicorp Holdings Ltd* [2011] NZCA 450; [2012] 1 N.Z.L.R. 5.

[*Add to n.177*] **2–064**

See also *North Shore City Council v Attornery-General* [2012] NZSC 49; [2012] N.Z.L.R. 341 and *Body Corporate No.207624* [2012] NZSC 83; [2013] 3 N.Z.L.R. 341 and, in particular, the judgment of Blanchard, McGrath and William Young JJ. at [147]–[161] for a helpful review of the approach adopted to deciding whether a duty of care is owed in a novel situation.

Canada

[*Add to n.199*] **2–071**

See also *Alberta v Elder Advocates of Alberta Society* 2011 SCC 24; (2011) 331 D.L.R. (4th) 257.

(c) *Particular Situations*

(i) *Public and Local Authorities: Duty of Care and Statute*

[*Add to n.305*] **2–093**

See also *Smeaton v Equifax plc* [2013] EWCA Civ 108; [2013] 2 All E.R. 959, at [73] per Tomlinson L.J.

(ii) *Directors and Employees*

[*Add to n.351*] **2–100**

However, there was no such assumption of direct responsibility in *Summit Advances Ltd v Bush* [2015] EWHC 665 (QB); [2015] P.N.L.R. 18: the terms of the report in issue made it clear that the views being expressed were of the limited liability partnership of surveyors and not by the employee of that partnership who had prepared the report.

[*Add to n.364*] **2–103**

In *Sainsbury's Supermarkets Ltd v Condek Holdings Ltd (formerly Condek Ltd)* [2014] EWHC 2016 (TCC) [2014] B.L.R. 574 at [19] Stuart-Smith J. suggested that there was no tension between the decisions in *Williams v Natural Life Health Foods Ltd* [1998] 1 W.L.R. 830 and in *Merrett v Babb* [2001] EWCA Civ 214; [2001] Q.B. 1174. This is because in the latter case the building society to whom the report was addressed was required by s.13 of the Building Societies Act 1986 to make arrangements to ensure that the person who provided it was competent to do so and not disqualified from doing so, so that the personal standing of the individual valuer was "an integral part of the assurance available to the building society". However, it is respectfully submitted that the tension remains: it was no doubt equally important to the claimant in *Edgeworth Construction Ltd v ND Lea Associates Ltd* [1993] 3 S.C.R. 206 (approved by Lord Steyn in *Williams v Natural Life Health Foods Ltd* [1998] 1 W.L.R. 830: see para.2–099, above) that the individual engineers who had attached their seals to the drawings were properly qualified to have produced the design. Stuart-Smith J. went on to strike out a claim against the individual behind a one-man company through an orthodox application of the decision in *Williams v Natural Life Health Foods Ltd* [1998] 1 W.L.R. 830.

(iii) *Sub-agents and Sub-contractors*

2–104 [*Add to n.370*]

It is for the person who is alleging that a duty of care was owed in such circumstances to prove the existence of a special relationship. That will not be shown if the contractual structure does not show "any particular or unusual feature": *Sainsbury's Supermarkets Ltd v Condek Holdings Ltd (formerly Condek Ltd)* [2014] EWHC 2016 (TCC) [2014] B.L.R. 574 at [45] per Stuart-Smith J.

(iv) *Immunity*

2–108 [*Add to n.383*]

See further *Smart v The Forensic Science Service Ltd* [2013] EWCA Civ 783; [2013] P.N.L.R. 32 and *Singh v Reading Borough Council* [2013] EWCA Civ 909; [2013] 1 W.L.R. 3052.

2–110 [*Add to n.389*]

See also *Crawford Adjusters v Sagicor General Insurance (Cayman) Ltd* [2013] UKPC 17; [2013] 3 W.L.R. 927, at [73] per Lord Wilson (but see also [82] per Lady Hale).

(e) *Liability to Third Parties*

(ii) *Analysis of Denning L.J.'s Dissenting Judgment*

2–123 [*Add to n.428*]

In the former case Gleeson C.J., Gummow and Hayne JJ. emphasised the importance of the following statements of principle by Barwick C.J. in *Mutual Life & Citizens' Assurance Co Ltd v Evatt* [1968] HCA 74; (1968) 122 C.L.R. 556, at 569–572, in the context of the giving of information or advice orally:

> "the speaker must realize or the circumstances be such that he ought to have realized that the recipient intends to act upon the information or advice in respect of his property or of himself in connexion with some matter of business or serious consequence".

And

> "the circumstances must be such that it is reasonable in all the circumstances for the recipient to seek, or to accept, and to rely upon the utterance of the speaker. The nature of the subject matter, the occasion of the interchange, and the identity and relative position of the parties as regards knowledge actual or potential and relevant capacity to form or exercise judgment will all be included in the factors which will determine the reasonableness of the acceptance of, and of the reliance by the recipient upon, the words of the speaker."

The second principle is an important factor in determining whether a duty of care is owed. Mere foreseeability of reliance is not sufficient (cf. *Sainsbury's Supermarkets Ltd v Condek Holdings Ltd (formerly Condek Ltd)* [2014] EWHC 2016 (TCC) [2014] B.L.R. 574 at [48]–[50] per Stuart-Smith J.).

As Tomlinson L.J. explained in *Hunt v Optima (Cambridge) Ltd* [2014] EWCA Civ 714 [2014] P.N.L.R. 29 at [110]:

> "The touchstone of the liability recognised by Denning L.J. in his dissenting judgment was either the showing of the report to a third party by the accountants themselves, or knowledge of the accountants when they prepared their report that their employer (or client) intended to show the report to a third party with a view to inducing that third party to invest money, or to take some other action, in reliance on the report—see at pages 180–181. In each case crucial to the formulation for the test for liability is an intention or a realisation that the report is reasonably to be relied upon as a statement made by a person with particular expertise in evaluating the matters to which the report relates, those being matters requiring expertise for their evaluation."

See also *Swynson Ltd v Lowick Rose LLP (in liquidation) (formerly known as Hurst Morrison Thomson LLP)* [2014] EWHC 2085 (Ch); [2014] P.N.L.R. 27 (no reliance by individual who owned the limited company which was the client of the defendant accountants other than through that company).

5. FIDUCIARY OBLIGATIONS

(a) *The Nature of Fiduciary Obligations*

[*Add to n.472*] **2–136**

So it is wrong to talk of a fiduciary owing a duty of disclosure. Disclosure of a fiduciary's interest is a defence, not a duty: *Blackmagic Design Pty v Overliese* [2011] FCAFC 24; (2011) 276 A.L.R. 646 at [106]–[108] per Besanko J. with whom the other members of the Federal Court of Australia, Full Court, agreed.

[*Add to n.497*] **2–141**

This sentence was cited with approval by Tomlinson L.J., with whom the other members of the Court of Appeal agreed, in *McWilliam v Norton Finance (UK) Ltd (t/a Norton Finance (In Liquidation))* [2015] EWCA Civ 186; [2015]

P.N.L.R. 22 at [46]. In that case the vulnerability of the claimants, even though the defendant was not offering to advise them, resulted in a finding that there was a fiduciary relationship. The relationship between the parties had the necessary element of reliance.

[*Add to n.498*]

For a helpful review of the authorities as to whether and when one party to a commercial joint venture will be under fiduciary obligations to another, see the judgment of Lloyd L.J. in *Ross River Ltd v Waveley Commercial Ltd* [2013] EWCA Civ 910 [2014] 1 B.C.L.C. 545 at [34]–[59].

6. CONFIDENTIALITY

(a) *Introduction*

2–164 [*Add to n.582*]

A helpful statement of the basic principles and consideration of the significance of any confidentiality agreement on the extent of equitable duties of confidence is to be found in the judgment of Hildyard J. in *CF Partners (UK) Ltd v Barclays Bank Plc* [2014] EWHC 3049 (Ch) at [118]–[142].

(c) *Elements of the Cause of Action*

Confidentiality of the information

2–177 [*Add to n.624*]

In *Wallace v Canadian Pacific Railway* 2011 SKCA 108; (2011) 340 D.L.R. (4th) 402, "vague assertions of the transfer of confidential information consisting of litigation strategies and general assertions of knowledge of risk management and tolerances" by a client to its solicitors were held not to constitute confidential information.

(d) *The Continuing Duty to Former Clients*

2–189 [*Add to n.654*]

See also *Walsh v Shanahan* [2013] EWCA Civ 411 [2013] 2 P. & C.R. DG7 at [40]–[53] per Rimer L.J., with whom the other members of the Court of Appeal agreed.

Bolkiah v KPMG (A Firm)

2–190 [*Add to n.658*]

As to whether the principles enunciated in *Bolkiah v KPMG (A Firm)* [1999] 2 A.C. 222 apply to in-house lawyers, see the discussion in *Generics (UK) Ltd v*

Yeda Research & Development Co Ltd [2012] EWCA Civ 726; [2013] Bus.L.R. 777.

Factors to consider

[*Add to n.659*] **2–191**

See also *Singla v Stockler* [2012] EWHC 1176 (Ch); [2012] B.P.I.R. 1061 (Briggs J.). In *Georgian American Alloys Inc v White & Case LLP* [2014] EWHC 94 (Comm) [2014] 1 C.L.C. 86 Field J. granted a permanent injunction restraining an international law firm from acting or advising a party to litigation proceeding in the Commercial Court and by way of litigation. While "ethical barriers" had been put in place within the firm, this was only done some time after it had started acting for the second client so that there was a real risk that confidential information relating to the first client had moved within the firm. Further the "ethical barriers" did not prevent communication of information orally as opposed to electronically. There had also been an absence of physical separation between fee earners acting for the two clients in one of the firm's offices. Field J. concluded that the firm had failed to discharge the evidential burden set down in *Bolkiah v KPMG (A Firm)* [1999] 2 A.C. 222.

[*Add to n.664*]

For a helpful discussion of the Canadian authorities, including the leading case of *MacDonald Estate v Martin* [1990] 3 S.C.R. 1235, see *Dow Chemical Canada Inc v Nova Chemicals Corp* 2011 A.B.Q.B. 509; (2011) 339 D.L.R. (4th) 119.

Chapter 3

REMEDIES

3. Equitable Remedies

(c) *Account of Profits*

3–019 [*Add to n.71*]

In *Walsh v Shanahan* [2013] EWCA Civ 411; [2013] 2 P. & C.R. DG7 at [37], Rimer L.J. stated that the ordinary remedy against a fiduciary who made profits in breach of his duty of loyalty was an account of profits and referred to his discussion of the authorities in his judgment in *O'Donnell v Shanahan and Another* [2009] EWCA Civ 751; [2009] 2 B.C.L.C. 666, at [51] ff.

[*Add at end of paragraph*]

Where the claim is for misuse of confidential information, it is a matter for the Court whether to order an account of profits rather than to make an award of damages. As Rimer L.J. said in *Walsh v Shanahan* [2013] EWCA Civ 411; [2013] 2 P. & C.R. DG7 at [64]:

> "The objective in any case is to identify the appropriate remedy for the circumstances of the wrongdoing—to make the remedy fit the tort."

On the facts the trial judge had been entitled to make an award of damages: the information used by the defendants was limited and they had used it in a venture which had involved risk on their part and from which the claimant had withdrawn (ibid at [70]). (See also the decision of Sales J. in *Vercoe v Rutland Fund Management Ltd* [2010] EWHC 424 (Ch); [2010] Bus. L.R. D141.)

Chapter 4

CONTRIBUTION BETWEEN DEFENDANTS

4. The Claim

(d) *Time for bringing a Claim for Compensation*

[*Add at end of paragraph*] **4–019**

When a claim is settled by an agreement as to the amount to be paid with the amount of costs payable to be determined or agreed at a later date, time runs from the date when damages are agreed and not from the later date when costs are determined or agreed: *Chief Constable of Hampshire v Southampton City Council* [2014] EWCA Civ 1541; [2015] P.I.Q.R. P5.

[*Add to n.80*]

The decision (but not necessarily the reasoning) in *Knight v Rochdale Healthcare NHS Trust* [2003] EWHC 1831 (QB); [2004] 1 W.L.R. 371 was approved by the Court of Appeal in *Chief Constable of Hampshire v Southampton City Council* [2014] EWCA Civ 1541; [2015] P.I.Q.R. P5.

CHAPTER 5

DEFENCES

1. EXCLUSION OR RESTRICTION OF LIABILITY

(a) *The Position at Common Law*

5–003 [*Add at end of paragraph*]

However, where the firm is in fact doing the very thing which the relevant clause states it is not obliged to do, the clause may not be an attempt to re-write history as between two contracting parties who wish to achieve contractual certainty but may depart from reality and, in effect, seeks to exclude liability which would otherwise arise: see in *Raiffeisen Zentralbank Österreich AG v Royal Bank of Scotland Plc* [2010] EWHC 1392 (Comm); [2011] 1 Lloyd's Rep 123 at [313] per Christopher Clarke J. (approved by Aikens L.J. in *Springwell Navigation Corp v JP Morgan Chase Bank* [2010] EWCA Civ 1221; [2010] 2 C.L.C. 705, at [181] and applied by Newey J. in *Avorva Fine Arts Investments Ltd v Christie, Manson & Woods Ltd* [2012] EWHC 2198 (Ch); [2012] P.N.L.R. 35 at [145]).

5–004A [*Add new paragraph to text*]

It is also possible to reduce the time in which a claim must be brought by including some other time limit in a contract: see, for example, *Inframatrix Investments Ltd v Dean Construction Ltd* [2012] EWCA Civ 64; [2012] 2 All E.R. (Comm) 377. However, it must do so clearly. So in *Elvanite Full Circle Ltd v Amec Earth & Environmental (UK) Ltd* [2012] EWHC 1191 (TCC); (2013) 148 Con. L.R. 127 (Coulson J.) a clause requiring "all claims by the Client shall be deemed relinquished unless filed within one year" did not require the client to have issued proceedings and a defence on that basis failed. But it did require the client to send "something akin to the Letter of Claim in the Pre-Action Protocols" and the client had not done so in the time allowed (ibid at [291]–[301]).

(b) *The Statutory Framework*

[*Add to n.51*] **5–017**

See also *Elvanite Full Circle Ltd v Amec Earth & Environmental (UK) Ltd* [2012] EWHC 1191 (TCC); (2013) 148 Con. L.R. 127 (Coulson J.) at [286]–[287].

(c) *Exclusion of Liability to Third Parties*

[*Add to n.80*] **5–022**

See also *Rehman v Jones Lang Lascelle Ltd* [2013] EWHC 1339 (QB) (HH Judge Belcher, sitting as a High Court Judge) at [72]–[79].

2. LIMITATION IN CONTRACT AND TORT

(a) *The Limitation Period*

[*Add to n.92*] **5–026**

A claim under s.2(1) of the Misrepresentation Act 1967 is "an action founded on tort" and so falls within s.2 of the Limitation Act 1980: *Green v Eadie* [2011] EWHC B24 (Ch); [2012] Ch. 363 (Mark Cawson QC, sitting as a Deputy High Court Judge).

[*Add at end of paragraph*]

The fact that time is running for breach by a professional in respect of one retainer or transaction does not mean that time is also running in respect of a similar or identical breach of another retainer or a different transaction. So in *St Anselm Development Company v Slaughter & May (A Firm)* [2013] EWHC 125 (Ch) (David Richards J.) solicitors were retained to act in relation to the leases of two flats in the same building. A failure to give relevant advice in relation to the lease of the first property was a separate cause of action for the subsequent failure to give the same advice in relation to the second property.

(b) *Date when Cause of Action in Contract Accrues*

[*Add to n.119*] **5–030**

This sentence was cited with approval by the Privy Council in *Maharaj v Johnson* [2015] UKPC 28; [2015] P.N.L.R. 27, where it was held that the defendant solicitors were under no continuing duty in contract after completion of the transaction in respect of which they had been retained.

See also *Green v Eadie* [2011] EWHC B24 (Ch); [2012] Ch. 363 (Mark Cawson QC, sitting as a Deputy High Court Judge) and *Integral Memory Plc v*

Haines Watts [2012] EWHC 342 (Ch) (Richard Sheldon QC, sitting as a Deputy High Court Judge). For a rare example of a retainer which did give rise to a continuing duty see *Capita (Banstead 2011) Ltd v RFIB Group Ltd* [2014] EWHC 2197 (Comm) (Popplewell J.) at [11]: retainer of specialist benefits consultancy (whose services included giving pension scheme advice) involved "considering the changes previously made, or purportedly made, and considering the implementation of the amendments in the context of subsequent dealings with the trustees".

(c) *Date when Cause of Action in Tort Accrues*

5–037 [*Add to n.141*]

See also *Co-operative Group Ltd v Birse Developments Ltd (In Liquidation)* [2014] EWHC 530 (TCC); [2014] B.L.R. 359 (Stuart-Smith J.) discussed in para.5–077A, below.

(i) *Claims against Solicitors*

Contingent liability or actual loss?

5–042 [*Add at end of paragraph*]

However, where, faced with notice of a potential claim, a trustee or other fiduciary pays away trust assets (his solicitors having failed to advise him against this course), actionable damage is suffered when the assets are paid away because he had altered his position to his detriment because he no longer had a fund from which he could satisfy a claim if and when made or from which he could be indemnified as to his costs of defending the claim: *Lane v Cullens Solicitors* [2012] EWCA Civ 547; [2012] Ce.B. 693.

Where client acquires less valuable rights than intended

5–043 [*Add at end of paragraph*]

The recent decision of the Privy Council in *Maharaj v Johnson* [2015] UKPC 28; [2015] P.N.L.R. 27 emphasises that it is not enough that the claimant has acquired different rights from those intended. The rights acquired must be less valuable than those which should have been acquired. On the facts, the failure to acquire the full legal title to land as well as the beneficial title resulted in the claimants having less valuable rights than should have been the case. It followed that time began to run in respect of their claim against their former solicitors in tort when legal title was not acquired.

[*Add to n.166*]

See also *Green v Eadie* [2011] EWHC B24 (Ch); [2012] Ch. 363 (Mark Cawson QC sitting as a Deputy High Court Judge): purchasers of property who had relied upon a misrepresentation which their solicitors allegedly negligently failed to discover, suffered actionable damage when contracts were exchanged to purchase the property. This was notwithstanding the existence of remedies against the vendors.

[*Add to n.167*]

Nouri v Marvi [2010] EWCA Civ; [2011] P.N.L.R. 7 was applied by Roth J. in *Edehomo v Edehomo* [2011] EWHC 393 (Ch); [2011] 1 W.L.R. 2217. In the latter case the claimant's estranged husband had forged her signature on the contract for sale and transfer of a house they owned. Damage was held to have occurred when contracts were exchanged: at that point the value of the claimant's interest in the house reduced because anyone considering buying the house would be deterred by the existence of a purported contract to sell it to someone else. Roth J. was not persuaded that loss was also suffered because the estranged husband's beneficial interest passed under the contract on the particular facts of the case.

Previous action dismissed for want of prosecution

[*Add at end of paragraph*] **5–047**

The same reasoning should apply where a claimant has settled a claim which was subject to striking out (or otherwise being unable to proceed) because of negligent inactivity on the part of the defendant solicitors. On the facts in *Berney v Saul* [2013] EWCA Civ 640; [2013] P.N.L.R. 26, the claimant had not suffered actionable damage before she settled her claim for personal injuries on the advice of her then current solicitors and barrister that, as a result of the failure of the solicitors she had first instructed to serve Particulars of Claim for a number of years, her claim was liable to be struck out. In fact because of one or more of (i) the admission of liability by the defendant to the original claim and (ii) assurances by solicitors acting for the defendant to the original claim that no point would be taken about delay, there was no more than a fanciful risk of the claim being struck out as at the time of settlement.

Where the client purchases a property

[*Add to n.181*] **5–048**

See also *Sullavan v Teare* [2010] QCA 70; [2011] 1 Qd.R. 291: a claim against solicitors: cause of action in tort complete when the claimant was contractually committed to pay more than the property was worth, following *HTW Valuers (Central Qld) Pty Ltd v Astonland Pty Ltd* [2004] HCA 54; (2004) 217 CLR 640, (a claim against valuers).

(v) *Claims against Financial Advisers*

[*Add to n.213*] **5–055**

A case which fell on the other side of the line is *British Telecommunications plc v Luck* [2014] 290 (QB). An employer was alleged to have given negligent advice to its employees in reliance on which they agreed to a transfer to another employer. While they remained within the pension scheme of the original employer, they could be removed from it. Teare J. held on the particular facts that loss was only suffered when the employees were removed from the scheme, not when they were exposed to the risk of being removed: until then the terms and conditions of their employment (including pension arrangements) were unchanged.

(vi) *Claims against Accountants*

Law Society v Sephton

5–057 [*Add to n.216*]

But a claimant who is exposed to a liability in tax as a result of his accountant's negligence suffers loss when he is so exposed and not when the tax authorities demand payment of the tax: *Integral Memory Plc v Haines Watts* [2012] EWHC 342 (Ch) (Richard Sheldon QC, sitting as a Deputy High Court Judge).

5–058 [*Add to n.218*]

Where a claimant has made a loan in reliance on advice of an accountant the principles set out in paragraph 5–052 of the main text apply. So, where the value of the security for the loan is less than the amount lent, time will run: *Arrowhead Capital Finance Ltd (in liquidation) v KPMG LLP* [2012] EWHC 1801 (Comm); [2012] P.N.L.R. 30 (Stephen Males QC, sitting as a High Court Judge).

(vii) *Claims against Construction Professionals*

5–077A *[Add new paragraph to text*]

A construction professional may, as a result of his negligence, expose his client to a claim under a construction contract. In *Co-operative Group Ltd v Birse Developments Ltd (In Liquidation)* [2014] EWHC 530 (TCC); [2014] B.L.R. 359 the client argued that in such a case time only runs when the claim is made under the contract, not when liability is incurred. Until then, it was submitted, there was merely a contingent liability (as to which see para.5–037 of the main text). Stuart-Smith J. rejected the argument, holding that the value of the claimant's rights under the contract had been rendered less valuable and that the claimant had acquired a package of rights which were less valuable then they should have been (as to which see para.5–043 of the main text). In doing so he declined to follow the earlier decision of Akenehad J. in *Linklaters Business Services v Sir Robert McAlpine Ltd* [2010] EWHC 2931 (TCC); (2010) 133 Con. L.R. 211.

(d) *Effect of the Latent Damage Act 1986*

Date of knowledge

5–084 [*Add to n.326*]

In *Schumann v Veale Wasbrough* [2015] EWCA Civ 441; [2015] P.N.L.R. 25 the majority of the Court of Appeal (Jackson and Longmore L.JJ.) held obiter that the relevant negligence was that of the current defendant or of some person for whose conduct that person was liable and not the negligence of some other person.

[*Add to n.330*] 5–085

See also *Renwick v Simon & Michael Brooke Architects* [2011] EWHC 874 (TCC); [2011] P.N.L.R. 31 (Akenhead J.): client who knew that building was poorly built and threatened legal action against the structural engineer had sufficient knowledge for time to run. See also *St Anselm Development Company v Slaughter & May (A Firm)* [2013] EWHC 125 (Ch) (David Richards J.): client received letter which was inconsistent with the advice they had been given by the defendant and which informed them that they had suffered the loss for which it was claiming. That was sufficient for time to run.

[*Add to n.332*]

See also *Hunt v Optima (Cambridge) Ltd* [2014] EWCA Civ 714; [2014] P.N.L.R. 29 (expenditure incurred to make good the consequences of leaks was sufficient for time to run).

[*Add at end of paragraph*] 5–086

In the same way, an investor who has been told that her investment will not fall in value is fixed with knowledge which a reasonable person in her position would have acquired by asking her investment advisor or reading the literature about the investment which she had and so discovered that what she had been told was incorrect: *Jacobs v Sesame Ltd* [2014] EWCA Civ 1410; [2015] P.N.L.R. 6. Constructive knowledge can be a two-stage process. First, it may be that the claimant should have acquired knowledge himself. Secondly, it may be that the acquisition of that knowledge would have reasonably led him to obtain expert advice. This was the result in *Seton House Group Ltd v Mercer Ltd* [2014] EWHC 4234 (Ch); [2015] Pens. L.R. 45. The claimant had been provided with a report which, when read with reasonable care, would have informed it of a problem with its pension fund in respect of which it should then reasonably have obtained expert advice. The result was that the claimant had constructive knowledge more than three years before the issue of proceedings. Where a claimant has sufficient information to be able to choose whether to seek expert advice or to let matters rest, a claimant who initially chooses to do the latter will be held to have acquired constructive knowledge at that point if, at a later date, he changes his mind: *Schumann v Veale Wasbrough* [2015] EWCA Civ 441; [2015] P.N.L.R. 25, following *Forbes v Wandsworth Health Authority* [1997] Q.B. 402.

(e) *Special Rules re Personal Injury and Death*

(i) *Primary Limitation Periods*

Application to clinical negligence

[*Add to n.354*] 5–091

See also the decision of the Supreme Court in *AB v Ministry of Defence* [2012] UKSC 9; [2013] 1 A.C. 78: claimants are likely to have first acquired knowledge of the facts needed for time to run under s.14 of the Limitation Act 1980 when they first reasonably believed that those facts existed. For the purposes of s.14 knowledge does not mean knowledge for certainty, but sufficient knowledge to justify embarking on the preliminaries to issuing proceedings. It is impossible for a claimant to lack the knowledge required for time to run under s.14 after he has issued proceedings. It followed that lack of proof that the claimants' injuries were caused as alleged by them was not a bar to time running against them.

5–095 [*Add to n.370*]

See also *Johnson v Ministry of Defence* [2012] EWCA Civ 1505; [2013] P.I.Q.R. P7: In relation to constructive knowledge, the Court asks "whether a normal adult in the position and with the knowledge of the claimant would have sought expert advice about the cause or attributability of his condition" (per Dame Janet Smith at [22]). On the facts the claimant should have sought the advice of his GP as to the cause of his increasingly serious deafness and, had he done so, would have known the cause more than three years before the issue of proceedings. In the same way in *Collins v Secretary of State for Business Innovation and Skills* [2014] EWCA Civ 717; [2014] P.I.Q.R. P19 it was held that a reasonable person in the position of the claimant would have asked his medical advisers about the possible causes of cancer from which he had suffered more than three years before the issue of proceedings. And in *Platt v BRB (Residuary) Ltd* [2014] EWCA Civ 1401; [2007] P.I.Q.R. P7) it was held that a reasonable person in the position of a claimant who was suffering from deafness would have asked his doctor whether it might have been caused by a noisy working environment (a topic discussed between them).

(ii) *Discretionary Exclusion of Time Limit*

Manner in which the discretion is exercised

5–098 [*Add to n.377*]

In *Aktas v Adepta* [2010] EWCA Civ; [2011] Q.B. 894 at [38] Rix L.J., with whom Longmore and Aikens L.JJ. agreed, explained that the decision of the House of Lords in *Horton v Sadler* [2006] UKHL 27; [2007] 1 A.C. 207 was not confined to its own special facts, but was "concerned with every aspect of the problem". It followed that the issue of a second claim form after the first had not been served as a result of negligence was not an abuse of the process.

[*Add to n.381*]

Less weight should be attached to delay before the claimant's date of knowledge under s.14 of the Limitation Act 1980 than to delay after that date: *Collins v Secretary of State for Business, Innovation and Skills* [2014] EWCA Civ 717; [2014] P.I.Q.R. P19 at [66] per Jackson L.J. with whom the other members of the Court of Appeal agreed.

[*Add at end of paragraph*]

While the burden is on the claimant in that it is the claimant who is seeking to be relieved from the usual consequences of failing to issue proceedings in time, it is not helpful to describe it as a heavy burden or as a light burden. Judges should exercise the discretion under s.33 in accordance with its words: *Sayers v Hunters (A Firm)* [2012] EWCA Civ 1715; [2013] 1 W.L.R. 1695, at [50]–[56] per Jackson L.J., with whom the other members of the Court of Appeal agreed.

[*Add to n.388*] **5–100**

While a claim against the former solicitors may be "second best" and be based upon loss of a chance, it is still something which a judge could (and usually should) take into account as best as he can: *Davidson v Aegis Defences Services (BVI) Ltd* [2013] EWCA Civ 1586; [2014] C.P. Rep. 17 at [13] per Longmore L.J. with whom the other members of the Court of Appeal agreed.

(f) *Fraud or Concealment*

[*Add to n.406*] **5–105**

See also *Ford & Warren v Warring-Davies* [2012] [EWHC] 3523 (QB) (Coulson J.): the claimant knew all the facts needed to plead his claim and did not need to know the facts of which he was ignorant. The "statement of claim" test was confirmed and applied in *Arcadia Group Brands Ltd v Visa Inc* [2015] EWCA Civ 883, dismissing suggestions that the decision in *Williams v Lishman, Sidwell, Campbell & Price Ltd* [2010] EWCA Civ 418; [2010] P.N.L.R. 25 involved some possible departure from that test.

3. LIMITATION IN EQUITY

(a) *Express Application of the Limitation Act 1980*

[*Add new paragraph to text*] **5–119A**

These decisions have been approved by the Supreme Court in *Williams v Central Bank of Nigeria* [2014] UKSC 10; [2014] A.C. 1189 (save that it is now clear that a claim against someone who has dishonestly assisted in a breach of trust does not fall within s.21 of the Limitation Act 1980).

(b) *Application of the Limitation Act 1980 by Analogy*

[*Add to n.466*] **5–127**

See also *Seaton v Seddon* [2012] EWHC 735 (Ch); [2013] 1 W.L.R. 3636 (Roth J.): six-year limitation period applied by analogy to a claim against solicitors for breach of fiduciary duty.

4. OTHER EQUITABLE DEFENCES: LACHES AND ACQUIESCENCE

5–131 [*Add to n.478*]

In *Byrnes v Kendle* [2011] HCA 26; (2011) 279 A.L.R. 212, French C.J. said at [27] that acquiescence as a defence to a claim for equitable relief is used in "at least two different senses". The first is where someone who is aware that an act is about to be done to his or her prejudice takes no step to object to it. The second is where a person who is aware of a violation of his or her rights which has already occurred fails to take timely proceedings to obtain equitable relief. The second founds the defence of laches.

(b) *Acquiescence*

5–143 [*Add at end of paragraph*]

What is required to found a defence of acquiescence is deliberate and informed inaction by the claimant which encouraged the defendant reasonably to believe that his wrongful conduct was accepted or not opposed by the claimant: *Byrnes v Kendle* [2011] HCA 26; (2011) 279 A.L.R. 212 at [79] per Gummow and Hayne JJ., applying the judgment of Deane J. in *Orr v Ford* [1989] HCA 4; (1989) 167 C.L.R. 316, at 337–338 and 340 (see also the judgment of Heydon and Crennan JJ. at [133]–[139]).

5. CONTRIBUTORY NEGLIGENCE

(a) *Contributory Negligence and Contract*

5–149 [*Add to n.542*]

See also *Co-operative Group (CWS) Ltd v Pritchard* [2011] EWCA Civ 329; [2012] Q.B. 330: contributory negligence is not a defence to a claim for assault and battery.

Chapter 6

LITIGATION

1. Group Actions

(c) *Procedure*

[*Add new footnote reference 23a to the word "litigation" in the seventh sentence*] 6–003

Note 23a. In *Holloway v Transform Medical Group (CS) Ltd* [2014] EWHC 1641 (QB), the Court held that where a claimant had failed to apply to join a group litigation register by a cut-off date set in court directions and sought to join out of time, it was necessary for her to satisfy the criteria for relief from sanctions under CPR r.3.9. The argument that the sanction did not apply to her because she was not a party to the group litigation at the time when the order was made was rejected.

[*Add to n.26*] 6–004

Or the issues may not be sufficiently common or sufficiently related to make a GLO. See *Various v Barking, Havering and Redbridge University Hospitals NHS Trust* QBD (May 21, 2014, unreported).

[*Add new footnote reference 26a at end of fourth sentence (ending "... tailored to the circumstances of the dispute.")*]

Note 26a. In general terms, the fact that a person is a claimant in group litigation, but not a test claimant, does not prevent him from successfully making an application for an interim payment of damages, if the conditions for such a payment are met. However, there may be terms of specific GLOs which preclude this form of interim relief. See *Test Claimants in the FII Group Litigation v Revenue and Customs Comrs* [2012] 1 W.L.R. 2375 at [47].

[*Add to n.27*]

When considering whether to order a preliminary trial of common or generic issues, the objective is to find the best means of dealing with a large number of claims in an expeditious, fair and proportionate way. The court should therefore be cautious about applying to the group litigation context principles which have been developed in ordinary private litigation about the ordering of preliminary issues. See *Varney v Ford Motor Co Ltd* [2013] EWHC 1226 (Ch).

[*Add to n.28*]

It is worth noting that where a judge decides for test cases to proceed, non-test claimants are not deprived of the opportunity to invoke the interim payment jurisdiction "merely because for good case management reasons the claimant had been enrolled in a GLO but had not been designated as a test claimant": *GKN Holdings Plc v Revenue and Customs Commissioners* [2013] EWHC 108 (Ch) at [22].

[*Add new footnote reference 28a to the word "active" to the final sentence (ending "... before the Woolf reforms.")*]

NOTE 28a. In *XYZ v Various Companies* [2014] Lloyd's Rep I.R. 431, the Court decided, in the context of group litigation relating to medical implants, that it had power to order a defendant to file a witness statement giving details of its ability to fund participation in the group litigation. This would assist the Court in managing the case and was therefore a step which could be taken under CPR r.3.1. However, in a subsequent hearing in the same litigation, the Court rejected an application by the insurer of one defendant to join the insurer of another defendant. The scope of insurance cover was not an issue connected to the matters in dispute in the proceedings, and so joinder could not be permitted under CPR r.19.2(2). While a general case management power could be exercised flexibly in group litigation, it could not be used to circumvent specific rules. See *XYZ v Various Companies* [2014] EWHC 4056 (QB).

[*Add at end of paragraph*]

Solicitors for claimants in group litigation are expected to behave professionally when advertising for and recruiting additional claimants.[28b]

[*Add new footnote*]

NOTE 28b. In *Saunderson v Sonae Industria (UK) Ltd* [2015] EWHC 2264 (QB) at [456]–[463], the Court made critical comments regarding the practices adopted by solicitors in this regard, observing that those adopted (which included leading questionnaires, pop-up shops and cold calling of potential claimants) failed to inspire any degree of confidence.

(d) *Costs*

6–005 [*Delete first sentence of text and n.29*]

[*Add text at beginning of paragraph, before sentence beginning "The fundamental rules are that . . . "*]

As a result of the Civil Procedure (Amendment) Rules 2013/262, the special costs rules applying where a court has made a GLO are now contained in CPR r.46.6.[29] The scheme under the old CPR r.48.6A, now repealed, remains exactly the same.

[*Replace n.29 with the following*]

NOTE 29. See further the notes to the *White Book* accompanying CPR r.46.6.

[*Add new footnote reference 29a at the end of the second sentence (ending "... an equal proportion of the common costs.")*]

NOTE 29a. The Court has considerable latitude to vary the default position: the broad question is what fairness demands in the particular situation. In *Greenwood v Goodwin* [2014] EWHC 227 (Ch), the Court considered, in the context of group litigation brought by shareholders of a company, how costs sharing should be managed, given that there was a range of different sub-groups of litigants and that there were significant disparities between the value of the various claimants' claims. The Court accepted that the default position under CPR r.46.6 involved equal sharing of costs, but noted that it should exercise latitude in adopting a solution that was fair to all the parties. A complex costs sharing scheme was ultimately decided upon, to reflect (inter alia) the value of the claims.

[*Add to n.30*]

In *Jones v Secretary of State for Energy and Climate Change* [2013] 2 Costs L.R. 230, the Court applied an overall percentage reduction of the costs recoverable by claimants in group litigation, to reflect failures on some issues of causation in some of the selected lead claims.

2. EXPERT EVIDENCE

(a) *The Functions of the Expert Witness*

[*Add to n.33*] **6–006**

In principle, a court or tribunal may reject uncontroverted expert evidence, or the common opinion of the experts of all parties, on an issue within the relevant scope of expertise. However, if this is to be done, then specific and adequate justification should be given. See *Al-Jedda v Secretary of State for the Home Department* [2012] EWCA Civ 358 at [102]–[107]; *Perkins v McIver* [2012] EWCA Civ 735 at [27]–[31]. There are some categories of case where the court can more readily take a middle position between experts, or adopt its own approach after considering expert evidence. In the valuers' negligence case of *Capita Alternative Fund Services (Guernsey) Ltd v Drivers Jonas (A Firm)* [2013] 1 EGLR 119, Gross L.J. said (at [43]):

> "It is as well to emphasise that a Judge is never bound by expert evidence (even, though that does not arise here, undisputed expert evidence). While a Judge must have a reasoned or rational basis for a decision—on issues of quantum as on other issues—the

Judge is in no way confined to the figures contended for by the experts. This is manifestly so in a typical valuation case where the figure arrived at by the Judge may well lie somewhere in between those advanced by the rival experts. Moreover, having regard to the true nature of quantum disputes and their history as jury questions, a Judge will sometimes find himself needing to do the best he can".

6–007 [*Add to n.34*]

In the Privy Council case of *Caribbean Steel Co Ltd v Price Waterhouse (A Firm)* [2013] P.N.L.R. 27, the Board upheld an appellate decision that a trial judge had been wrong to find accountants negligent on a question of share valuation on a supposed "common sense" basis and without carefully scrutinising the evidence of the firm's expert (who was the only qualified accountant called as an expert in the case). The Court of Appeal of Jamaica had founded its reasoning on the passage from the *Sansom* case.

(b) *Cases where Expert Evidence is Not Required*

6–011 [*Add to n.56*]

This proposition was acknowledged by Akenhead J. in *Whessoe Oil & Gas Ltd v Dale* [2012] P.N.L.R. 33, but the judge there explained that it was limited in its application to claims for breach of duties by professionals to whose work the *Bolam* test might be applied. It did not extend to a claim against a managing director for breach of contractual duties owed under a business agreement.

[*Add new footnote reference 56a at end of paragraph*]

NOTE 56a. However, in the recent case of *ACD (Landscape Architects) Ltd v Overall* [2012] P.N.L.R. 19, Akenhead J. said that there was no immutable rule of practice that a party could not allege professional negligence in a pleading without having secured supportive expert evidence. Even in a case where an allegation is of a character that it can only be made good with expert evidence, there may be good reason for such evidence not to be available at the stage when a statement of case is drafted.

(c) *The Civil Procedure Rules*

6–012 [*Add new footnote reference 57a at end of second sentence (ending "... without the court's permission.")*]

NOTE 57a. This provision concerns permission to adduce the evidence of a witness. Similar permission is not required to rely upon technical literature, although of course the court may be unable to interpret or place reliance on such literature without relevant expert evidence on the subject: *Interflora Inc v Marks and Spencer Plc* [2013] EWHC 936 (Ch) at [14]–[20].

[*Add to n.58*]

Decisions as to the scope of expert evidence which is reasonably required to resolve relevant issues are matters of case management and will accordingly be difficult to disturb on appeal: *Blair-Ford v CRS Adventures Ltd* [2012] EWHC 1886 (QB). However, such decisions must be made in accordance with the overriding objective, and can be challenged where the court has been over-zealous in excluding potentially valuable evidence in the interests of saving costs: *British Airways Plc v Spencer* [2015] EWHC 2477 (Ch) at [19]. *Evans v Frimley Park Hospital NHS Trust* QBD May 24, 2012, unrep, provides an instance where a defendant made a successful application to adduce additional expert evidence. The Court found that an additional haematologist's report which supported the defendant's reasoning "was likely to radically affect the outcome of a trial or have an impact on potential negotiations", and therefore granted the application.

[*Add new footnote reference 58a to "control of the court" in fourth sentence (ending ". . . adduced in writing only.")*]

NOTE 58a. In *Rogers v Hoyle* [2014] 3 W.L.R. 148, the Court of Appeal held that an Air Accident Investigation Branch report was admissible in a negligence action against a pilot who had crashed an aircraft. The narrative portions of the report were admissible as factual evidence and the opinion sections as expert evidence. In admitting the report, the Court of Appeal rejected the submission that the opinion sections had to be admitted under CPR Pt 35 and subject to its provisions. The report was not within the scope of Pt 35; it was admissible documentary evidence, but the court had a discretion under CPR r.32.1 to exclude it if justice and proportionality so dictated. The Court of Appeal drew a distinction with quasi-judicial reports, the factual findings of which are generally inadmissible. This is a significant case and it may be applied directly or by analogy in relation to many forms of report in negligence actions.

[*Add to n.60*]

However, it should be recognised that a judge who attempts to decide between competing expert opinions is faced with a very difficult task unless the experts are called to give oral evidence, a common sense proposition recently acknowledged in *Preece v Edwards* [2012] EWCA Civ 902 and in *Rengasamy v Homebase Ltd* [2015] EWHC 618 (QB).

[*Add new footnote reference 61a at end of sub-paragraph (iii) (ending ". . . the sums at stake ("proportionality")."*)]

NOTE 61a. In *Proton Energy Group SA v Public Company Orlen Lietuva* [2013] EWHC 334 (Comm) at [30], the Court approved and applied this approach when exploring whether the admission of an expert's evidence would "genuinely assist" the trial judge in the determination of the issues. This composite "genuine assistance" test was taken from Aikens J.'s formulation of the judge's approach under CPR r.35.1 in *JP Morgan Chase Bank v Springwell Navigation Corp* [2007] 1 All ER (Comm) 549. In that case, he stated at [19] that "[i]t is well established that in order to fulfil the requirement of CPR r. 35.1, a court must be satisfied that the expert evidence is properly admissible and will genuinely assist the trial judge in determining the matters which are in issue. The burden of establishing these two requirements rests upon the party that seeks permission to adduce the expert evidence concerned". See also *British Airways Plc v Spencer* [2015] EWHC 2477 (Ch) at [21]–[24]. The case of *Mitchell v News Group Newspapers Ltd* [2014] EWHC 3590 is a good illustration of the test in practice. Having regard to the importance and value of a high-profile defamation claim, the Court permitted expert evidence on phonetics to help determine whether words could be said in a given time and evidence from an optometrist and a scene reconstruction expert to help determine what could be seen from a given position. In giving permission for this evidence, the Court in substance applied the test of genuine assistance, and rejected a test of absolute necessity.

[*Delete final sentence of paragraph (beginning "Further guidance . . .) and replace with the following.*]

Further assistance concerning expert evidence in civil proceedings is to be found in the Guidance for the Instruction of Experts to give Evidence in Civil Proceedings which took effect in December 2014. It replaced a Protocol which had been in place, subject to amendments, since 2005 and which had been cited with approval by the Court of Appeal in *General Medical Council v Meadow*.[62] The document gives detailed guidance on the instruction and responsibilities of experts, and their role in modern litigation. In its latest form, it contains new sections on sequential exchange of expert evidence and on concurrent oral evidence from multiple experts, and it stresses the need for solicitors to keep experts informed about the evidential status of material supplied to them.

6–012A [*Add new paragraph to text*]

Further reforms to the rules governing expert evidence have been introduced following Lord Justice Jackson's Review of Civil Litigation Costs, as part of the package of procedural reforms which have resulted from that Review. As from April 1 2013, parties applying for permission to call expert evidence must identify the issues which the evidence will address, as well as the expert discipline.[62a] Where practicable, the expert should be identified by name.[62b] If permission for expert evidence is granted, the order may specify the issues which the evidence can address.[62c] The court has specific power to limit the amount of a party's expert's fees and expenses which can be recovered from any other party,[62d] in addition to its broader powers of costs management. The Final Report of Lord Justice Jackson's Review stresses the benefits of good case management in controlling the extent and cost of expert evidence and explains the rationale underlying the changes.[62e] A further innovation which has followed on from a recommendation in the Review is an amendment of the Practice Direction to CPR Pt 35, which now provides a power to receive concurrent evidence from multiple experts (a practice known colloquially as "hot-tubbing"). The new provisions[62f] envisage that the evidence will follow an agenda and will be led by questions from the Judge addressed to each witness in turn, followed by questioning by the parties' advocates.

NOTE 62a. CPR r.35.4(2).
NOTE 62b. CPR r.35.4(2)(b).

NOTE 62c. CPR r.35.4(3).
NOTE 62d. CPR r.35.4(4).
NOTE 62e. Final Report of the Review (2010), paras 3.1–3.24.
NOTE 62f. Paras 11.1–11.4 of the Practice Direction to Pt 35.

[*Add new footnote reference 62fa at end of first sentence (ending "... with pre-action protocols.")*] 6–013

NOTE 62fa. A number of cases in the professional liability field have considered whether an application to introduce expert evidence late is to be treated as one seeking relief from sanction, and thus engaging the principles discussed in *Mitchell v News Group Newspapers Ltd* [2014] 1 W.L.R. 795 and *Denton v TH White Ltd* [2014] CP Rep 40. In *Bank of Ireland v Donaldsons LLP* [2014] EWHC 1957 (Ch), the claimant was permitted, in the context of a valuer's negligence claim, to adduce a supplementary expert report despite having delayed in doing so. The Court rejected the submission that the request to introduce the report outside the time set in an order had to be addressed as if it were an application for relief from sanction. In *Warners Retail Ltd v National Westminster Bank plc* [2014] EWHC 2818 (Ch), when a party in an interest rate swaps mis-selling action sought to introduce expert evidence late in the day and an adjournment of the trial would have been required to accommodate the new evidence, the Court refused the application. It was not necessary to decide whether the *Mitchell* approach applied, since ordinary application of the overriding objective dictated the answer. In *Gladstar Ltd v Layzells* [2014] EWHC 1449 (Ch), which involved a claim for breach of a solicitor's undertaking, the claimant sought unsuccessfully to adduce expert evidence seriously out of time. Sales J. concluded that the order requiring filing/service of expert evidence by a set date included an implicit sanction against non-compliance and that therefore the application to introduce the evidence late had to be treated as one for relief from sanction. In *Ellison v University Hospital of Morecombe Bay NHS Trust* [2015] EWHC 477 (QB), the Court identified variable treatment of this issue in the case law, with some cases treating any late application to introduce expert evidence as engaging the robust approach in *Mitchell* and others taking a different view. On the facts of that case, it was unnecessary to decide the point.

[*Add new footnote reference 62g at end of second sentence (ending "... will be discouraged.")*]

NOTE 62g. However, the practical effect of a refusal to admit new expert evidence must be taken into account. In *Adams v Allen & Overy* ChD July 11, 2013, unreported, Foskett J. found that a Master had erred in not considering the practical effect of his refusal of permission for a party to rely on a new valuation expert where the initial expert had expressed an unwillingness to continue. The reality was that the applicant party (X) had a witness unwilling to support their case, and X therefore would not wish to call this witness. A refusal of permission to call a new expert would leave X without any effective expert evidence. In reaching his conclusions, Foskett J. concluded that authorities dealing with the use of experts in personal injury cases were applicable across all fields of litigation; however, that some features which served to restrict the use of expert evidence were to be borne in mind as essential to personal injury cases owing to the volume of the litigation and the stringency of the pre-action protocol.

[*Add after end of second sentence (ending "... will be discouraged.")*]

In *Guntrip v Cheney Coaches Ltd*,[62h] the Court of Appeal rejected an attempt by a claimant to introduce a substitute expert after his original expert had signed a joint statement, the effect of which would have been seriously adverse to the claimant's case. Lewison L.J. pointed out that an expert might modify or change his opinion during a meeting with his opposite number, and stated that it was best for the revised opinion to be brought to the attention of the parties and the Court as soon as possible. Such a change of mind by an expert did not necessarily have the consequence that the instructing party would be permitted to rely upon evidence from a new expert. It was necessary for the Court to consider all the circumstances, including the stage at which the substitution was attempted, the nature of any change of view and the cogency of the newly expressed opinion. In *Lee v Colchester Hospital NHS Foundation Trust* [2015] EWHC 1766 (QB), the Court acknowledged that *Guntrip* explained the relevant principles for such an application. However, the Court permitted late substitution of an expert on the ground that his evidence had been compromised by his having been dismissed from employment. There was a very genuine reason for seeking to change expert and a prospective application would plainly have been allowed.

NOTE 62h. [2012] C.P. Rep. 26.

[*Add new paragraph to text*]

While these cases establish that the Court will exercise its powers in favour of a principle of openness, it does not follow that conditions will always be imposed requiring reports of currently or formerly instructed experts to be disclosed. In *Odedra v Ball*,[64a] the claimant received two reports at the same time from an expert valuer, each addressing different issues, and only chose to disclose one. The Court recognised that the interest in openness might in some cases trump privilege, but said that this was not always the case. Since the experts appeared to have become confused about the task facing them, the parties would not be ordered to provide previously undisclosed reports.

In *BMG (Mansfield) Ltd v Galliford Try Construction Ltd*[64b] which involved a claim against a contractor and architects, the claimants' expert was nearing retirement age. He participated in a mediation and shortly thereafter withdrew from the case. The claimants were permitted to substitute in a new expert, and were not required as a condition to disclose communications with the previous expert. It was not possible to say for certain what had motivated the expert's decision to withdraw but the case was not apparently one of "expert shopping". In any event, the circumstances did not justify the invasion of privilege involved in ordering disclosure of attendance notes and the like.

NOTE 64a. [2012] BLR 434.
NOTE 64b. [2014] C.P. Rep. 3.

(d) *Relevance and Admissibility of Expert Evidence*

[*Add after first sentence of paragraph (ending "... both before and at trial".)*] **6–014**

Expert evidence should not be admitted if the issue to which it is directed can readily be resolved by the Court without resort to expert assistance.[64c] Furthermore, expert evidence should be directed to assisting in the resolution of issues, and it should not ordinarily be admitted on the basis of a vague and generalised appeal to the assistance it might give the court.[64d]

[*Add new footnotes*]

Note 64c. See *Liddell v Middleton* [1996] P.I.Q.R. P36 at P41–P44; *Barings Plc v Coopers & Lybrand* [2001] Lloyd's Rep. P.N. 379 at [45]; *Esure Insurance Ltd v Direct Line Insurance Plc* [2008] EWCA Civ 842. In *Team Tex SAS v Wang* [2015] EWHC 1909 (QB), the Court rejected an attempt to adduce evidence of an ergonomist on the issue of whether instructions for a child car seat were sufficiently clear and unambiguous. In the partnership dispute case of *Bagga v Nagpal* [2015] EWHC 398 (Ch), a party was refused permission to adduce expert evidence on the terms on which the partnership was entered into, although it was recognised that an expert might need to be called at a later stage if accounts and inquiries were ordered to be made.

Note 64d. See *British Airways Plc v Spencer* [2015] EWHC 2477 (Ch) at [21]–[24]. The judge added that, where there are technical matters requiring uncontentious explanation, that should be provided by way of agreed summary rather than by calling an expert solely to educate the Court.

[*Add new footnote reference 64e to end of second sentence (ending "... as soon as possible.")*]

Note 64e. In *Acamar Films Ltd v Microsoft Corporation* [2012] EWHC 2682 (Pat), a late application was made which challenged the admissibility of the respondent's expert evidence. Although Arnold J. found that there was room to doubt the admissibility of some passages of the report in question, he held (at [5]) that "bearing in mind the lateness with which the point has been raised, as a result of which not only have I read the evidence in question but also the parties are ready to cross-examine to it, and in particular the difficulty of disentangling that which is properly admissible from that which is inadmissible, it seems to me that the better course is to admit all of the evidence and to allow any question over the evidence to be taken as one of weight rather than admissibility". Note also *Teva Pharmaceutical Industries Ltd v Actavis UK Ltd* [2015] EWHC 2605 (Pat), where the Court considered admissibility of written expert evidence filed in support of an interim injunction application. Objection was taken to the evidence on the ground that it did not contain the prescribed form of declaration. The Court accepted that the provisions of CPR Pt 35 governing the form of reports applied to evidence in interlocutory applications, but admitted the evidence because as a matter of substance the report was suitable for admission as expert evidence.

[*Add at end of paragraph*]

6–016 While an expert is entitled to express opinions which would, if accepted, resolve issues in the proceedings, it is important that the expert's role should be limited to providing assistance within the scope of his or her particular expertise.[69a]

[*Add new footnote*]

NOTE 69a. See the discussion in the Privy Council criminal appeal of *R. v Pora* [2015] UKPC 9 at [23]–[27].

(iv) *Impartiality*

6–020 [*Add to n.86*]

In *Rowley v Dunlop* [2014] EWHC 1995 (Ch) a party's expert was a partner in a firm the owner of which was also the sole director of the claims management company pursuing the party's claim. The Court held that this was not enough to render the expert's evidence inadmissible. No financial interest in the litigation and no conflict could be established such as would justify excluding the evidence.

[*Add to n.88*]

In *Meat Corp of Namibia Ltd v Dawn Meats (UK) Ltd* [2011] EWHC 474 (Ch), Mann J. reviewed the line of authority considered in this paragraph and concluded that the question whether a prior interest or connection with a party will disqualify an expert is a question of fact and degree the resolution of which will depend on all the facts of the case. An expert who has acted as a consultant for a party, performing limited functions, will not necessarily be debarred from giving evidence against that party.

[*Add to n.89*]

In *Matchbet Ltd v Openbet Retail Ltd* [2013] EWHC 3067 (Ch), an expert was not disqualified from giving evidence in circumstances where he had personal and professional links with the CEO of a company connected to the party instructing him. The connections simply went to the weight of the expert's evidence. In the circumstances, weight was not significantly reduced, not least because the expert had been open about the links. Where an expert's connection with a party is not voluntarily disclosed and emerges late in the day, that may adversely affect the weight to be given to his or her evidence. In the clinical negligence case of *EXP v Barker* [2015] EWHC 1289 (QB), an expert's prior professional connection with the defendant only came to light at trial. The judge said that he had come close to excluding the evidence and was left with reservations about the expert's independence and objectivity.

[*Add at end of paragraph*] 6–021

While an expert may be precluded from accepting instructions because he has received privileged or confidential information from another party to the litigation, this will depend on the nature of the information, the capacity in which it has been received and the relationship between expert and client. The receipt of such information does not place the expert in a position analogous to that of a former solicitor of a party. See *Meat Corp of Namibia Ltd v Dawn Meats (UK) Ltd* [91a] where Mann J. rejected the argument that an expert who had been approached by the claimant and had received confidential information of limited importance should later be precluded from giving evidence for the defendant.

Note 91a. [2011] EWHC 474 (Ch) at [25]–[42].

(e) *The Single Joint Expert*

[*Add to n.94*] 6–023

In *Stratton v Patel* [2014] EWHC 2677 (TCC) at [424]–[428], the Court rejected an attack which was mounted against an expert on the basis that he had communicated unilaterally with one party, since the communication had been procedural and innocuous. The Deputy Judge said that the usual rule needed to be "tempered with common sense."

[*Add to n.99*]

The authorities on this topic were reviewed in *Bulic v Harwoods* [2012] EWHC 3657. Eady J. deprecated the use of any one test to decide whether a party could withdraw instructions from a joint expert and adduce further expert evidence. A flexible approach was required, taking proper account of the scale of the case, the nature of the expert evidence and its effect on the issues.

[*Add new footnote reference 103a at end of paragraph (sentence ending "... set out in CPR 35.6")*] 6–026

Note 103a. Where a party finds reason to disagree with a single joint expert's conclusions, the remedy is to seek permission to instruct a separate expert. This proposition is illustrated by the decision of the Court of Appeal in *Gilruth v Harding* unreported July 21, 2015, where it was held that a party wishing to dispute a single joint expert's opinion about the effect of a back defect on the value of an eventing horse should have sought permission to instruct their own expert.

(f) *Experts' Immunity from Suit*

[*Add new footnote reference 114a at end of first sentence (ending "... in respect of defamation claims.")*] 6–030

Note 114a. In general terms, the participants in a trial continue to enjoy a "core immunity" in respect of their conduct during the trial. The *Arthur JS Hall* and

Jones cases established that that immunity should not extend to protect advocates and experts respectively against claims from their own clients. In *A v Chief Constable of Hampshire* [2012] EWHC 1517 (QB), a case concerning the liability of the police to informants for disclosures made by prosecuting counsel in a trial, Spencer J. (at [15]–[34]) rejected the submission that the "core immunity" had been weakened more generally by these decisions.

[*Add to n.117*]

In *X Local Authority v Trimega Laboratories Ltd* [2014] P.N.L.R. 7 experts in a laboratory had made a serious mistake in a blood test relevant to family proceedings. In those circumstances, the parties to the proceedings succeeded in a s.51 application for a non-party costs order against the laboratory (i.e. an application based on the *Philips v Symes* jurisdiction).

[*Add at end of paragraph*]

Finally, it should be borne in mind that serious shortcomings in the evidence of an expert can result in costs sanctions against the party who instructed that expert.[118] A party penalised in this way might now seek to bring a claim against the expert, since the abolition of experts' immunity.

NOTE 118. See *Siegel v Pummell* [2015] EWHC 195 (QB) at [37]–[39].

CHAPTER 7

HUMAN RIGHTS AND PROFESSIONALS

1. INTRODUCTION

[*In n.1 after "R. (on the application of Johnson, Thomas, Manning) v Havering LBC [2006] EWHC 1714 (Admin)" add the following*] **7–001**

The decision was upheld in the Court of Appeal [2007] 2 W.L.R. 109 and the House of Lords [2007] 3 W.L.R. 112.

2. RELEVANT CONVENTION RIGHTS

(a) *Article 6*

[*Add to n.27*] **7–011**

In *Popivčák v Slovakia* (App. No.13665/07, December 6, 2011) the European Court rejected a complaint that the applicant had not been provided with access to a court, in violation of his rights under art.6(1), to bring a claim for damages in connection with undisputed malpractice by his lawyer. Judge 8Aikuta and Judge Myjer powerfully dissented stating that there appeared to be a total structural and systematic impossibility for such claims as the present one (which arose out of lost litigation) even to be argued before a Slovakian court, let alone to succeed, and that this could not be in keeping with art.6(1) and the rule of law in general. In *Malik v Sir Robin Wales* (unreported July 11, 2012 H.H. Judge Mackie QC reported on Lawtel July 12, 2012 ex tempore), a complaint by a claimant that preventing a claimant management company to conduct litigation on his behalf was a breach of his art.6 rights was rejected. Whilst the claimant had a right to a fair and public hearing, he did not have a right to go to court through a company not permitted to conduct litigation under local law.

3. NEGLIGENCE AND DUTY OF CARE

(f) *Further Developments since Z*

7–037 [*Add at end of paragraph*]

In *Michael v Chief Constable of South Wales & Chief Constable of Gwent* [2012] EWCA Civ 981, the Court of Appeal granted summary judgment to the defendant chief constables of two police forces in respect of claims for damages in negligence by the family of a woman who was killed by her ex-partner, having made an emergency call to the police which was not given immediate priority. Any police action in the course of investigating or suppressing crime could not generally be made the subject of an action and it was neither necessary nor appropriate for the factual issues in the case to be determined at trial. However, the Court considered that there could be no case of non-actionability in relation to the merits of the family's claim under art.2 and this would have to be determined at trial. Davis L.J. dissented on the Convention issue considering that the positive obligation arising under art.2 was breached only if the authorities had known or ought to have known, on the facts at the relevant time, that there existed a real and immediate risk to the life of an identified individual. However he considered the facts did not show any realistic prospect of satisfying that test. In *Robinson v Chief Constable of West Yorkshire Police* [2014] EWCA Civ 15; [2014] P.I.Q.R. P14 the Court of Appeal declined to give exhaustive guidance of such special circumstances, but indicated, obiter, that they would include claims which do not relate to core police functions (such as negligent traffic management decisions) and claims where police officers have assumed responsibility for a claimant. In *C (A Person Under A Disability) v The Chief Constable of the Police Service of Northern Ireland* [2014] NIQB 63, the plaintiff alleged that she had suffered psychiatric losses as a result of an inadequate police investigation into her alleged rape. Gillen J. upheld the dismissal of an application to strike out her claim on the basis of *Hill*, finding that a full trial was necessary in order to consider whether special circumstances existed so as to impose a duty of care. The fact that there was a potential breach of art.3 and that this was a developing area of the common law in light of the Convention rights was held a particularly important reason for not striking the claim out.

4. IMMUNITIES

7–040 [*Add to n.91*]

See also *Dobson v Thames Water Utilities Ltd & Water Services Regulation Authority (Intervenor)* [2011] EWHC 3253 (TCC) where Ramsey J. considered that Thames Water could not escape liability under art.8 for failing to control odour from its sewerage facility using the statutory duty defence under the Water Industry Act 1991 s.94(1)(b) as it had failed to have reasonable regard for others. It had therefore committed unlawful acts for the purposes of s.6(1) HRA.

5. LAWYERS

(b) *Lawyer/Client Confidentiality and the Convention*

[*Add at end of paragraph*] **7–044**

In *Michaud v France* (2014) 59 E.H.R.R. 9 the European Court of Human Rights held that an obligation under European Community and French law for lawyers to report suspicions about their clients' involvement in money laundering interfered with lawyers' art.8 rights. The obligation forced lawyers either to report suspicions, and thus breach legal professional privilege; or to refuse to comply and thus expose themselves to disciplinary sanctions and even disbarment. There was therefore an interference both with the right to respect for correspondence and the right to respect for private life, which was held to include *"activities of a professional or business nature"*. However, there was no violation of art.8 because the interference was in accordance with law, had a legitimate aim, and was proportionate. Requiring lawyers to report suspicions did not amount to disproportionate interference with the fundamental right to professional confidentiality given the general interest in combating money laundering. Furthermore, lawyers were only required to report suspicions in certain defined situations, which did not include acting for clients in judicial proceedings, and thus did not go to the very essence of the lawyer's *"defence role"* which formed the basis of legal professional privilege.

[*Add at end of paragraph*] **7–046**

The decision of the Court of Appeal was upheld by the Supreme Court [2013] 2 W.L.R. 325, albeit on grounds other than those arising from the HRA or art.8. Lord Neuberger, who gave the leading judgment for the majority, stated (at [74]) that he did not consider that the HRA took the case any further and that a determination that legal advice privilege would apply to communications with professional lawyers but not other professional people would not infringe art.14 or art.8 read together with art.14.

(c) *Freedom of Expression/Association*

[*Add at end of paragraph*] **7–053**

In *Richard Craven v Bar Standards Board* unreported January 30, 2014 the Visitors to the Inns of Court (Silber J., Mr Kenneth Crofton-Martin, Ms Amanda Savage) dismissed an appeal against a finding by the Bar Standards Board that a barrister who had sent an offensive email about a colleague to other colleagues was guilty of conduct which was likely to bring the legal profession into disrepute. Amongst other findings, they rejected the submission that the BSB proceedings against him for sending the email constituted an infringement with the appellant's art.10 right to freedom of expression. In any event, even if there was such an interference, there was no infringement of art.10 because the proceedings were in accordance with the law, necessary in a democratic society, particularly for the protection of the reputation of others, namely the legal professional, and were proportionate. A related argument based on art.8 was also dismissed.

6. MEDICAL PRACTITIONERS

(b) *Relevant Articles in relation to Medical Practitioners*

(i) *Article 2*

Examples of the application of art.2

7–059 [*In (a) Abortion, add to n.152*]

The decision is considered in further detail in "What's the consensus? The Grand Chamber's Decision on Abortion in A, B and C v Ireland" [2011] E.H.R.L.R. 200. See also *RR v Poland* (2011) 53 E.H.R.R. 31 in which the European Court held that Poland had violated arts 3 and 8 where an applicant had been denied access to the prenatal genetic testing prior to the time limit for abortion for foetal abnormality. The woman subsequently gave birth to a baby with Turner's Syndrome and her husband left her. She was awarded €45,000 in relation to non-pecuniary damage.

[*In (b) Euthanasia, add to n.159*]

In *R. (on the application of AM) v (1) DPP (2) Solicitors Regulation Authority (3) General Medical Council* [2012] EWHC 470 the Court granted a declaration that solicitors retained by a terminally ill person wishing to end his life would not be encouraging or assisting suicide within the meaning of the Suicide Act 1961 by obtaining information from third parties to place before the Court in support of their client's case.

[*Add at end of paragraph (b)*]

In *R. (on the application of Tony Nicklinson) v Ministry of Justice & DPP* [2012] EWHC 2381 (Admin); (2012) 109 (32) L.S.G. 18 the English Court relied on *Haas* as authority for the proposition that whilst an individual's right to decide how and when to end his life was an aspect of art.8, the state had a wide margin of appreciation in this area. The Court clarified that the ruling in *Pretty* that a blanket ban on assisted suicide was not incompatible with art.8 also applied to voluntary euthanasia and that it would be wrong to conclude that art.8 required voluntary euthanasia to afford a possible defence to murder. The Court reiterated that it was for Parliament to decide whether to change the law on voluntary euthanasia.

The *Nicklinson* case has now been considered by the Court of Appeal [2013] EWCA Civ 961 and by the Supreme Court [2015] A.C. 657. The Court of Appeal upheld the lower court's ruling that the blanket legal prohibition on providing assistance to those wishing to die was not a disproportionate interference with art.8. In support of the appeal, an attempt was made to rely upon a recent decision of the ECHR in *Koch v Germany* [2013] 1 F.C.R. 595; (2013) 56 E.H.R.R. 6

(application No.497/09). However *Koch* was distinguished on the basis that the German courts had not made a ruling on the relationship between art.8 and the German law regulating the accessibility of drugs capable of terminating life despite it being incumbent on them to do so. By contrast, in the *Nicklinson* case the Divisional Court had expressly addressed this issue.

A majority of the Supreme Court dismissed the appeal reiterating that states which were parties to the Convention had a wide margin of appreciation regarding whether assisted suicide should be lawful and that a prohibition on assisted suicide such as that imposed by s.2 of the Suicide Act 1961 was within that margin of appreciation. The interference with the claimants' right to private life caused by that prohibition had to be balanced against the interests of society in protecting vulnerable people from being pressured into suicide, and on the evidence available it was impossible for the Court to make such an assessment. It was also emphasised that whether and to what extent assisted suicide should be lawful, and whether the risks to vulnerable people could be mitigated was inherently a matter for determination by the elected legislature rather than the court.

This decision has been upheld by the European Court (2015) 61 E.H.R.R. SE7 who declared the application inadmissible. The ECHR made clear that it did not consider it appropriate to extend art.8 so as to impose on the Contracting States a procedural obligation to make available a remedy requiring the courts to decide on the merits of a claim. In any event, the ECHR found that the majority of the Supreme Court had dealt with the substance of the first applicant's claim concluding that she had failed to show that developments since *Pretty* meant that the ban could no longer be considered a proportionate interference with art.8 rights.

[*In (f) Duty of Care in relation to Patients Detained under the Mental Health Act, add to n.187*]

But see now the Supreme Court's decision reported at [2012] UKSC 2; [2012] 2 W.L.R. 381.

[*Add new bullet point at end of paragraph (e) Inquests*]

In *R. (on the application of Kent CC) v HM Coroner for Kent* [2012] EWHC 2768 (Admin); (2013) 177 J.P. 82 the Divisional Court held that a coroner had been wrong to decide that the inquest was required to be conducted as an art.2 inquest because the evidence did not justify a conclusion that any general or operational duty was arguably breached. Where there was an allegation that the authorities had violated their positive general duty to protect the right to life, it must be established that the authorities knew or ought to have known at the time of the existence of a real and immediate risk to the life of an identified individual and that they failed to take measures within the scope of their powers which, judged reasonably, might have been expected to avoid that risk.

[*Add at end of paragraph (f)*]

The Supreme Court has now overruled the Court of Appeal's decision holding that art.2 does impose an operational obligation on states to protect mentally ill patients who were not detained under the Mental Health Act where there was a real and immediate risk of suicide: see *Rathbone v Pennine Care NHS Trust* [2012] UKSC 2; [2012] 2 W.L.R. 381. The Court relied on the Strasbourg jurisprudence in *Osman* and the UK case of *Savage* to hold that a duty existed to protect persons from a real and immediate risk of suicide where they were under the state's control (although it also noted that the ECHR had stated that in most cases involving medical negligence, there was no operational duty under art.2).

The Court held that the deceased had been admitted to hospital as a real suicide risk, that she was extremely vulnerable and that the hospital had assumed responsibility for her. If she had insisted on leaving the hospital, the authorities could and should have exercised their powers under the 1983 Act to prevent her. Lord Dyson stated that the standard required for proper performance of the operational duty was reasonableness, which included "consideration of the circumstances of the case, the ease or difficulty of taking precautions and the resources available" but also made clear that "it is more difficult to establish a breach of the operational duty than mere negligence". On the facts, the decision to allow the deceased two days' home leave was one that no reasonable psychiatric practitioner would have made. The Court also permitted the deceased's parents to bring an art.2 claim despite having settled the negligence claim and awarded them £5,000 each.

In *Selwood v Durham CC* [2012] EWCA Civ 979 the Court of Appeal refused to strike out a claim by a girl who was attacked by her mentally ill father with a knife when he left hospital on the basis that it was arguable following *Rathbone* that the respondents might have breached her rights under art.2.

In *R. (on the application of L) v West London Mental Health Trust* [2012] EWHC 3200 (Admin); [2013] A.C.D. 15 the Divisional Court held that art.6 was not engaged in relation to a decision to transfer a patient detained under the 1983 Act from a medium security hospital to a high security hospital as that decision did not determine any civil rights (there being no dispute about the claimant's civil rights at the time of the decision).

[*Add to n.188*]

In *Reynolds v United Kingdom* (App. No.2694/08) the European Court held that an applicant whose schizophrenic son had committed suicide whilst in the care of a local council psychiatric unit was entitled to damages against the United Kingdom for failing to provide an effective remedy (namely civil proceedings to establish any liability and compensation due to the non-pecuniary damage suffered by her on her son's death) and was awarded £7,000. This lacuna has now been corrected by the decision in *Rathbone* (which was decided after Mrs Reynolds' application was made but before the judgment of the European Court).

(ii) *Article 3*

7–060 [*Add to n.192*]

See also *A Local Authority v (1) E (by her litigation friend the Official Solicitor (2) A Health Authority (3) E's parents* [2012] EWHC 1639 (COP); [2012] 2

F.C.R. 523 (it was found to be in the best interests of a young woman suffering from anorexia nervosa to be fed, forcibly if necessary: any resulting interference with her rights under arts 3 and 8 was proportionate and necessary in order to protect her right to life).

(iv) *Article 8*

[*Add at end of sub-paragraph (i)*] **7–065**

The European Court has now overturned the Chamber's decision in *SH v Austria* [2012] E.H.R.L.R. 211 holding that the margin of appreciation to be afforded to Austria was a wide one because in vitro fertilisation, at the time of the Austrian court's decision, involved sensitive ethical issues against a background of fast-moving scientific developments. However the Court also emphasised that this area of the law was continuously evolving and was subject to particularly dynamic developments in science and law as a result of which it needed to be kept under review by Contracting States.

[*Add a new sub-paragraph (o)*]

In *A NHS Trust v DE* [2013] EWHC 2562 (Fam) King J. granted declarations to an NHS Trust to permit the non-therapeutic sterilisation of a 37-year-old man with learning disabilities who was unable to consent to such a procedure. A vasectomy was found to be "overwhelmingly" in his best interests under the Mental Capacity Act 2005 as, amongst other things, he did not want any more children, it would allow him to continue his long-term relationship with the mother of his child and would restore to him his lost skills and independence. Article 8 was noted to involve competing rights which the court had to balance and consider.

[*Add a new sub-paragraph (p)*]

In *R. (on the application of IM and MM) v Human Fertilisation and Embryology Authority* [2015] EWHC 1706 (Admin) Ousley J. dismissed a challenge by the parents of a deceased woman against the refusal of the HFEA to allow their deceased daughter's eggs to be exported to a treatment centre in New York to be fertilised by an anonymous sperm donor and implanted in the mother. The basis for the refusal was the lack of any written consent from the deceased as required by the HFE Act 1990. The Court held that the claimants did not have any art.8 rights to use the gametes. The deficiencies in the consent by the donor (it having been found that there was no settled consent), meant that it did not amount to a sufficiently informed consent for the HFE's refusal to engage the claimants' art.8 rights. It was further stated that even if that was wrong, any interference was one justified by the public interests underlying the structure and procedures in the HFE Act (the lawfulness of that Act not having been challenged). Gametes were permitted to be exported if there was effective consent of the donor but that was missing here.

[*Add a new sub-paragraph (q)*]

In *A NHS Foundation Trust v Mrs X* [2014] EWCOP 35 (Court of Protection) Cobb J. held that arts 3 and 8 were particularly prominently engaged in the case of a young woman with a 14 year history of anorexia nervosa. He held that repeated forcible feeding over a long period of time against her clearly expressed wishes, most especially with the use of physical restraint, was likely to amount to inhuman or degrading treatment and would certainly amount to a severe interference with her private life and autonomy.

(v) *Article 9*

7–066 [*Add at end of paragraph*]

In *Doogan v Greater Glasgow and Clyde Health Board* [2012] CSOH 32, Lady Smith dismissed a petition by midwives for review of the decision of the local health board that s.4(1) of the Abortion Act 1967 did not confer on midwives any right to refuse to delegate to, supervise or support staff in the provision of nursing care to patients undergoing medical termination of pregnancy. The midwives were Roman Catholics who objected, on religious grounds, to participating in abortions. They had each undertaken the role of a labour ward co-ordinator which did not require direct involvement in medical termination but raised a conscientious objection following all medical terminations being moved to the labour ward. The Court found that the midwives were sufficiently removed from direct involvement to afford appropriate respect for their beliefs.

7. PARTICULAR ISSUES ARISING UNDER THE HRA IN RELATION TO MEDICAL PRACTITIONERS

(a) *Clinical Negligence and the Bolam Test*

7–069 [*Add at end of paragraph*]

Nevertheless, the potential for using the Human Rights Act in clinical negligence cases to challenge the *Bolam* test continues to be advocated at an academic level: see *Professional Negligence and Liability*, 1st edn, Ch.14 section viii "Clinical Practitioners: The Impact of the Human Rights Act 1998".

(b) *Right to Treatment*

7–071 [*Add at end of paragraph*]

In *R. (on the application of Rose) v Thanet Clinical Commissioning Group* [2014] EWHC 1182 (Admin) Jay J. reiterated that the state was under no positive duty to fund medical treatment pursuant to art.8 (in that case NHS funding for oocyte cryopreservation before chemotherapy began). He also dismissed a challenge under art.14 holding that there had been no discrimination in the decision not to provide treatment.

[*Add at end of paragraph*] **7–073**

In *R. (on the application of Tracey) v Cambridge University Hospital NHS Foundation Trust and others* [2012] EWHC 3860 (Admin) the court declined to hold a substantive hearing to investigate a hospital's non-resuscitation policy. It was emphasised that where ethical questions were concerned, the court should not enunciate general propositions of principle outside the particular factual context in which the issues arose.

(c) *Withdrawal of Treatment*

[*Add at end of paragraph*] **7–076**

In *An NHS Foundation Trust v R* [2013] EWHC 2340 (Fam); [2014] Fam. Law 294 Jackson J. sanctioned the withdrawal of ventilation to a 14-month-old profoundly handicapped child contrary to his family's wishes. He emphasised that a court making such a decision should not only consider the child's medical condition but also weigh the emotional, social and existential factors underpinning the child's right to respect as a unique individual, a member of his family and a member of society which considerations were protected by arts 2, 3 and 8 of the Convention. However, having considered all such factors, the Judge concluded that it would be in the child's best interests for treatment to be stopped because continued ventilation would be futile and would progressively cause him more and more suffering whilst giving him very little in terms of any positive experience of the life being preserved.

In *Aintree University Hospitals NHS Foundation Trust v James* [2013] 3 W.L.R. 1299 the Supreme Court stated that the fundamental question in cases relating to withdrawal of treatment was whether it would be in the patient's best interests, and therefore lawful, to have the treatment, rather than whether it would be in his best interests to withhold or withdraw it. If the treatment was not in the patient's best interests, the court would not be able to give consent on the patient's behalf and, since it would then be unlawful to give such treatment, its withholding or withdrawal would be lawful. The Supreme Court also set out that: (a) in considering the best interests of a particular patient the patient's welfare in the widest sense had to be considered, including not just medical but also social and psychological welfare; and (b) the test to be applied was a subjective and not an objective one, namely the decision maker had to try and put itself in the position of what the individual patient's view of the proposed treatment would be.

The key principles to be derived from *Aintree* are usefully summarised at [24] of the decision in *Kirklees Council v RE, SE and Leeds Teaching Hospital* [2014] EWHC 3182 (Fam). Moor J. made clear that such principles apply to cases concerning children who lack capacity just as they apply to adult patients. The fundamental question was described as being whether it is in the best interests of the patient, and therefore lawful, to give medical treatment. The purpose of the best interests test is to consider matters from the patient's point of view rather than applying an objective test.

7–077 [*Add at end of paragraph*]

In *Newcastle upon Tyne Hospitals Foundation Trust v LM* [2014] EWHC 454 (COP), a declaration was granted that it would be lawful to withhold a blood transfusion from LM, a gravely ill 63-year-old Jehovah's Witness. Jackson J. emphasised in his judgment that the right to life contained in art.2 was fundamental but not absolute. There was no obligation on a patient with decision-making capacity to accept life-saving treatment, and doctors were neither entitled nor obliged to give it.

7–078 [*Add at end of paragraph*]

In *W (by her litigation friend B) v (1) M (by her litigation friend the Official Solicitor) (2) S (3) a NHS Primary Care Trust* [2011] EWHC 2443 (Fam); [2012] 1 W.L.R. 1653, it was emphasised that all cases relating to withdrawal of artificial nutrition and hydration should be referred to the court and that the test to be applied was an objective one, namely what would be in the patient's best interests. The court had to identify the factors on each side which were relevant to the patient's best interests and carry out a balancing exercise. A balance sheet approach should be adopted in every case save where the patient was in a vegetative state and treatment was futile. Provided this occurred, there would be no breach of arts 3 and 8.

In *R. (on the application of Tracey) v Cambridge University Hospitals NHS Foundation Trust* [2014] EWCA Civ 822; [2014] Med. L.R. 273 the Court of Appeal granted a declaration that the Trust had violated Mrs Tracey's art.8 right to respect for private life in failing to involve her in the process which led to a decision to introduce a Do Not Attempt Cardio-Pulmonary Resuscitation Notice onto her notes. The Court made clear that since a DNACPR decision was one which will potentially deprive the patient of life-saving treatment, there should be a presumption in favour of patient involvement.

In *Gloucestershire Clinical Commissioning Group v (1) AB (2) CD* [2014] EWCOP 49 Baker J. reiterated that in making a decision concerning life sustaining treatment, the court must have regard to the ECHR, and in particular arts 2 and 8. Article 2 imposed a positive obligation to give life sustaining treatment if this was in the best interests of the patient but did not impose an absolute obligation to treat if treatment was futile. Article 8 encompassed considerations of a patient's personal autonomy and quality of life.

(d) *Consent to Treatment*

7–081 [*Add at end of paragraph*]

In *VC v Slovakia* [2012] E.H.R.L.R. 214, the government was found to have acted in violation of arts 3 and 8 by permitting a Slovakian national of Roma ethnic origin to be sterilised during the delivery of her second child by Caesarean section without first obtaining her informed consent. Sterilisation was held to have a significant bearing on physical and mental well-being as well as upon emotional, spiritual and family life. The manner in which the applicant had been requested to agree to sterilisation was liable to arouse feelings of fear, anguish and inferiority in her and to entail lasting suffering. She was awarded £31,000.

See also *A Local Authority v (1) E (by her litigation friend the Official Solicitor (2) A Health Authority (3) E's parents* [2012] EWHC 1639 (COP); [2012] 2 F.C.R. 523 in which it was held to be in the best interests of a young woman suffering from anorexia nervosa not having the capacity to consent, to be fed, forcibly if necessary: any resulting interference with her rights under arts 3 and 8 was said to be proportionate and necessary in order to protect her right to life.

By contrast in *A NHS Foundation Trust v Mrs X* [2014] EWCOP 35 (Court of Protection) Cobb J. held that arts 3 and 8 were particularly prominently engaged in the case of a young woman with a 14 year history of anorexia nervosa. He held that repeated forcible feeding over a long period of time against her clearly expressed wishes, most especially with the use of physical restraint, was likely to amount to inhuman or degrading treatment and would certainly amount to a severe interference with her private life and autonomy.

In *An NHS Trust v Dr A* [2013] EWHC 2442 (COP) Baker J. made an order authorising artificial nutrition and hydration to be provided to a 50-year-old Iranian doctor who was found to be incapacitated. Dr A had sought to go on hunger strike in order to protest against the refusal of asylum. The Judge found that he was under an operational duty under art.2 to protect Dr A in light of his lack of capacity. This decision was applied in *A Local Health Board v AB* [2015] EWCOP 31.

In *Nottinghamshire Healthcare NHS Trust v RC* [2014] EWCOP 1317; [2014] Med. L.R. 260, Mostyn J. emphasised the importance of judicial scrutiny in cases where the approved clinician in charge of treatment in respect of a patient detained under the Mental Health Act decides not to impose potentially life-saving treatment given that art.2 was likely to be engaged which was described as *"the most fundamental of the convention rights"*.

(g) *Right of Access to Confidential Information*

[*Add at end of paragraph*] **7–084**

In *Jovanovic v Serbia* (2015) 61 E.H.R.R. 3 the ECHR held that there had been a violation of art.8 in relation to the state's failure to provide information to the applicant regarding the death of her new born son in hospital shortly after his death, the applicant having simply been told that the cause was unknown and the records had been destroyed in a flood. The applicant had also been denied access to the room her son had been in after being told he had died and the hospital had refused to release his body to her on the grounds an autopsy was to be performed. The state was ordered to pay a sum in respect of non pecuniary damage, costs and expenses and to establish a mechanism to provide individual redress to all parents in a similar position to the applicant's from one year on which the judgment became final.

(g) *Disclosure of Medical Records and Confidentialitys*

7–089 [*Add at end of paragraph*]

In *O'Hara v Belfast Health and Social Care Trust* [2012] NIQB 75 the disclosure of medical records for the purpose of an inquiry into the deaths of children in hospital was justified under art.8(2). There was held to be a strong public interest in the records being produced and it was hoped the Inquiry would help restore public trust and confidence in the quality and standards of the care being provided. Reasonable steps had been taken to confine to a minimum the number of people seeing the documents and the documents themselves would be heavily redacted to ensure the minimum intrusion into the private lives of the patients. No less intrusive method was available.

In *JR60's Application for Judicial Review* [2013] NIQB 93 it was held that trusts in Northern Ireland had not acted unlawfully in retaining the applicant's records relating to a period when she was a resident of children's homes and a training school between 1978 and 1991, and in intending to keep those records for a period of up to 75 years. Such retention was found to be proportionate and lawful and in accordance with the Code of "Good Practice, Good Management, Good Records 2011", adequate training having been given to staff to ensure the policy was followed and proper safeguards being in place to ensure that it could not be circumvented.

In *LV v Latvia* (2015) 61 E.H.R.R. 17 the ECHR held that there has been a violation of art.8 when an administrative inquiry was initiated into the applicant's care between 1996 and 2003 following a request from the director of the hospital, the applicant having had tubal ligation performed on her without her consent after giving birth by caesarean section. Following the inquiry a report had been issued containing medical details of a particularly private and sensitive character.

8. PROFESSIONAL DISCIPLINARY PROCEEDINGS

(a) *Introduction*

7–097 [*Add at end of paragraph*]

In *Dowland v Architects Registration Board* [2013] EWHC 893 (Admin) Simon J. held that the erasure of the appellant from the Register of Architects did not engage art.1 of Protocol No.1 as that article was concerned with deprivation of possessions, not the right to earn future income as a registered architect. Furthermore, the relevant provisions of the Architects Act 1997 satisfied the requirements that deprivations should be in the public interest and subject to conditions provided for by law.

(b) *Procedural Guarantees*

Independence and impartiality

[*Add at end of paragraph*] 7–100

Heather Moor & Edgcomb Ltd had made a complaint to the European Court arising out of earlier related proceedings before the Court of Appeal ([2008] EWCA Civ 642) in which, inter alia, it raised a complaint that the Financial Ombudsman Service was not independent and impartial: *Heather Moor & Edgecomb Ltd v United Kingdom* (2011) 53 E.H.R.R. SE18. The Court rejected this complaint because it noted from the Court of Appeal judgment that the applicant had not raised this complaint before the Court of Appeal. In *Holmes v Royal College of Veterinary Surgeons* [2011] UKPC 48, the Board held that the disciplinary procedures of the Royal College of Veterinary Surgeons did not give rise to any appearance of bias arising out of the fact that the membership of the committee dealing with the prosecution of charges and that dealing with the determination of charges was drawn from the College's governing body, in whose name any charges were brought. Although it was hamstrung by the Veterinary Surgeons Act 1966 which required that members of both committees should be drawn from the council, the College had made strenuous efforts to separate the preliminary investigation committee from the disciplinary committee. It was held that a fair-minded observer would not conclude that a member of the disciplinary committee might, as a result of prior service on the preliminary investigation committee, remain predisposed to uphold a complaint irrespective of its intrinsic strength. Nor was there any real possibility of bias in previous membership of the disciplinary committee by a member of the preliminary investigation committee (albeit the Board noted that it was not being asked to appraise a complaint of apparent bias on the part of the preliminary investigation committee). By contrast, in *R. (on the application of Darsho Kaur) v Institute of Legal Executives Appeal Tribunal* [2012] 1 All E.R. 1435 the Court of Appeal held that the vice-president of the Institute of Legal Executives (ILEX), due to her leading role in the body and her inevitable interest in its policy of disciplinary regulation, was disqualified from sitting on its disciplinary or appeal tribunal. This was the conclusion either applying the doctrine of automatic disqualification or the doctrine of apparent bias. The same conclusion would embrace all ILEX council members and directors. The Court held that, whatever the means by which regulations and representation were kept separate, the necessary insulation was undermined if those principally concerned in governance were permitted to move from representation to regulatory functions as ex officio members of disciplinary or appeal tribunals.

Right to a public/oral hearing

[*Add at end of second paragraph*] 7–103

In *Miller v General Medical Council* [2013] EWHC 1934 (Admin) a direction of the General Medical Council's Fitness to Practice Panel (FTPP) that a substantive hearing be held in private was quashed as having violated the claimant's art.6 rights. The FTPP had failed to remind itself that the clear default position under art.6 is that the hearing should be in public. There was also a burden on the FTPP to show that derogation from the claimant's art.6 rights was necessary and proportionate. The evidence before the FTPP did not discharge that burden as it did not show that a witness really had a settled intention not to give evidence unless the hearing was in private, nor that such a position was objectively justifiable.

[*Add at end of paragraph*]

In *Heather Moor & Edgecomb Ltd v United Kingdom* (2011) 53 E.H.R.R. SE18, the European Court considered whether there was any duty on the Financial Ombudsman Service to convene an oral hearing in relation to determination of a disputed complaint which was said to "closely resembl[e] professional negligence proceedings" ([36]). The Court considered that the general practice of FOS, whatever it may be, was beyond the scope of the application before it ([40]). It stated that the key consideration is the overarching principle of fairness embodied in art.6 (*Jussila v Finland* (2007) 45 E.H.R.R. 39) but reiterated that the fact that proceedings are of considerable significance for an applicant is not decisive of the necessity of a hearing. The Court held that in the instant case, the applicant was afforded ample opportunities to present its case, to know and respond to the arguments put forward by the complainant and to make final representations on the basis of the Ombudsman's provisional decision. Further, the relevant issues of fact and law could be adequately addressed in, and decided on the basis of, written submissions. The requirements of fairness were therefore complied with and there was no need for an oral hearing before the Ombudsman. In any event, the Court of Appeal did consider on their merits each of the grounds raised by the applicant without ever having to decline jurisdiction ([40]–[41]). The applicant also complained that the Ombudsman's decision was not made public. Whilst the Court decided that there was no compelling reason to withhold the Ombudsman's decisions from publication and noted Rix L.J.'s remarks in the Court of Appeal that its register of decisions should be a public register, the Court determined that the Court of Appeal's judgment (which quoted at length from the Ombudsman's final decision in relation to the applicant) achieved the purpose of art.6(1) ([45]).

The giving of reasons

7–105 [*Add at end of paragraph*]

In *Perry v Nursing & Midwifery Council* [2012] EWHC 2275 (Admin), the decision of a fitness to practice panel of the Nursing and Midwifery Council to make an interim suspension order was quashed because the panel had not adequately explained why such an order was appropriate rather than a decision to instead impose conditions of practice.

Hearing within a reasonable time

7–106 [*Add at end of third paragraph*]

Article 6 was violated where there had been a four and a half year period between the notification to the appellant of allegations against her and the final hearing before the Nursing and Midwifery Council's Conduct and Competence Committee: *Okeke v Nursing and Midwifery Council* [2013] EWHC 714 (Admin). Although the hearing on liability had not been unfair, the case was remitted for reconsideration of sanction. The panel was directed to consider whether a reduction in sentence was appropriate given: (i) that the appellant's suspension from practice had been prolonged as a result of the delay; (ii) that the delay may have affected the appellant's attitude to her defence, leading her to make an unjustified counter-attack; and (iii) the need for a remedy for the breach of the appellant's art.6 rights. By contrast in *O'Connor v Bar Standards Board* [2014] EWHC 4324 (QB) a period of 18 months from the start of proceedings to a determination at a Tribunal hearing was not so unreasonable as to violate the respondent's Article 6 rights, notwithstanding that there were three to four months of inadequately explained delay.

Legal representation

[*Add to second paragraph, line 17 (after ". . . for legal representation in the disciplinary proceedings.")*] **7–107**

On appeal, the Supreme Court ([2012] 1 A.C. 167) held unanimously that the Court of Appeal had applied the correct test for whether art.6 was engaged. However, it held by a majority that it had wrongly applied the test to the particular facts and that art.6 was not in fact engaged by the disciplinary hearing. See para.7–095, above.

[*Replace "By contrast, in R (on the application of Martina K) . . ." with the following*]

Similarly, in *R. (on the application of Martina K)* . . .

Existence of a procedure to challenge interim suspensions

[*Add at end of paragraph*] **7–109**

However, arts 6 and 8 do not give the professional the right at the interim stage to call evidence which addresses the substance of the allegations against him: *Perry v Nursing and Midwifery Council* [2013] EWCA Civ 145. (For the purpose of its decision, the Court of Appeal assumed, without deciding, that arts 6 and 8 applied to an Interim Orders hearing of the Investigating Committee of the Nursing and Midwifery Council.)

Sanctions

[*Add at end of first paragraph (after ". . . Law Society v Salsbury.")*] **7–111**

Although there is no requirement mechanically to set out and answer a list of questions when considering whether arts 6 and 8 have been breached, the articles themselves should be expressly mentioned: *Robinson v Solicitors Regulation Authority* [2012] EWHC 2690 (Admin).

Appeals

7–112 [*Add at end of paragraph*]

Time limits for appeals against disciplinary decisions are also to be interpreted consistently with art.6. In *Adesina v Nursing and Midwifery Council* [2013] EWCA Civ 818 the Court of Appeal held that the prima facie absolute 28-day time limit for appealing against a disciplinary decision of the Nursing and Midwifery Council was to be read down in a manner compatible with art.6, so as to allow for an extension in exceptional circumstances. However, on the facts, the appellants failed to demonstrate that their cases were exceptional. The adverse decisions were announced in their presence and subsequent delays were largely or entirely the fault of the appellants. In *Parkin v Nursing and Midwifery Council* [2014] EWHC 519 (Admin) Eder J., applying *Adesina*, held that the reading down was limited to the minimum extent necessary to secure ECHR compliance. Extensions of time should therefore only be granted in *"very limited"* circumstances. Although the notice of appeal was lodged less than a day late, the applicant had instructed solicitors in time to prepare the case, and the reason for the delay was that his solicitors had not been aware of the deadline for lodging, these were not sufficiently exceptional matters to justify an extension of time for lodging the appeal. In *Nursing and Midwifery Council v Daniels* [2015] EWCA Civ 225 the Court of Appeal overturned the High Court's extension of time for appealing against a decision of the Nursing and Midwifery Council. It held that held that in circumstances where the appellant did not contact her lawyers until the last day before the expiry of the 28-day time limit and those lawyers acted expeditiously to file an appellant's notice, there were no exceptional circumstances justifying an extension. Jackson L.J. noted that if the court had had a general discretion to extend time, the decision below would have been without fault. However, they did not, and could only do so in exceptional circumstances, which there were not on the facts.

(c) *Law Society Interventions and Investigations*

7–113 [*Add at end of paragraph*]

In *Sheikh v United Kingdom* (2011) 53 E.H.R.R. SE19, the European Court dismissed as inadmissible various complaints made by an applicant relating to an intervention by the Law Society which was subsequently ordered to be withdrawn. She had complained under art.6(1) that she did not receive a fair hearing in that: (i) she was not given the opportunity to answer the allegations against her before a decision to intervene was taken; and (ii) she was not advised of the Law Society's reasons for intervention. She also contended that the proceedings in which she applied for withdrawal of the intervention were subject to unreasonable delay by reason of a three and a half month period between lodging her application and the date when judgment was handed down in her favour. She said that this was also a violation of art.13 since as a result of the delay she was deprived of an effective remedy in respect of the intervention into her practice. She also complained under art.1 of Protocol 1 that there had been an unjustifiable interference with her right to peaceful enjoyment of her possession. The European Court dismissed the complaints of delay under art.6(1) and art.13 as out of time. In relation to her other complaints of unfairness, the Court was satisfied that she was given ample opportunity to respond to the allegations against her and was not persuaded that her ignorance of the reasons for the intervention could be attributed to any failure of the Law Society to provide her with information. Her consistent failure to reply to requests from the Law Society for further information or her response to the allegations made denied her an opportunity to present her side of the case to the Law Society and to dispel concerns regarding her professional conduct. Has she opened papers sent to her, she would have realised that intervention was a possibility and could have sought timely legal advice as to her available remedies. She further failed to apply for an interim order requiring the Law Society to state the grounds on which the application to withdraw the intervention was resisted if she considered that the reasons given were inadequately explained. Accordingly, the Court concluded that the applicant had failed to exhaust domestic remedies in respect of her art.6(1) complaints regarding the intervention procedure. In relation to her complaint under art.1 of Protocol No.1, the Court reiterated its findings in relation to her art.6(1) complaints and repeated the applicant's responsibility for her failure to engage with the Law Society as requested in the period leading to the intervention and her failure to take steps to obtain an interim injunction or other relief. It also considered that by failing to raise the Convention arguments in the context of the domestic proceedings or commence any separate proceedings for damages for the alleged breach of art.1 of Protocol No.1, she had again failed to exhaust domestic remedies.

[*Add new paragraph to text*] **7–116**

In *Adams v Law Society* [2012] EWHC 980 (QB), Foskett J. held that individual Law Society investigators who prepared a forensic investigation report leading to an intervention were not "public authorities" under s.6(3)(b) HRA.

CHAPTER 8

PROFESSIONAL INDEMNITY INSURANCE

2. REGULATORY REQUIREMENTS

(a) *Insurance Brokers*

8–003 [*Revise first sentence to read*]

Insurance brokers are now regulated by the FCA and are therefore subject to the requirements set out in Ch.3 of the Prudential Sourcebook for Mortgage and Home Finance Firms, and Insurance Intermediaries (MIPRU).

(d) *Accountants*

8–009 [*Revise paragraph to read*]

The ICAEW Minimum Approved Policy Wording 2015 provides an indemnity against both civil liabilities[21] and awards by any ombudsman to whose jurisdiction the insured is subject by virtue of contract or law.[22] It also provides for payment of defence costs incurred with insurers' written consent (such consent not unreasonably to be withheld or delayed) in the investigation, defence or settlement of any claim or circumstance in addition to the sums payable under the primary insuring clauses;[23] the indemnity payable for defence costs will be prorated where the ultimate value of an ascertained liability exceeds the limit of indemnity.[24] The costs cover also now extends to costs of proceedings for recovery in respect of a claim as well as costs incurred in reducing or avoiding a claim against the insured.[25] Any self-insured excess is subject to an annual aggregate limit.[26] Although insurers were previously entitled to stipulate an aggregate limit on their liabilities under the insurance,[27] the limit of indemnity must now be expressed on an each and every claim basis.[27a] Where the insured is unable to obtain a replacement insurance policy, the existing insurer must now provide cover during an "Extended Policy Period" (EPP) which ends on the earlier of: (1) the insured obtaining replacement cover; or (2) 30 days from receipt by the relevant Institute of written notice from the insurer of the commencement of the EPP. [27b]

NOTE 21. ICAEW's Minimum Approved Policy Wording 2015 cl.A1.
NOTE 22. ibid. cll.A2 and B11.
NOTE 23. ibid. cll.A3 and B4.
NOTE 24. ibid. cl.A3.
NOTE 25. ibid. cl.B4.
NOTE 26. ibid. cl.C3.3.
NOTE 27. ICAEW's Minimum Approved Policy Wording 2010 cl.C1.
NOTE 27a. ICAEW's Minimum Approved Policy Wording 2015 cl.C1.
NOTE 27b. ICAEW's Minimum Approved Policy Wording 2015 cll.D3 and B6.

(e) *Solicitors*

[*Revise paragraph to read*] **8–011**

Solicitors are under a statutory obligation to obtain professional indemnity cover in accordance with the relevant Minimum Terms and Conditions for the year in which cover is sought.[28] Until September 1, 2000, solicitors' compulsory cover was effected through the Solicitors Indemnity Fund (SIF). Since that date, solicitors' practices have been required to take out professional indemnity insurance on the open market from one of an approved list of insurers (now known as "participating insurers"). SIF continues to exist, but only to run off claims which had been notified prior to September 1, 2000. From September 1, 2007 SIF also started to provide extended run-off cover for firms which ceased to practise on or after September 1, 2000 without a successor practice, following the completion of the six-year run-off period provided by their qualifying insurance.

[*Revise paragraph to read*] **8–012**

From October 1, 2011, responsibility for the formulation of the Solicitors Indemnity Insurance Rules has formally passed from the Law Society to the Solicitors' Regulatory Authority. Rule 4.1 of the Solicitors Indemnity Insurance Rules 2013 requires insurance to be effected in accordance with the SRA Minimum Terms and Conditions. The minimum levels of cover are £2,000,000 for ordinary firms and £3,000,000 for bodies corporate.[29] Although insurance may be subject to an excess, such an excess cannot operate to reduce the limit of indemnity payable.[30] Defence costs are payable in addition to the limit of indemnity[31] and must not be the subject of any monetary limit[32] or excess.[33]

NOTE 29. SRA's Minimum Terms and Conditions 2014 cl.2.1.
NOTE 30. ibid. cl.3.2.
NOTE 31. ibid. cll.1.2 and 2.1.
NOTE 32. ibid. cl.2.2.
NOTE 33. ibid. cl.3.3.

8–013 [*Revise paragraph to read*]

In order to provide temporary cover[34] for firms which cannot afford or obtain open market cover, the Law Society established an Assigned Risks Pool. The ARP was underwritten by the qualifying insurers in proportion to their premium income from open market business. Firms covered by the ARP had to pay premiums calculated as a percentage of turnover which are markedly higher than would *normally* apply in the open market. However, the ARP closed with effect from September 30, 2013: from that date it was replaced by the last insurer of record retaining the risk for a 90-day extended policy period (EPP) split between a 30-day extended indemnity period and a 60-day cessation period[34a]; during the cessation period the firm would only be permitted to handle existing instructions.[34b] Any firm unable to obtain a new policy before the end of the EPP would have to close.[34c]

NOTE 34. For up to 24 months in any four-year period, and for no more than six months in any indemnity period: SRA Indemnity Insurance Rules 2011 r.12.2.
NOTE 34a. SRA Indemnity Insurance Rules 2013 r.4.2.
NOTE 34b. SRA Indemnity Insurance Rules 2013 r.5.2.
NOTE 34c. SRA Indemnity Insurance Rules 2013 r.4.2.

8–014 [*Revise paragraph to read*]

Prior to September 30, 2013, qualifying insurers were required to enter into a qualifying insurer's agreement with the Law Society, by which they agreed inter alia to underwrite the ARP.[34d] Since September 30, 2013, the SRA Minimum Terms and Conditions require the insurer to provide run-off cover for the 30-day extended indemnity period and 60-day cessation period referred to in the preceding paragraph.[34e]

NOTE 34d. See, e.g., Schedule 1 to the Qualifying Insurer's Agreement 2012.
NOTE 34e. SRA's Minimum Terms and Conditions 2014 cl.5.

(f) *Barristers*

8–015 [*Revise paragraph to read*]

Rule C76 of the Second Edition of the *BSB Handbook* (2015) requires all self-employed practising barristers to have adequate insurance in place, taking into account the nature of the barrister's business. Rule C77 requires that (save in very limited circumstances) all self-employed barristers must be members of the Bar Mutual Indemnity Fund (BMIF). Under the BMIF scheme, premiums are calculated by reference to turnover which is weighted according to practice area.

Limits of indemnity depend upon the premium payable, and vary between £500,000 and £2,500,000. Excess of loss cover in excess of £2,500,000 is underwritten by open market insurers.

[*Revise paragraph to read*] **8–016**

Under the BMIF Terms of Cover, defence costs are payable in addition to the Limit of Cover,[35] but will be pro-rated where a sum in excess of the Limit of Cover is paid to dispose of a claim.[36]

3. THE NATURE/SCOPE OF PROFESSIONAL INDEMNITY INSURANCE

[*Add to n.42*] **8–018**

In *The 'Kos'* [2012] 2 Lloyd's Rep. 292 there was a lively debate (in the context of a standard employment and indemnity clause in a charterparty) about whether it was legitimate to search for concurrent causes of the owners' loss. It is possible to read Lord Mance's dissenting speech as encouraging a search for a single proximate cause; conversely, the speeches of Lords Sumption and Clarke reflect a view that there can readily be more than one effective cause of a loss.

[*Add new footnote reference n.44a at end of first sentence*] **8–019**

NOTE 44a. For a review of the relevant jurisprudence, see *AstraZeneca Insurance v XL Insurance* [2013] Lloyd's Rep. I.R. 290 at [41] and following.

[*Revise n.49 to read*]

As in *Mabey & Johnson Ltd v Ecclesiastical Insurance Office* [2004] Lloyd's Rep. I.R. 10 and *ACE European Group v Standard Life* [2013] Lloyd's Rep. I.R. 415.

[*Add to end of main paragraph*]

Where, however, insurers have agreed to indemnify the insured in respect of expense incurred in avoiding an insured liability, the amount payable under such an extension will not (in the absence of appropriate wording) fall to be reduced because the sums were paid also to avoid an uninsured liability.[50a]

NOTE 50a. *ACE European Group v Standard Life* [2013] Lloyd's Rep. I.R. 415.

[*Add to n.59*] **8–022**

In *AstraZeneca Insurance v XL Insurance* [2014] Lloyd's Rep. I.R. 509, the Court of Appeal (whose lead judgment was delivered by Christopher Clarke L.J.) upheld Flaux J.'s decision at first instance [2013] Lloyd's Rep. I.R. 290 and endorsed and followed the approach which had been taken by Christopher Clarke J. in *Omega Proteins*.

8–025 [*Revise paragraph to read*]

Professional indemnity insurance will often exclude cover in respect of any liability which arises purely by reason of a contractual term and which would not attach in the absence of that term. It might be thought, therefore, that such insurance would not ordinarily provide cover against a liability to a third party which could not be established in negligence (or for breach of trust).[63] However, the Court of Appeal has held that cl.6.6 of the SRA Minimum Terms and Conditions (which excludes liability for trading and personal debts as well as liabilities arising from breach of a contract or arrangement for the supply of goods or services in the course of the Insured Firm's practice) did not exclude the insured's contractual liability to a third party which had provided loans to the insured's clients to cover disbursements in litigation.[63a]

NOTE 63a. *Impact Funding Solutions Ltd v Barrington Support Services Ltd* [2015] Lloyd's Rep. I.R. 371 at [19]–[22]. The Court of Appeal reasoned that obligations in respect of such loan agreements were part and parcel of the obligations assumed by a solicitor in respect of his professional duties to his client rather than being (as capital expenditure would be) personal to the solicitor: it is suggested that such a distinction may be difficult to sustain in practice, and that—in many instances—the Court of Appeal's decision may result in insurers underwriting their insured's solvency. The Supreme Court has granted permission to appeal the Court of Appeal's decision.

7. THE PRE-CONTRACTUAL DUTY OF UTMOST GOOD FAITH

(a) *The Duty*

8–042 [*Replace n.97 with the following*]

[2003] Lloyd's Rep I.R. 131 at [59], [62], [187] and [215].

8. RULES OF CONSTRUCTION

(a) *Generally*

8–055 [*Add to n.136*]

In the *Employer's Liability Trigger Litigation* [2012] Lloyd's Rep. I.R. 371 at [19], Lord Mance stressed the need to (1) avoid over-concentrating on single words or phrases viewed in isolation; and (2) consider and construe a policy in its entirety.

[*Add new sub-paragraph (2A) after existing sub-paragraph (2)*]

Where there are two possible constructions of a contract, the Court is entitled to adopt the option which is consistent with business common sense and to reject the other: there is no requirement that the most natural meaning must be applied unless it can be said that the meaning produces a result so extreme as to suggest it was unintended.[139a]

NOTE 139a. See *Rainy Sky v Kookmin Bank* [2012] 1 Lloyd's Rep. 34 at [20]–[21] per Lord Mance.

[*Add to n.150*] **8–056**

See also *AstraZeneca Insurance v XL Insurance (Bermuda) Ltd* [2013] Lloyd's Rep. I.R. 290 at [33].

(b) *Exclusion Clauses and Insuring Clauses*

[*Add to n.157*] **8–060**

In *British Waterways v Royal & Sun Alliance Insurance* [2012] Lloyd's Rep. I.R. 562 at [47], Mr Justice Burton concluded that (although they might signify a weaker—but still significant—relationship when used in other contexts (see para.8–108, below) the words "arising out of" in an exclusion clause also import a requirement that the excluded peril should be a proximate cause.

[*Add new paragraph to text*] **8–060A**

It would appear that a condition precedent to liability should be treated as a form of exclusion clause, on the basis that it operates as an exemption to prima facie liability. The effect of this approach is that an insurer can only rely on the clause if its words are clear on a fair construction of it.[158a]

NOTE 158a. See *Royal & Sun Alliance v Dornoch* [2005] Lloyd's Rep. I.R. 544 at [19]; *Beazley v Al Ahleia* [2013] Lloyd's Rep. I.R. 561 at [70].

9. CLASSIFICATION OF TERMS/CONSEQUENCES OF BREACH

(a) *"Warranties"*

[*Add new footnote reference 165a to sub-para.(c)*] **8–066**

NOTE 165a. In *Argo Systems FZE v Liberty Insurance* [2012] Lloyd's Rep. I.R. 67 at [44]–[51], the Court of Appeal rejected a suggestion that insurers' failure expressly to rely on a breach of a hold harmless warranty when sending a letter denying liability under the policy amounted to a waiver of the breach of that warranty (as had been held at first instance). The Court of Appeal observed that insurers had expressly reserved their rights to rely on all the terms and conditions of the policy and concluded that—in such circumstances—it could scarcely be said that they were thereby unequivocally representing that they would forego their rights to rely on the hold harmless warranty. We would suggest that the Court of Appeal's decision was plainly right, both for the reasons given by the Court of Appeal and also because insurers' reliance (at a later date) on the hold harmless warranty could not be said to be inconsistent with the earlier repudiation of liability for the claim; in addition, it does not appear that the Court at first instance really grappled with the question of whether the insured in fact understood that insurers were foregoing a right to repudiate on the basis of a breach of the hold harmless warranty: that question was, in the light of the Court of Appeal's reasoning in the *HIH v Axa* case, one which it was essential should be answered in the insured's favour if any plea of waiver was to be sustainable.

(d) *Collateral Promise and Innominate Terms*

8–073A [*Add new paragraph to text*]

In *Milton Keynes BC v Nulty,*[184a] Edwards-Stuart J. derived encouragement from [33] of Mance L.J.'s judgment in *Friends Provident* to quantify insurers' counterclaim for damages for breach of an innominate term as to notification on the basis of a loss of a chance of successfully defending the third party's claim.[184b] The judge assessed that insurers had been deprived of a 15 per cent chance of successfully defending the third party's claim. Insurers were entitled to raise a defence of set-off to the extent of that proportion of their liability to indemnify the insured.

NOTE 184a. [2012] Lloyd's Rep. I.R. 453 (Edwards-Stuart J.). There was no appeal against the judge's findings on this issue.
NOTE 184b. The judge concluded that the principles set out in para.11–302 of the 6th edition of this book (para.11–314 of the current edition) were analogous to the position of an insurer who asserted that late notification had deprived it of the opportunity of successfully defending a claim against its insured. It should not be forgotten that the law does not compensate for the loss of chances which are only speculative: see *Allied Maples v Simmons & Simmons* [1985] 1 W.L.R. 1602 at 1641C–D per Stuart-Smith L.J.

12. CLAIMS NOTIFICATION AND CO-OPERATION CLAUSES

(a) *Generally*

8–085 [*Add to n.223*]

Such an approach would not of itself be inconsistent with an effective "laundry list" notification, for example where based on a perception of the existence of a "can of worms"—see the slightly inchoate analysis in *McManus v European Risk Insurance* [2013] Lloyd's Rep. I.R. 533.

[*Add to end of main paragraph*] **8–089**

In *Ted Baker Plc v Axa Insurance UK Plc (No.2)*, Eder J. indicated (obiter) that there might be limits as to the information which it might be reasonable for insurers to seek where there was a serious issue (unrelated to the information sought) as to the engagement of the policy.[236a]

Note 236a. [2015] Lloyd's Rep. I.R. 325 at [108]: Eder J. suggested that the time and expense involved in providing the requested information will be relevant considerations where there is an unrelated dispute as to the engagement of the policy.

14. Deductibles and Limits of Indemnity; Aggregation of Claims

(a) *Generally*

[*Add new paragraph to text*] **8–101A**

Where the insured faces a number of claims which, in the aggregate, would exceed the available limit of indemnity, it may be important to identify the priority in which the claims should be allocated to the limit of indemnity. In *Cox v Bankside*, Phillips J. held that vested rights to indemnity would occur only (1) where defence costs were incurred to which insurers had consented and (2) upon the establishment of a quantified liability to a third party.[251a] In the same case, the Court of Appeal considered that Phillips J. had been "plainly correct" to consider that the basic rule for the attribution of claims to the available cover was on the basis of chronological priority.[251b] This approach has now been endorsed and applied by the UK Supreme Court (in the context of a dispute about excess of loss insurance) in *Teal Assurance Co v W R Berkley Insurance*.[251c] In a subsequent decision in the same litigation, Eder J. held that payments made by an insured pursuant to a settlement agreement into an escrow account did not themselves "ascertain" the insured's liability, since the extent of the liability was not actually quantified until as and when the third party became entitled to draw down the funds in the escrow account.[251d]

Note 251a. See [1995] 2 Lloyd's Rep. 437 at 441 col.2.
Note 251b. See [1995] 2 Lloyd's Rep. 437 at 457 col.1.
Note 251c. [2014] Lloyd's Rep. I.R. 56.
Note 251d. [2015] EWHC 1000 (Comm).

[*Add new paragraph to text*] **8–107A**

In *AIG Europe Ltd v OC320301 LLP*,[260a] Teare J. was asked to determine whether a number of different claims against a firm of solicitors could be characterised as arising from "similar acts or omissions in a series of related matters or transactions" for the purposes of limb (iv) of the aggregation provision within the SRA Minimum Terms and Conditions.[260b] He held that the words "series of related matters or transactions" were intended to limit the scope of what would otherwise be a very wide aggregation clause and concluded that they applied only to a series of transactions which were related by reason of being interdependent on each other.[260c] It is suggested that, contrary to the judge's approach, there is no obvious reason why transactions should not be "related" without being interdependent. The judge gave permission to appeal.

NOTE 260a. [2015] EWHC 2398 (Comm).
NOTE 260b. The same provision can be found at cl.2.5(iii) of the SRA Minimum Terms and Conditions 2014.
NOTE 260c. See [40].

8–108 [*Add to n.262*]

While there is a requirement for a significant causal relationship, that relationship does not require that the aggregating event should be the proximate cause of the loss—see *Beazley* at [128]. Cf. the position which might apply where the words "arising from" relate to an excluded cause: see *British Waterways v Royal & Sun Alliance Insurance* [2012] Lloyd's Rep. I.R. 562 at [47].

16. THIRD PARTY RIGHTS

8–120 [*Add new paragraph to text*]

In a written ministerial statement made on April 25, 2013, it was announced that the 2010 Act would not be brought into force until it had been amended to: (1) add further insolvency situations to the Act which are within the scope of the 1930 Act but not the 2010 Act; and (2) provide a power for the Secretary of State to add further insolvency situations by order should the need arise. The necessary amendments were contained within Pt 6 of the Insurance Act 2015 and it is anticipated that the 2010 Act will be brought into force imminently. The 1930 Act will continue to apply to claims where both the relevant insolvency event *occurred* and the insured's liability was *incurred* prior to the date on which the 2010 Act comes into force.[286]

NOTE 286. See para.3 of Sch.3 to the 2010 Act.

CHAPTER 9

CONSTRUCTION PROFESSIONALS

1. INTRODUCTION

(a) *The Construction Professionals*

Architects

[*Add to note 5*]

See also *Woodman-Smith v Architects Registration Board* [2014] EWHC 3639 (Admin) (the Architects Code: Standards of Conduct and Practice 2010 and therefore the disciplinary jurisdiction of the Board extends to an architect acting as a surveyor under the Party Wall etc. Act 1996). **9–002**

Project managers

[*Add at end of paragraph*] **9–006**

The role of project manager is often undertaken by persons who are also qualified as quantity surveyors. In *William Clark Partnership Ltd v Dock St PCT Ltd* [2015] EWHC 2923 (TCC), a claim for unpaid professional fees made by quantity surveyors and project management was met by a (largely unsuccessful) counterclaim alleging breach in the claimant's advice to its client during the pre-construction and the construction phases of its development.

[*Add to n.17*]

In *Ampleforth Abbey Trust v Turner & Townsend Project Management Ltd* [2012] EWHC 2137 (TCC), project managers were in breach of duty in failing to procure an executed building contract and allowing construction works to proceed on the basis of letters of intent. An attack on the suitability of the claimant's expert witness failed.

[*Add to note 17*]

See also *Lloyds Bank Plc v McBains Cooper Consulting Ltd* [2015] EWHC 2372 (TCC) for consideration of the obligations of a "monitoring surveyor" (a construction professional who is appointed to inspect and report throughout the stages of a construction project, normally for the benefit of a finance lender as in this case, but sometimes for others).

(b) *Claims against Construction Professionals*

[*Add new paragraph after 9–006*]

Planning consultants

9–006A In *Middle Level Commissioners v Atkins Ltd* [2012] EWHC 2884 (TCC) and in *Elvanite Full Circle Ltd v AMEC Earth & Environmental (UK) Ltd* [2013] EWHC 1191 (TCC), the court accepted that there was not an established profession of "planning consultant" (notwithstanding the existence of the Royal Town Planners Institute, a chartered institute which seeks to maintain professional standards among planners).

9–007 [*Add to n.21*]

Since the parties must consider the Protocol in the context of the overriding objective that cases are to be determined justly, they must not use it as a weapon or tactic and must co-operate in its implementation: *Higginson Securities (Developments) Ltd v Hodson* [2012] EWHC 1052 (TCC). In *Amec Foster Wheeler Group Ltd v Morgan Sindall Professional Services Ltd* [2015] EWHC 2012 (TCC) it was held that the Protocol does not apply to a CPR Pt 8 claim for the production of documents but that, even if it did, the defendant was seeking to use it as a tactical device.

The Technology and Construction Court

9–008 [*Add to n.26*]

The new practice of the TCC as regards allocation of cases between County Courts, High Court centres outside London which have designated TCC judges and the High Court in London is described and explained in the judgment of Akenhead J. in *West Country Renovations Ltd v McDowell* [2012] EWHC 307 (TCC).

[*Add to n.28*]

The current edition of the TCC Guide is the 3rd revision of the 2nd edition, effective from March 3, 2014.

2. DUTIES

(a) *Duties to Client*

(i) *Contractual Duties*

Limitation of liability

[*Add to n.58*] **9–020**

A contractual limitation period which was substantially shorter than the statutory period was upheld in *Inframatrix Investments Ltd v Dean Construction Ltd* [2012] EWCA Civ 64 (a building contract case).

[*Add to n.60*]

See also *West v Ian Finlay and Associates* [2014] EWCA Civ 316, discussed at para.9–023 below.

[*Add at end of paragraph*] **9–022**

A challenge to a financial limitation of liability clause succeeded in *Ampleforth Abbey Trust v Turner & Townsend Project Management Ltd* [2012] EWHC 2137 (TCC). A project manager's appointment sought to limit its maximum liability for breach of the appointment to the amount of the fees paid to it under the appointment. It was held that this was unreasonable for the purposes of the Unfair Contract Terms Act 1977 because the same appointment required the project manager to maintain professional indemnity insurance cover of £10 million, the cost of which would have been passed on to the claimant as part of those fees. By contrast, in *Elvanite Full Circle Ltd v AMEC Earth & Environmental (UK) Ltd* [2013] EWHC 1191 (TCC), Coulson J. (obiter) held that each of a range of contractual clauses which limited the liability of the defendant planning consultants withstood challenge under the 1977 Act.

[*Add at end of paragraph*] **9–023**

A challenge under the Regulations to a net contribution clause in a standard form appointment failed in *West v Ian Finlay and Associates* [2014] EWCA Civ 316. It was held that the defendant architect was entitled to rely upon a clause in the RIBA Conditions of Appointment for Small Works which purported to limit his liability to the amount that it was reasonable to pay given the contractual responsibilities of "other consultants, contractors and specialists" appointed by the client. On its correct construction, the clause did not fall foul of either the Unfair Contract Terms Act 1977 or the Unfair Terms in Consumer Contracts Regulations 1999.

The duty to review a design

[*Add at end of paragraph*] **9–038**

The professional duty to review previous advice or services normally arises in relation to work done under the same contract of engagement, so that a professional engaged under successive appointments to perform different pieces of work will not owe a duty to review work done under its prior engagements: *Shepherd Construction Ld v Pinsent Masons LLP* [2012] EWHC 43 (TCC). This was a claim against solicitors but Akenhead J. illustrated his reasoning by referring to the position of construction professionals. The situation may be different where a professional is engaged under a general retainer, rather than a series of separate commissions.

(ii) *Duties Independent of Contract*

The Defective Premises Act 1972

9–043 [*Add at end of paragraph*]

In *Rendlesham Estates Plc v Barr Ltd* [2014] EWHC 3968 (TCC), Edwards-Stuart J. examined a number of important issues arising under the Defective Premises Act 1972 and in the particular context of a building in multiple ownership. He held that a "dwelling" is the place where a person or household lives to the exclusion of members of another household. Thus each apartment in a block of flats, together with its balcony, comprised a dwelling but the common parts were not included. However, the construction of the structural and common parts would amount to "*work . . . in connection with the provision of a dwelling*" within the meaning of s.1 of the Act if those parts were physically or functionally connected with the relevant dwelling (the apartment), especially when the apartment-owner had an obligation under its lease to share the cost of maintenance and repair of the structural and common parts.

9–044 [*Add at end of paragraph*]

The Defective Premises Act 1972 does not impose a duty upon persons who build a dwelling for their own occupation, even if they later sell it on, where the development is not part of a business venture: *Zennstrom v Fagot* [2013] EWHC 288 (TCC).

9–045 [*Add to n.118*]

This finding was not challenged on the appeal in *Harrison v Shepherd Homes Ltd* [2012] EWCA Civ 904.

9–046 [*Add to end of paragraph*]

In *Rendlesham Estates Plc v Barr Ltd* [2014] EWHC 3968 (TCC), Edwards-Stuart J. held that the question of fitness for habitation is to be judged by the standards prevailing at the time when the building was completed. For a dwelling to be fit for habitation within the meaning of the Act, it must on completion be capable of occupation and access via the common parts for a reasonable time without risk to the health or safety of the occupants and without undue inconvenience or discomfort to the occupants. What is a reasonable time will be a question of fact and, depending on the defect, may or may not be as long as the design life of the building. For example, a boiler in a building with a 20-year design life would not be expected to last 20 years; but the structural frame of the building would. Thus a risk of structural failure within the design life of the building may make it unfit for habitation.

[*Add to n.120*]

This finding was not challenged on the appeal in *Harrison v Shepherd Homes Ltd* [2012] EWCA Civ 904.

The Construction (Design and Management) Regulations

[*Add at end of paragraph*] **9–049**

With effect from April 6, 2015, the Construction (Design and Management) Regulations 2015 replaced the 2007 Regulations. The new regulations widen the range of projects affected (and include those which had already begun on April 6, 2015). The role of the CDM co-ordinator is replaced by that of the "principal designer", who must be the designer with control over the pre-construction phase. The principal designer's duties include planning, managing and monitoring the pre-construction phase to ensure that, as far as is reasonable practicable, the project is carried out without risks to health or safety, and coordinating the work of all designers on the project with a view to delivering the project safely. A designer must not start work on a project unless satisfied that the client knows of its duties under the 2015 Regulations, and his duties include preparing a design which, as far as is reasonably practicable, eliminates foreseeable risks to the health and safety of those working on the project, cleaning or maintaining the completed project or using the completed project as a workplace.

(b) *Duties to Third Parties*

Collateral warranties

[*Add at end of paragraph*] **9–061**

Collateral warranties commonly provide that the warrantee shall be treated as if it had been an employer under the professional's appointment and that the professional's liability under the warranty shall be no greater than the liability he could have had under the appointment. Ramsey J. considered the meaning of such a clause in *Oakapple Homes (Glossop) Ltd v DTR (2009) Ltd* [2013] EWHC 2394 (TCC). Architects were obliged under their appointment to execute collateral warranties in favour of the tenants of a building which they had designed. The appointment had been novated to the building contractor. Relying on the "no greater liability" clause, the architects argued that they could rely on the building contractor's breaches to reduce damages payable on a claim by the tenants. The argument failed because the warranty was construed as referring to the pre-novation appointment and, in any event, the contractor's negligence could not be imputed to the tenants even although they were to be treated as joint employers.

[*Add to n.171*]

A collateral warranty may amount to a construction contract for the purposes of adjudication under the Housing Grants, Construction and Regeneration Acts: see para.3–363, below.

(ii) *Recovery by Third Parties in respect of Personal Injury and Damage to "Other Property"*

Personal injury

9–074 [*Add at end of paragraph*]

Foreseeability of harm is not sufficient to establish a duty of care: it remains necessary to satisfy the requirement of proximity or "neighbourhood". In *Harrison v Technical Sign Co Ltd* [2013] EWCA Civ 1569, a building surveyor inspected a shop front on behalf of the landlord and for the limited purpose of investigating the tenant's complaint that the awning had been damaged by the landlord's workmen. Unlike the inspector in *Perrett v Collins* (considered in the main work), the purpose of the building surveyor's involvement was not to protect the safety of passers-by. Accordingly, the Court of Appeal held, the building surveyor owed no duty of care to a passer-by who was injured when the shop's sign fell.

[*Add to n.219*]

Clay v Crump (discussed in the main work) is not authority for the proposition that a professional or a contractor cannot delegate its duty to guard against personal injury arising out of the activity which it has agreed to perform: *Cleightonhills v Bembridge Marine Ltd* [2012] EWHC 3449 (TCC). The duty to warn in respect of a danger arises when there is an obvious and significant danger either to life and limb or to property; it arises when a reasonably careful and competent professional would have appreciated the danger, but probably not when there is a mere possibility of future danger: see *Goldswain v Beltec Ltd (t/a BCS Consulting Ltd)* [2015] EWHC 556 (TCC). The cases in this area all concern a professional's duty to warn as part of his implied contractual duty of care to his client; it is likely that a duty to warn a third party will rarely be found.

9–078 [*Add at end of paragraph*]

The limited purpose of the construction professional's involvement and the relationship between his client and the claimant meant that there was no duty of care to guard against economic loss in *Harrison v Technical Sign Co Ltd* [2013] EWCA Civ 1569. A building surveyor inspected a shop front on behalf of the landlord for the purpose of investigating the tenant's complaint that the awning had been damaged by the landlord's workmen. The Court of Appeal held that the surveyor owed no duty of care to the tenant in respect of loss suffered when the sign fell and a passer-by was injured. The surveyor's instruction by the landlord meant that his relationship with the tenant was adversarial, and it would not have been reasonable for the tenant to rely upon his report. Therefore the surveyor had not assumed responsibility to protect the tenant against loss caused by features of the shop front which were unsafe.

(iv) *The English Exceptions to the Exclusionary Rule*

The Hedley Byrne or reliance principle

[*Add at end of paragraph*] 9–098

In *Hunt v Optima (Cambridge) Ltd* [2013] EWHC 681 (TCC), property consultants engaged by a property developer to carry out periodic inspections of a residential building during construction and to certify that the work had been carried out to a reasonable standard were held to owe a *Hedley Byrne* duty of care to first purchasers of the apartments. Further, the certificates were enforceable as contractual warranties because the purchasers had given consideration for them in entering into the purchase agreements. Finally, the purchasers' reliance on the certificates gave rise to a cause of action against the property consultants for negligent misstatement. The Court of Appeal reversed all three findings: [2014] EWCA Civ 714. It held that the purchasers placed no relevant reliance upon any statement made to them in the certificates, because the certificates were issued only after completion of the purchases. Further, the certificates did not constitute any form of warranty. Finally, any duty of care owed to a third party by a person appointed to certify matters (in this case, the satisfactory construction of a building) arises from the making of statements in a certificate. The certifier does not also owe to those to whom his certificates might later be issued a duty of care in carrying out the work which he does in order to issue the certificate.

[*Add at end of paragraph*] 9–103

In *Sainsbury's Supermarkets Ltd v Condek Holdings Ltd* [2014] EWHC 2016 (TCC) Stuart-Smith J. approved paras 9–102 and 9–103 in the main work. The judge struck out as having no real prospect of success a claim that structural engineers engaged by a building contractor owed a *Hedley Byrne* duty of care to the employer under the building contract.

(v) *The Position in Other Jurisdictions*

New Zealand

[*Delete n.366 after the first sentence and replace it with the following*] 9–118

In *North Shore City Council v Body Corporate 188529* [2010] NZSC 158; [2011] 2 N.Z.L.R. 289 (*Sunset Terraces*) the Supreme Court confirmed the long-standing New Zealand case law that councils owed a duty of care to building owners when inspecting residential buildings. In *Body Corporate No.207624 v North Shore Council* [2012] NZSC 83, the Supreme Court held by a majority that this duty of care is not limited to residential dwellings but applies regardless of the nature of the buildings.

(d) *The Standard of Care and Skill*

(ii) *General Practice and Knowledge as Evidence of the Standard*

9–139 [*Add at end of paragraph*]

Where a multidisciplinary partnership agrees to provide architectural, engineering and quantity surveying services in connection with a building project, it will be necessary to identify into which category each of the services falls and assess performance using the standard of the relevant profession: see *Pickard Finlason Partnership Ltd v Lock* [2014] EWHC 25 (TCC) at [221].

9–139A [*Add new paragraph 9–139A*]

The roles of project manager and party wall surveyor do not represent professions which are recognised as such. Those roles are commonly undertaken by members of the established construction professions. It seems likely that, for example, an architect accepting appointment as a party wall surveyor will be judged by the standards of a reasonably competent architect who has agreed to perform such an appointment. Similarly, in *Middle Level Commissioners v Atkins Ltd* [2012] EWHC 2884, Akenhead J. observed that there is a range of qualifications and/or experience against which the court must seek to judge whether a planning consultant has fallen below the standard to be expected of a reasonably competent planner. The court in that case and in *Elvanite Full Circle Ltd v AMEC Earth & Environmental (UK) Ltd* [2013] EWHC 1191 (TCC) accepted that there was not an established profession of "planning consultant". It is unclear whether, in either case, the court's attention was drawn to the existence of the Royal Town Planners Institute, a chartered institute which seeks to maintain professional standards among planners.

9–142 [*Add to n.427*]

For an example of a category (ii) case involving construction professionals see *Ampleforth Abbey Trust v Turner & Townsend Project Management Ltd* [2012] EWHC 2137 (TCC): the court did not need expert opinion evidence to conclude that project managers were in breach of duty in failing to secure the execution of a building contract and instead allowing a substantial construction project to proceed under letters of intent.

9–145A [*Add new paragraph to text*]

The *Bolam* test does not apply in a case where there is no body of relevant professional opinion. In *199 Knightsbridge Development Ltd v WSP UK Ltd* [2014] EWHC 43 (TCC), the mechanical services engineering profession generally had not identified the risk of catastrophic "water hammer" in a boosted cold water system at the time of the defendant's design. There was no body of professional opinion as to how best to guard against that risk. In that situation, Edwards-Stuart J. held, evidence of general practice in the profession was not highly persuasive. The evidential burden passed to the defendant to show the reasoning behind his design. That reasoning would then be subject to scrutiny by the court, with the assistance of expert evidence, to check whether there was a rational and logical basis for it. On the facts, it was held that a competent engineer in the defendant's position who gave proper consideration to the design process would have foreseen the risk and advised that steps be taken to deal with it. Similarly, if a design professional is in fact aware of a risk which he could design to guard against, it is no defence that the risk has not yet been recognised by his profession generally. An example of this kind of case is *Greenwich Millennium Village Ltd v Essex Services Group Plc* [2013] EWHC 3059 (TCC), where mechanical services engineers were aware of the risk of water hammer and consequent flooding in a boosted cold water system and that measures could be taken which would prevent it. They failed to incorporate such measures in their design for the system. Coulson J. held that the engineers were negligent even although the mechanical services engineering profession generally was not yet aware that such measures could be taken.

(iii) *Expert Evidence*

[Add at end of paragraph] **9–147**

Certainly, while it may be reasonable in some circumstances to plead allegations of professional negligence without supporting expert evidence, if proof of those allegations will require such evidence then a party which continues the claim without it risks the allegations being struck out: see *ACD (Landscape Architects) Ltd v Overall* [2012] EWHC 100 (TCC) and *Whessoe Oil and Gas Ltd v Dale* [2012] EWHC 1788 (TCC).

[Add to n.453] **9–151**

See also *Pickard Finlason Partnership Ltd v Lock* [2014] EWHC 25 (TCC) where the judge criticised both architectural expert witnesses for "descending into the arena and arguing the case for their respective clients".

(ix) *Special Steps and Warranty of Reasonable Fitness*

[Add at end of paragraph] **9–174**

The Court of Appeal in *Platform Funding v Bank of Scotland Plc* [2008] EWCA Civ 930 (discussed at para.2–017) concluded that the "default" obligation of a professional is limited to the exercise of reasonable care and that clear language or special facts are required to impose a stricter obligation. The same approach was applied in *Trebor Bassett Holdings Ltd v ADT Fire and Security Plc* [2012] EWCA Civ 1158, where it was held that a contract to design and supply a bespoke fire suppression system for a particular manufacturing process did not impose an absolute obligation to provide an effective system. A tailor-made system could not be regarded as "goods", so as to attract the statutory requirements of satisfactory quality and fitness for purpose terms implied by the Supply of Goods and Services Act 1982. On the true construction of the contract, the contractor's obligation was merely to exercise reasonable skill and care in the design of the system. Similarly, in *Sweett (UK) Ltd v Michael Wight Homes Ltd* [2012] E.W. Misc. 3 (CC) it was held that a consultant appointed to act as a quantity surveyor and employer's agent did not owe an absolute obligation to ensure that the main contractor entered into a performance bond. The decision in *MT Hojgaard v E.ON Climate & Renewables UK Robin Rigg East Ltd* [2015] EWCA Civ 407 illustrates the importance of correctly construing the contract to determine the standard of care required. A contractor engaged to design and install wind turbines relied in its foundations design upon an international standard. Unknown to the industry, the standard contained a fundamental error. The contract included an express term requiring the contractor to exercise reasonable skill and care in design; but it also included a requirement for foundations with a 20-year service life. The designer's reliance on the standard, albeit consistent with the exercise of due skill and care in design, meant that the foundations did not have the required service life. The Court of Appeal held that, properly construed, the requirement for a 20-year service life was not a guarantee that the foundations would operate for 20 years. Accordingly, the contractor was not liable for the cost of remedial works. It does not follow that express contractual requirements are irrelevant to the question whether a construction professional has complied with his duty to apply reasonable skill and care. In *MW High Tech Projects UK v Haase Environmental Consulting GmbH* [2015] EWHC 152 (TCC), the design consultant's overriding obligation was to design a waste plant using reasonable skill and care and, subject to that, to comply with a specification and delivery plan. Coulson J. granted declarations to the effect that, if it was possible to comply with the specification and delivery plan by way of a non-negligent design, then that was the consultant's obligation; but if it was not possible, then the consultant was not obliged to comply with the specification or delivery plan.

(b) *Costs Estimates and Budgets*

9–200 [*Add at end of paragraph*]

By contrast, in *William Clark Partnership Ltd v Dock St PCT Ltd* [2015] EWHC 2923 (TCC) a claim that quantity surveyors and project managers were negligent in their costs monitoring advice during the construction phase of development succeeded (although the claim failed for want of causation between particular breaches and overspend on the development as a whole).

3. LIABILITY FOR BREACH OF DUTY

(c) *Compliance with Legislation, Planning and Building Control Requirements and Codes of Practice*

9–203 [*Add at end of paragraph*]

Claims that planning consultants were in breach of their obligations to exercise reasonable skill and care failed in *Middle Level Commissioners v Atkins Ltd* [2012] EWHC 2884 (TCC) and in *Elvanite Full Circle Ltd v AMEC Earth & Environmental (UK) Ltd* [2013] EWHC 1191 (TCC).

(d) *Design and Specification*

[*Add at end of paragraph*] **9–204**

A professional who has undertaken design obligations must make sure that it has a detailed understanding of the extent of those obligations. In *National Museums and Galleries on Merseyside Board of Trustees v AEW Architects and Designers Ltd (No.1)* [2013] EWHC 2403 (TCC), the defendant architects mistakenly supposed that it was the building contractor's responsibility to design elements of the new Museum of Liverpool when, in fact, it was their own.

Assessment of risk

[*Add to note 594*] **9–208**

In *Goldswain v Beltec Ltd (t/a BCS Consulting Ltd)* [2015] EWHC 556 (TCC), structural engineers engaged to design basement underpinning avoided liability for the collapse of the building because their design was capable of construction by a competent contractor without threat to the stability of the building.

Buildability

[*Add to n.622*] **9–217**

In *Pickard Finlason Partnership Ltd v Lock* [2014] EWHC 25 (TCC) at [198], it was said that a designer must consider not only technical buildability (i.e. whether a design is capable of being constructed from a technical engineering perspective) but also practical buildability (i.e. whether its construction would be too risky, difficult, expensive or time-consuming). See also *Goldswain v Beltec Ltd (t/a BCS Consulting Ltd)* [2015] EWHC 556 (TCC) (structural engineering design for basement underpinning was capable of being constructed by a competent contractor using appropriate propping, which was part of the temporary works for whose design the contractor was responsible).

Coordination of Design

[*Add at end of paragraph*] **9–219**

A design professional needs to understand where his own design responsibilities start and end and to coordinate his design with those of specialist subcontractors with design responsibility. *Board of Trustees of National Museums and Galleries on Merseyside v AEW Architects & Designers Ltd (No.1)* [2013] EWHC 2403 (TCC) concerned the construction of a landmark museum in Liverpool. The architect wrongly assumed that the design of steps, seats and terraces were entirely the responsibility of the specialist reinforced concrete subcontractor, whereas they were architectural features and within the architect's contractual sphere of design responsibility; and in any event it was the architect's duty to provide the requisite design criteria (including the design life of the building) to which the subcontractor would work in designing the reinforcement detailing and placing. Furthermore, the architect failed competently to discharge its design coordination responsibilities by failing to appreciate that the safe and secure installation of ceiling tiles would be prevented by elements of the lighting design.

(g) *Advice on Choice and Terms of a Building Contract*

9–229 [*Add at end of paragraph*]

Failure to attend to the formalities of agreeing a building contract may also lead to liability for a construction professional. In *Ampleforth Abbey Trust v Turner & Townsend Project Management Ltd* [2012] EWHC 2137 (TCC), project managers were in breach of duty in failing to procure an executed building contract and instead allowing substantial construction works to proceed on the basis of letters of intent. They were liable for loss suffered because their client lacked the protections against contractor's claims offered by a standard form building contract.

(h) *Administration of the Building Contract*

9–238 [*Add at end of paragraph*]

In *Walter Lilly & Co Ltd v Mackay* [2012] EWHC 1773 (TCC), Akenhead J. concluded that it was not open to a contract administrator operating a JCT Standard Form of Building Contract under the law of England and Wales to apportion responsibility for concurrent delays in accordance with the approach outlined in *City Inn Ltd v Shepherd Construction Ltd* (discussed in the main work).

(i) *Supervision or Inspection of the Works*

Confidence in the contractor

9–249 [*Add to end of paragraph*]

In *Goldswain v Beltec Ltd (t/a BCS Consulting Ltd)* [2015] EWHC 556 (TCC), Akenhead J. observed obiter that the scope of the duty of a professional retained to supervise or inspect building works may well involve a consideration of how safely the works are being carried out by the contractor.

The contractor's method of working

[*Add to note 719*]

9–253 The particular terms of a construction professional's engagement may require him to assess the contractor's safety precautions: in *Goldswain v Beltec Ltd (t/a BCS Consulting Ltd)* [2015] EWHC 556 (TCC), Akenhead J. observed obiter that the scope of the duty of a professional retained to supervise or inspect building works may well involve a consideration of how safely the works are being carried out by the contractor.

(j) *Certification*

[*Add at end of paragraph*] **9–259**

In *National Museums and Galleries on Merseyside Board of Trustees v AEW Architects and Designers Ltd (No.1)* [2013] EWHC 2403 (TCC), Akenhead J. rejected the submission that a competent inspecting architect might miss even obvious defects in a high ceiling. An architect with a responsibility to inspect with reasonable skill and care must put himself in a position (physically) where he can inspect, even if that means using a scaffold tower or ladder, or binoculars.

[*Add n.735a*]

For discussion of the meaning of "practical completion" in various contracts, see *Westminster Corporation v J Jarvis & Sons Ltd* [1970] 1 WLR 637, *Menolly Investments 3 Sral v Serep Sarl* [2009] EWHC 516 (Ch) and *Elmbid Ltd v Burgess* [2013] EWHC 1489 (Ch).

[*Add at end of paragraph*] **9–260**

In *Scheldebouw BV v St James Homes (Grosvenor Dock) Ltd* [2006] EWHC 89 (TCC) at [35], Jackson J. distilled from the authorities the following three principles as to the role of a professional engaged to perform the various roles involved in the administration of a building contract (the "decision-maker"):

> "(1) The precise role and duties of the decision-maker will be determined by the terms of the contract under which he is required to act. (2) Generally the decision-maker is not, and cannot be regarded as, independent of the employer. (3) When performing his decision-making function, the decision-maker is required to act in a manner which has variously been described as independent, impartial, fair and honest. These concepts are overlapping but not synonymous. They connote that the decision-maker must use his professional skills and his best endeavours to reach the right decision, as opposed to a decision which favours the interests of the employer."

4. DAMAGES

(a) *The Scope of the Duty*

[*Add at end of paragraph*] **9–274**

In *ACD (Landscape Architects) Ltd v Overall* [2012] EWHC 100 (TCC), an architect was engaged to make a planning application for a limited development with a view to establishing the principle that development of the land was acceptable: the clients intended to seek permission for a wider development if the first application were granted. It was held that losses referable to lack of the wider permission were outside the scope of the architect's duty under its engagement to seek the limited permission.

9–276 [*Add to end of paragraph*]

By contrast, the Court of Appeal in *John Grimes Partnership Ltd v Gubbins* [2013] EWCA Civ 37 readily held that a consulting engineer who delayed in completing design work was liable for losses attributable to downward movement in property values. The engineer knew (and anyway could reasonably foresee) that delay on his part would delay completion of the development and so cause the developer loss if the property market fell in the interim. There was nothing in his contract of engagement, nor was there any general understanding or expectation in the property world, which indicated that the engineer had not assumed responsibility for such losses. The case is discussed at [2013] PN 128.

(b) *Remoteness*

(i) *Causation*

Advice to the claimant

9–279 [*Add at end of paragraph*]

Similarly, in *199 Knightsbridge Development Ltd v WSP UK Ltd* [2014] EWHC 43 (TCC), the claimant called no evidence to show that, had it been properly advised by the defendant mechanical services engineers, it would have taken (or taken in time) the steps necessary to prevent flooding of its premises. Accordingly, its claim failed on causation. It was significant that the claimant did not take the relevant measures even after the flooding and offered no evidence to explain why it did not do so.

Concurrent causes

9–283A [*Add new paragraph to text*]

Where each of two concurrent causes was sufficient to cause the loss and those causes operated independently of each other, the "but for" test of causation is unhelpful. That test would allow the author of each cause to avoid liability on the basis that the loss would have been suffered in any event, and lead to the absurd conclusion that neither cause was effective. In such cases, the court may depart from the "but for" test and regard the causes as equally efficacious. In *Greenwich Millennium Village Ltd v Essex Services Group Plc* [2013] EWHC 3059 (TCC), Coulson J. adopted that approach in holding that each of two separate workmanship defects was sufficient to cause the flooding in an apartment block.

Intervening act of a third party

9–287 [*Add to n.816*]

See also *Flanagan v Greenbanks Ltd* [2013] EWCA Civ 1702 (a thermal insulation company's negligent failure to establish that houses were suitable for installation did not break the chain of causation from a surveyor's prior negligence in failing to identify that the houses were unsuitable).

Intervening act of the claimant

[*Add to n.822*] **9–289**

The finding that the claimant's failures to guard against fire and to deal with fire when it occurred did not break the chain of causation from a poorly designed fire suppression system was upheld on appeal in *Trebor Bassett Holdings Ltd v ADT Fire and Security Plc* [2012] EWCA Civ 1158. A submission that the conduct or decisions of the claimant broke the chain of causation failed, similarly, in *Harrison v Technical Sign Company Ltd* [2012] EWHC 2887 (TCC) and in *Howmet Ltd v Economy Devices Ltd* [2014] EWHC 3993 (TCC); but succeeded (obiter) in *Elvanite Full Circle Ltd v AMEC Earth & Environmental (UK) Ltd* [2013] EWHC 1191 (TCC).

[*Add to n.823*]

For an example of such a response in an emergency, see *Trebor Bassett Holdings Ltd v ADT Fire and Security Plc* [2012] EWCA Civ 1158.

[*Add to n.825*]

These findings survived on appeal: [2012] EWCA Civ 1158.

(ii) *Foreseeability*

[*Add at end of paragraph*] **9–293**

That the risk in question was not generally foreseen by the relevant profession may assist a defence of "no foreseeability" but it is not conclusive. The defence failed in *199 Knightsbridge Development Ltd v WSP UK Ltd* [2014] EWHC 43 (TCC): the mechanical services engineering profession generally had not identified the risk of catastrophic "water hammer" in a boosted cold water system at the time of the defendant's design, but a competent engineer in the defendant's position who properly thought through the design process would have foreseen that risk.

(c) *The Measure of Damages*

[*Add to n.844*] **9–297**

Note that the Late Payment of Commercial Debts (Interest) Act 1998 does not apply to an award of common law damages arising for breach of contract through failure to exercise reasonable care and skill: *Board of Trustees of National Museums and Galleries on Merseyside v AEW Architects & Designers Ltd (No.3)* [2013] EWHC 3025 (TCC).

[*Add at end of paragraph*] **9–300**

Damages for loss of a chance were awarded in *Ampleforth Abbey Trust v Turner & Townsend Project Management Ltd* [2012] EWHC 2137 (TCC). In breach of duty, the defendant project managers failed to procure an executed standard form building contract and instead allowed substantial construction works to proceed on the basis of letters of intent. The works were completed late and a dispute arose between the claimant and the building contractor. Had a contract been executed, it would have entitled the claimant to recover liquidated damages from the contractor in respect of its delay. The claimant recovered damages for its lost opportunity to settle the dispute with the benefit of that entitlement.

(d) *Heads of Damage*

(i) *Costs of Rectification*

9–306 [*Add to n.873*]

The Court of Appeal upheld the manner in which the judge assessed damages for diminution in value, and held that his additional award for the costs of immediate and future minor repairs was not double recovery because the need for such repair had been excluded in the assessment of diminution in value: see *Harrison v Shepherd Homes Ltd* [2012] EWCA Civ 904.

9–312 [*Add at end of paragraph*]

The same principles were applied to determine the measure of damages in *West v Ian Finlay and Associates* [2014] EWCA Civ 316. The need for remedial works was a foreseeable result of the defendant architect's breach of duty, but disagreement between the claimants' advisers as to the correct approach to those works, which caused delay and additional expense, was not. Edwards-Stuart J. awarded half of the costs attributable to the delay to the claimants. This part of the decision was not a subject of the appeal at [2014] EWCA Civ 316.

[*Add to n.899*]

Compare the analysis in *Board of Trustees of National Museums and Galleries on Merseyside v AEW Architects & Designers Ltd (No.1)* [2013] EWHC 2403 (TCC) at [99] (claimant entitled to recover cost of second leakproof membrane because remedial works necessitated by designer's negligence created an inevitable risk of damage to the existing membrane).

(ii) *Diminution in Value*

9–314 [*Add at end of paragraph*]

There is a rebuttable presumption that the cost of repair of a damaged chattel represents its diminution in value; further, events which occur after the damage are irrelevant: see *Waterdance Ltd v Kingston Marine Services* [2014] EWHC 224 (TCC). For example, a fire which occurs after the damage and prevents repairs being carried out will not reduce the amount recoverable for diminution in value. However, where the value of property at the date of diminution in value depends upon the outcome of a future contingency, the court may take into account its knowledge of how that contingency turned out in assessing the diminution in value: see *Ageas (UK) Ltd v Kwik-Fit (GB) Ltd* [2014] EWHC 2178 (QB).

[*Add at end of paragraph*] **9–315**

Similarly, a principal award of damages for diminution in capital value may be supplemented on appropriate facts by an award of damages for the costs of repairs, provided that diminution of value is assessed in a way which ignores the need for repair so that there is no element of double recovery: *Harrison v Shepherd Homes Ltd* [2012] EWCA Civ 904.

(iv) *Excess Expenditure*

[*Add at end of paragraph*] **9–317**

Although an employer is entitled to claim excess expenditure on a "global" basis, by comparing the development's actual cost with what it ought to have cost, he must still show that the defendant's breaches of duty caused the overspend. Failure to do so in circumstances where there are other potential explanations for the excess expenditure (such as legitimate variations to the works) will mean that no recovery is made: see for example *William Clark Partnership Ltd v Dock St PCT Ltd* [2015] EWHC 2923 (TCC).

(vi) *Consequential Losses*

[*Add to n.924*] **9–322**

On the evidence, the court was willing to infer an equivalence between diverted staff time and lost revenue in *National Museums and Galleries on Merseyside Board of Trustees v AEW Architects and Designers Ltd (No.1)* [2013] EWHC 2403 (TCC). Akenhead J. reviewed the authorities applying *Aerospace Publishing Ltd v Thames Water Utilities Ltd* (referred to in the main work) and awarded the claimant its payroll costs for reasonable time spent dealing with the consequences of the defendant's negligence.

(vii) *Liability to Third Parties*

[*Add at end of paragraph*] **9–323**

Where the claimant's liability to a third party has not been ascertained by the time of trial, the court has three options: it may make a very broad damages assessment in relation to that head of loss, it may postpone assessment until further information is available or it may grant a declaration that the defendant is to indemnify the claimant against its liability once ascertained. Having identified those options, Akenhead J. chose the latter in *Board of Trustees of National Museums and Galleries on Merseyside v AEW Architects & Designers Ltd (No.1)* [2013] EWHC 2403 (TCC) at [111]–[118], where the claimant employer's liability to a building contractor for delay related losses caused ultimately by the defendant architect's breaches remained to be determined in an arbitration between the claimant and the contractor. In the same case, at [124]–[130], the judge held that the claimant's costs of defending certain claims referred by the contractor to adjudication were recoverable as damages from the architect. But for the architect's failure to acknowledge its design responsibility, the claimant would not have defended the contractor's claims. The judge commented that construction adjudication is well-established; it was reasonably foreseeable by the architects that the contractor would press its case on design responsibility (which case the court in this judgment upheld) via adjudication. Similarly, in a subsequent judgment dealing with further quantum issues, the claimant was awarded a declaration that the defendant architect should indemnify it against any liability it might have to a person injured by the defective works: *Board of Trustees of National Museums and Galleries on Merseyside v AEW Architects & Designers Ltd (No.2)* [2013] EWHC 2576 (TCC) at [60].

(ix) *Inconvenience, Distress and Loss of Amenity*

9–327 [*Add to n.940*]

This finding was not challenged on the appeal in *Harrison v Shepherd Homes Ltd* [2012] EWCA Civ 904.

[*Add to note 941*]

See also *West v Ian Finlay and Associates* [2014] EWCA Civ 316 (sums of £7,000, £5,000 and £2,000 awarded to different family members for just under two years' physical inconvenience and consequent distress were reduced on appeal to £2,000, £1,500 and £500); and *Rendlesham Estates Plc v Barr Ltd* [2014] EWHC 3968 (TCC) (in a claim under the Defective Premises Act 1972, occupiers of a block of apartments recovered general damages for distress and inconvenience of £750 per annum for a non-functioning intercom system and walkways subject to ponding of water, rising to £2,250 per annum where the occupier also suffered damp and mould inside his apartment).

(f) *Abatement of Fees*

9–332 [*Add at end of paragraph*]

That abatement is not available as a defence to a claim for professional fees was confirmed in *Pickard Finlason Partnership Ltd v Lock* [2014] EWHC 25 (TCC); however in *William Clark Partnership Ltd v Dock St PCT Ltd* [2015] EWHC 2923 (TCC) the same judge pointed out that this does not prevent a client being relieved of the obligation to pay fees for a service which was not performed at all or was performed so poorly as to be worthless.

5. SHARED RESPONSIBILITY

(a) *Apportionment of Liability*

9–334 [*Add new para.9–334A after para.9–334*]

9–334A Section 1(3) of the 1978 Act states that a person remains liable to make contribution in respect of the claimant's damage even although he ceased to be liable to the claimant before the contribution proceedings began, except where he ceased to be liable because of the expiry of a period of limitation which extinguished the right of action against him. The expiry of most limitation periods imposed by the Limitation Act 1980 does not extinguish the right of action, so that it is normally irrelevant to D1's contribution claim that C's claim against D2 is statute-barred. Contracts of appointment of construction professionals and collateral warranties given by professionals often include a clause which sets a time limit after which no claim against the professional may be brought, such as "No proceedings shall be commenced against the Consultant after the expiry of twelve years from the date of practical completion of the Project." In *Blomberg LP v Sandberg and Buro Happold Ltd* [2015] EWHC 2858 (TCC), Fraser J. considered whether a contractual limitation clause of this kind had the effect of extinguishing the right of action. The defendant professionals and a subcontractor had all given collateral warranties to the tenant of a development which they had been involved in building. When the professionals claimed contribution from the subcontractor, it argued that this clause in the collateral warranty which it had given to the claimant meant that the defendants' contribution claims were out of time. Fraser J rejected the subcontractor's argument. The clause imposed a merely procedural bar upon claims by the tenant. It did not extinguish the tenant's right of action against the subcontractor. Accordingly, under s.1(3), the subcontractor remained a person potentially liable for contribution in respect of the tenant's damage.

[*Add new footnote reference 974a after second sentence*] **9–348**

NOTE 974a. An example of a case where the designer's responsibility was significantly greater than the contractor's was *Board of Trustees of National Museums and Galleries on Merseyside v AEW Architects & Designers Ltd (No.1)* [2013] EWHC 2403 (TCC) (75 per cent liability apportioned to architect, 25 per cent to contractor).

6. ADJUDICATION

Construction contracts

[*Add to n.1009*] **9–363**

In *Parkwood Leisure Ltd v Laing O'Rourke Wales & West Ltd* [2013] EWHC 2665 (TCC), it was held that a collateral warranty given by a contractor (to the effect that it had carried out, and would carry out and complete, certain construction works in accordance with a building contract) amounted to a construction contract within the meaning of s.104(1) of the 1996 Act.

[*Add to n.1011*] **9–364**

In *Sprunt Ltd v London Borough of Camden* [2011] EWHC 3191 (TCC), Akenhead J. held that a construction contract was an agreement in writing within the meaning of the 1996 Act since it had been recorded in a letter and had been accepted by the parties' subsequent conduct. For a consideration of whether an allegation in a referral notice concerning the existence of an agreement made otherwise in writing was sufficient to satisfy the requirements of the 1996 Act, see *Glendalough Associated SA v Harris Calnan Construction Co Ltd* [2013] EWHC 3142 (TCC).

Enforcement of adjudicator's decisions

9–368 [*Delete the last sentence of n.1020 and replace it with the following*]

The Supreme Court has decided that a party who has made a payment pursuant to the decision of an adjudicator has a right, arising at the time of the payment, to have the dispute finally determined, and is entitled to six years from the date of payment to commence proceedings: *Aspect Contracts (Asbestos) Ltd v Higgins Construction Plc* [2015] UKSC 38.

[*Add to n.1021*]

Thameside Construction Co Ltd v (1) J Stevens (2) JL Stevens [2013] EWHC 2071 (TCC) provides a useful summary of the case law concerning a losing party's right to set off other claims against sums payable pursuant to an adjudicator's decision.

Challenging the adjudicator's decision

9–371 [*Add at end of paragraph*]

For two examples of the court severing parts of an adjudicator's decision but allowing the balance to be enforced see *Working Environments Ltd v Greencoat Construction Ltd* [2012] EWHC 1039 (TCC) and *Beck Interiors Ltd v UK Flooring Contractors Ltd* [2012] EWHC 1808 (TCC).

The adjudicator's jurisdiction

9–373 [*Add to n.1033*]

In *Beck Interiors Ltd v UK Flooring Contractors Ltd* [2012] EWHC 1808 (TCC), Akenhead J. held that a recipient's silence during a five-day period from the time that a claim was put forward to a notice of an intention to refer to adjudication would usually be sufficient to give rise to an inference that the claim was disputed, particularly in circumstances where there had been previous claims which had been disputed. On the facts of that case, however, as the five-day period included a four-day holiday weekend, the gap of one working day was not sufficient to infer that a dispute had crystallised.

[*Add to n.1036*]

For consideration of the term "construction operations", see *(1) Savoye (2) Savoye Ltd v Spicers Ltd* [2014] EWHC 4195 (TCC).

[*Add to n.1039*]

KNN Colburn LLP v GD City Holdings Ltd [2013] EWHC 2879 (TCC) provides a reminder of the need for objections to adjudication timetables to be made without delay: a failure to object could affect any future enforcement challenge based on late delivery of a decision.

[*Add to n.1040*]

For a list of factors to be considered by the court when deciding whether the same or substantially the same dispute has been referred to or resolved in an earlier adjudication see *Carillion Construction Ltd v Stephen Andrew Smith* [2011] EWHC 2910 (TCC).

[*Add to n.1042*] **9–374**

In *Eurocom Ltd v Siemens Plc* [2014] EWHC 3710 (TCC), summary judgment to enforce an adjudicator's decision was refused as the nomination of the adjudicator was invalid, the respondent having established a strong prima facie case of fraudulent misrepresentation on the part of those acting on behalf of the applicant when making the application for the appointment of an adjudicator.

Natural justice

[*Add to n.1044*] **9–375**

In *PC Harrington Contractors Ltd v Systech International Ltd* [2012] EWCA Civ 1371, the Court of Appeal held that the adjudicator involved in *PC Harrington Contractors Ltd v Tyroddy Construction Ltd* [2011] EWHC 813 (TCC) was not entitled to his fees as his unenforceable decision was of no value to either party.

[*Add to n.147*]

A fair-minded observer would conclude that an adjudicator had been biased as a result of his failure to disclose that one party had telephoned his office two months prior to the referral and had a lengthy discussion about the dispute (including previous adjudications with which he had been involved) with his office manager: *(1) G Paice (2) Kim Springhall v MJ Harding (T/A M J Harding Contractors)* [2015] EWHC 661 (TCC).

[*Add to n.1050*] **9–376**

Contrast *Berry Piling Systems Ltd v Sheer Projects Ltd* [2012] EWHC 241 (TCC) (in which it was held that as a point made by the adjudicator but not raised with the parties before its inclusion in his decision had not made a material difference to the outcome of the decision, there had been no material breach of natural justice) with *Herbosh-Kiere Marine Contractors Ltd v Dover Harbour Board* [2012] EWHC 84 (TCC) (in which it was held that the adjudicator's decision would not be enforced on grounds including that there had been a material breach of the rules of natural justice. The adjudicator had decided the case on a basis not argued by either party which made a very real difference to quantum, and had not given each party the opportunity to make submissions on his intended method of assessment.) For further examples of failed attempts to challenge enforcement based on allegations of breaches of the rules of natural justice see: *Lidl UK GmbH v RG Carter Colchester Ltd* [2012] EWHC 3138 (TCC); *Arcadis UK Ltd v May & Baker Ltd (t/a Sanofi)* [2013] EWHC 87 (TCC); *Farrelly (M&E) Building Services Ltd v Byrne Brothers (Formwork) Ltd* [2013] EWHC 1186 (TCC), and *CG Group Ltd v Breyer Group Plc* [2013] EWHC 2722 (TCC). A successful challenge was, however, made in *ABB Ltd v BAM Nuttall Ltd* [2013] EWHC 1983 (TCC): it was held that there had been a serious breach of the rules of natural justice when an adjudicator decided an issue by reference to a clause in a sub-contract which had neither been relied upon nor referred to by either party, and on which neither party had been given an opportunity to address the adjudicator.

The Human Rights Act 1998

9–377 [*Add to n.1055*]

The Scots Court of Session (Outer House) refused to enforce the adjudicator's decision in *Whyte and Mackay Ltd v Blyth & Blyth Consulting Engineers Ltd* [2013] ScotCS CSOH 54 (concerning the design of foundations at a bottling plant and allegations of professional negligence). It did so because of a breach of natural justice (the adjudicator's failure to address a key defence). Enforcement was also refused on the grounds that it would violate the Convention, as there was no general or public interest served by the pursuers taking the dispute to adjudication, particularly as the bulk of the claimed losses would not occur for several years.

Impecuniosity

9–378 [*Add to n.1057*]

Herschel [2000] B.L.R. 272 was applied in *Nap Anglia Ltd v Sun-Land Development Co Ltd* [2011] EWHC 2846 (TCC).

[*Add to n.1059*]

For an application of the principle identified in *Wimbledon Construction* that a stay of execution will not usually be granted on the basis of the claimant's financial position if this is the same or similar to its financial position at the time that the contract was made see *Westshield Civil Engineering Ltd and Westshield Ltd v Buckingham Group Contracting Ltd* [2013] EWHC 1825 (TCC). A stay of execution was granted in *FG Skerritt Ltd v Caledonian Building Systems Ltd* [2013] EWHC 1898 (TCC) as a result of the claimant's insolvency and the defendant's grounds for an equitable set-off against the sums due to the claimant. The stay would be lifted if an appropriate guarantee was provided by the claimant's parent company.

In *Alexander & Law Ltd v Coveside (21 BPR) Ltd* [2013] EWHC 3949 (TCC) the existence of a winding-up petition did not defeat a summary judgment application. In *Maguire & Co v Mar City Developments* [2013] EWHC 3503 (TCC), Edwards-Stuart J. ordered an interim stay of enforcement of the judgment sum in excess of a specified amount, holding that a fairly cautious approach should be adopted in cases concerning potential insolvency of the receiving company. For an example of a case in which the high hurdles set in *Wimbledon Construction* were overcome, resulting in a defendant obtaining a stay of execution, see *Pioneer Cladding Ltd v John Graham Construction Ltd* [2013] EWHC 2954 (TCC).

Chapter 10

SURVEYORS

1. General

10–008 [*Add to end of para:*]

In *Titan Europe 2006-3 PLC v Colliers International Plc* [2014] EWHC 3106 (Comm), Blair J. considered a challenge which each side made to the other's expert valuer. The case concerned the valuation of commercial property in Germany where the claimant called an expert with no valuation experience in that country whilst the defendant called a man with considerable expertise but where a similar valuation by the expert was under attack by the same claimant. The Judge rejected both attacks although considered that both could go to the weight which could be attached to the respective evidence. The Judge was particularly critical of the failure of the expert called by the defendant to disclose that a relevant valuation of his own was said to be negligent. On appeal, [2015] EWCA Civ 1083, the Court of Appeal over-turned the Judge's finding as to liability, but held that the Judge's treatment of the criticisms was "impossible to criticise".

(a) *Bases of Liability*

10–017 [*Add to end of para:*]

The basis of liability for an individual surveyor was considered by H.H. Judge Seymour Q.C. in *Summit Advances Ltd v Bush* [2015] EWHC 665 (QB); [2015] P.N.L.R. 18 where the Judge struck out a claim by a lender against an individual valuer employed by an LLP. The Judge held, following the guidance issued by the House of Lords in *Williams v Natural Life* [1998] 1 W.L.R. 830 that there was no basis for finding that the individual had assumed responsibility to the lender. Although the valuer had signed the report personally, he had done so on behalf of the LLP and there were numerous references throughout the report showing that the report was not a personal document. The Judge referred only briefly to the decision of the Court of Appeal in *Merrett v Babb* in finding that the decision was of limited application.

(b) *Duties to Client*

(i) *Contractual Duties*

[*Add new paragraph to text*] **10–023A**

It is, of course, possible for a surveyor to assume contractual obligations to a person who is not, originally, his client. However clear words will be necessary in order to support the existence of such contractual obligations. In *Hunt v Optima* [2014] EWCA Civ 714, the Court of Appeal considered a case where a firm of surveyors had been hired by a developer to carry out inspections of flats in the course of development and to produce certificates for the benefit of potential purchasers and lenders. The certificates were described as such and stated that the relevant flats had been inspected, and insofar as could be determined by visual inspection, the properties had been properly constructed; and acknowledged that reliance would be placed by the first purchaser. The trial Judge found that these certificates amounted to contractually enforceable warranties in the hands of purchasers but the Court of Appeal rejected this conclusion holding that appropriate contractual language had not been used. The position would almost certainly have been different if the certificates had been described as warranties or guarantees and language appropriate to promises rather than representations had been used.

[*Add at end of paragraph*] **10–024**

An interesting example of the way in which the Court will approach resolution of a valuer's contractual duty is provided by the decision of Coulson J. in *Webb Resolutions v E. Surv Ltd* [2012] EWHC 3653 (TCC); [2013] P.N.L.R. 253. The Claimant lender required both compliance with RICS standards and that all information be provided on its "tick-box" forms which had no provision for further information to be provided. The Claimant's guidance notes warned that any additional information would not be read by its underwriters. The Judge concluded that if a valuer could not fulfil his duties without the provision of additional information, he had to provide it even if it was unlikely to be read. On the other hand, if he would, in ordinary circumstances, have provided elaboration but properly felt that, given his instructions, such elaboration was not required, the lender could scarcely complain if such elaboration were not provided.

[*Add new paragraph to text*] **10–027A**

In *Platform Funding Ltd v Anderson & Associates Ltd* [2012] EWHC 1853, H. H. Judge Thornton QC considered an unusual case where an entire development had been subverted in South East London. The original developer and builder had sold all the flats in one block to an intermediary. There had then been "sales" of flats purportedly by the original developer but in fact by the intermediary. The purchase of the flats by the intermediary had been purchased by the proceeds of sub-sales which were obtained with the assistance of mortgages granted to purchasers who were never intended to be genuine. There had been necessary, dishonest, involvement by the solicitors purportedly acting for the lender and the original seller but, in truth, acting at all times in the interests of the intermediary.

When a valuer sought to value a flat he was given "comparable" evidence which was, in fact, wholly contrived. The Judge rejected the claim against the valuer holding that the valuation had been required to be undertaken with the relevant Practice Standards. These Standards specifically required a willing buyer and seller and excluded an estimated price inflated or deflated by special terms or circumstances. The Judge found that although the valuer had poor valuation skills and did not, apparently, undertake proper enquiries, there was no readily available way of ascertaining the true value of the property at the valuation date. The valuer had not been retained to value a flat which was not being sold on the open market and where comparable evidence had been dishonestly inflated. It followed that the entire loss suffered by the lender was caused by a combination of the dishonesty of the intermediary; the way in which the conveyancing had been undertaken for the exclusive benefit of the intermediary and the apparent collusion of the original vendor in the marketing of the flats.

10–028A [*Add a new paragraph*]

The precise nature of instructions will be particularly relevant where the Court has to consider liability for failing to carry out proper monitoring of a project. In *Bank of Ireland v Faithful & Gould Ltd* [2014] EWHC 2217 (TCC); [2014] P.N.L.R. 28, a project monitor made a claim for contribution against a valuer. The project monitor had settled a claim brought by a lender but its own liability was relevant to the extent of contribution. The developer was seeking finance in relation to substantial sums for off-site materials which were said to be required for the project. The applications for payment which the monitor was required to approve had to be supported by a detailed list of materials together with a certificate vesting title in the lender. In fact no detailed list of materials was supplied and the certificate was defective in that it was not in the approved form and did not vest any title. The Judge had no difficulty in finding that the project monitor had, accordingly, failed to fulfil its instructions.

(c) *Duties to Third Parties*

(i) *General Principles*

10–038 [*Add at end of paragraph*]

A rare example of a case where a surveyor sought to be made liable for personal injury was considered by the Court of Appeal in *Harrison v Technical Sign Co Ltd* [2014] P.N.L.R. 15 where a surveyor had been instructed by a landlord to inspect the awning of a shop in Putney as a result of a tenant claiming that the landlord was liable to repair it. The awning subsequently collapsed and members of the public sued the tenants of the shop. The Court of Appeal rejected the suggestion that a duty of care was owed in such circumstances relying particularly on the lack of proximity of the surveyors to the Claimants and the fact that the surveyor had been instructed by the landlord who was in an adversarial relationship with the tenant. It is respectively suggested that such reasoning may not be sufficient in the case of physical injury if a professional person realises that something is dangerous. If a professional person realises or should realise that physical injury will occur, the policy considerations behind imposing liability are substantially greater than those for imposing liability for economic loss. Many professional bodies recognise duties on persons to do what they can to avoid physical injury to persons if they appreciate something is dangerous. On the facts the Court of Appeal also found that the surveyor was not negligent so it necessarily follows that the basis of a finding that the awning was dangerous was not present.

[Add new paragraph to text] **10–038A**

In *Hunt v Optima* [2014] EWCA Civ 714 (for facts, see para.10–023A, above), the Court of Appeal rejected a contention that the carrying out of inspections in the knowledge that certificates would be given to subsequent purchasers meant that surveyors owed duties to those purchasers not merely in relation to the giving of the certificates but also in the carrying out of the inspections. Tomlinson L.J. emphasised that the postulated duty arose from the certificates which the surveyor issued. Those certificates could give rise to a tortious claim for negligent misstatement but there was no separate duty in relation to the inspections themselves. Thus if a surveyor negligently carried out an inspection and subsequently realised this and so issued no certificate (or qualified it appropriately) he would not be in breach of duty to a subsequent purchaser.

(d) *The Standard of Care and Skill*

(i) *Reasonable Standard*

[*Add to n.221*] **10–056**

In *Webb Resolutions v E. Surv Ltd* [2012] EWHC 3653 (TCC); [2013] P.N.L.R. 253, Coulson J. rejected submissions that express requirements within a valuer's contract to provide a prudent valuation expanded the scope of a valuer's duty. He also rejected a submission that a valuation should have been provided on the basis of an assumed re-sale simply because the valuer knew that the lender would be seeking to re-sell in the event of a default. Absent special instructions, the valuer's job was to value the property being purchased at the time of the purchase.

(ii) *General Practice and Knowledge as Evidence of the Standard*

[*Add at end of paragraph*] **10–062**

In *Phimister v DM Hall LLP* [2012] CSOH 169; [2013] P.N.L.R. 95, Lord Glennie rejected a claim by a purchaser against a value instructed to provide a residential mortgage application that he had wrongly failed to point out that a property only had an area of about 0.6 acres rather than the 1.16 acres advertised on sale particulars. There was no suggestion that the property was not worth the amount of the valuation and the Judge found that there was no obligation imposed to measure the property when carrying out such a valuation.

(iv) *The Relevance of "the bracket"*

10–066 [*Add at end of paragraph*]

In *Paratus AMC Ltd v Countrywide Surveyors Ltd* [2011] EWHC 3307 (Ch); [2012] P.N.L.R. 12, H H Judge Keyser QC found that a bracket of eight per cent was applicable to the valuation of a residential flat bought in a rising market. The factors which the Judge expressly took into account in arriving at this bracket included the lack of consistency amongst available comparable sales; the buoyancy of the market and the particular circumstances whereby a "glut" of desirable properties had disappeared at the time of valuation. The Judge also recorded evidence showing that there was uncertainty as to the true earlier purchaser price of the property in question making any valuation based upon the application of indices inherently uncertain. On the facts, the Defendant's valuation was within the applicable margin and, accordingly, not negligent. In *Webb Resolutions v E. Surv Ltd* [2012] EWHC 3653 (TCC); [2013] P.N.L.R. 253, Coulson J. reiterated his earlier conclusions in *K/S Lincoln v CB Richard Ellis Hotels Ltd* [2010] EWHC 1156, summarised in para.10–065 above. In *Bank of Ireland v Faithful & Gould Ltd* [2014] EWHC 2217 (TCC); [2014] P.N.L.R. 28, Edwards-Stuart J. considered a claim for contribution by a project monitor against a valuer in relation to negligent valuations of a development site and the gross development value of the site. The experts on either side had contended for a "bracket" of either +/– 15 per cent or +/– 10 per cent but this, in the event, became irrelevant when the valuer's expert accepted that the valuation fell outside even the wider bracket.

In *Titan Europe 2006-3 Plc v Colliers International Plc* [2015] EWCA Civ 1083, the Court of Appeal considered a case concerning the valuation of a very substantial commercial property in Germany. Although the Court over-turned the Judge's finding as to the true value of the property (with the consequence that the valuer was not liable), there was no challenge to the finding that the appropriate "bracket" was 15 per cent either side of such correct figure.

2. LIABILITY FOR BREACH OF DUTY

(c) *Failing to Inspect Properly*

10–086 [*Add new footnote reference 378a at end of first sentence (ending "... complaint against surveyors.")*]

NOTE 378a. It is perhaps wholly unsurprising that a valuer who fails to inspect a property at all will be found to have been negligent. In *Webb Resolutions v E. Surv Ltd* [2012] EWHC 3653 (TCC), [2013] P.N.L.R. 253, Coulson J. found that a valuer who had not inspected a property before providing a report had no excuse by reason of the form that he was filling in or the fact that the property concerned had not been completed. He should have made clear that he had not inspected the property.

(iv) *Limited Survey*

[*Add at end of paragraph*] **10–101**

For a recent example of a case where the Court of Appeal found that a valuer was not negligent given the limited nature of his inspection, see *Hubbard v Bank of Scotland* [2014] P.N.L.R. 23. In that case, a valuer employed by a lender considered a small crack which showed no signs of recent movement not to be indicative of structural problems. In fact there was subsequently substantial movement. The Court of Appeal found that the valuer was not negligent in forming a view that no further report was necessary and pointed out that the necessity for recommending a full structural survey in every such case would be unlikely to be welcome. The valuer had let it be known that fuller surveys could be carried out if a purchaser wished it.

(e) *Failing to Make a Proper Appraisal*

[*Add at end of paragraph*] **10–110**

In the Northern Irish case of *Helm Housing v Myles Danker Associates Ltd* [2015] NIQB 73, Horner J. found the defendant valuers liable for providing a residual valuation of £10 million for a development site. The development had been prepared on a residual basis and ignored: (a) the fact that the site had been purchased for considerably less; (b) sales of comparable adjoining properties. The valuer should also have disclosed that he had valued the site previously for the bank that had funded the site on the basis that he had a conflict of interest which should have been disclosed.

3. DAMAGES

(a) *Has the Claimant Sustained the Loss Claimed?*

[*Add new paragraph to text*] **10–115A**

In *Paratus AMC Ltd v Countrywide Surveyors L*td [2011] EWHC 3307 (Ch); [2012] P.N.L.R. 12 (for facts see para.10–066 above), an argument was advanced that no loss could be claimed where a loan had been made and then, with other loans, "securitised". The original lender continued to hold legal title to the loans but the equitable title was held by an SPV financed by investors. The investors subscribed capital which enabled the value of the loans to be purchased. On its facts the claim against the Defendant valuer failed but the Judge held, obiter, that had it succeeded, the fact of the transfer would not have affected the ability to recover substantial damages. Either the original lender was obliged to assign the legal right to sue the valuer to the SPV or it had to account to the SPV for the proceeds of any cause of action. The Judge held that he would, if necessary, have been prepared to apply the maxim that where there was a right there was a remedy so as to avoid the disappearance of an otherwise valid claim.

A similar argument arose in *Titan Europe 2006-3 Plc v Colliers International Plc* [2015] EWCA Civ 1083, where the Court of Appeal considered, obiter, a situation where the claimant had issued non-recourse notes to note-holders. The defendant mounted an argument that no loss had been suffered by the claimant and that the true claimants were the note holders who had suffered loss. Having upheld the appeal on other grounds, the Court did not have to give a decision on the point but nonetheless made clear that it did not consider the argument to be correct. The Court emphasised that the claimant had title to sue for substantial damage in relation to suits of action in relation to loans and the securities underlying them. It rejected contentions that the claimant had suffered no loss or that it had to give credit for any rights that the note-holders had.

Arguments have also been made in situations where successive loans have been made. In *Preferred Mortgages v Bradford & Bingley Estate Agencies Ltd* [2002] EWCA Civ 336, the Court of Appeal considered a situation where a lender loaned money against the security of a property which had been valued by Valuer A. The borrower then sought an increased loan on the strength of a valuation from Valuer B. Instead of proceeding by way of an additional loan, the lender redeemed the charge and made a new loan for the increased amount to the borrower. When the borrower defaulted and sought to sue Valuer A, the valuer successfully argued that no loss had followed any negligence. The loan for which the valuation had been sought had been redeemed in full. In *Tiuta v De Villiers Surveyors Ltd* [2015] EWCH 773 (Ch); [2015] P.N.L.R. 23, the defendant valuer provided successive valuations in February 2011 and December 2011 of a residential development site. The first valuation was for £2.3 million with a GDV of £4.465 million whilst the later one was of £3.5 million with a GDV of £4.9 million. The lender lent £2.221 million in relation to the initial valuation and then a new advance was made on the later valuation of which £2.84 million was used to discharge the original indebtedness. On a summary judgment application, the Deputy Judge held that the lender was only entitled to claim the additional sums loaned flowing from the later valuation. No claim was made in respect of negligence in respect of the first valuation with the consequence that the lender was exposed to the initial sums lend in any event. The Judge accepted that the lender could have included a claim that, as a result of the negligent second valuation, he had lost the right to make a claim in respect of the first valuation but that was not how the claim was pleaded. He accordingly granted the defendant summary judgment save only in respect of the additional monies lent following the second valuation.

It is submitted that the decisions are correct in principle. It will, accordingly, be important to see whether a loan has been redeemed. If it has not, a claim can still be made in respect of the first valuation. It may also be possible, even if the loan has been redeemed, to sue a second valuer for the loss caused by the redemption of the first mortgage.

(b) *Is the Loss Claimed within the Scope of the Defendant's Duty?*

[*Add at the end of para.10–124*]

In the unusual case *Freemont (Denbigh) Ltd v Knight Frank LLP* [2014] EWHC 3347 (Ch), the owner of development property secured a report from the defendant for secured lending purposes. The owner sought to sue the valuer on the basis that, in reliance on the report, it had considered and rejected subsequent offers for the land and, as a result, lost value. On a trial of preliminary issues, the Judge found that the claimant had manufactured certain passages in disputed conversations whereby the claimant had let the defendant know of alternative uses for the valuation. On that basis he had no hesitation in finding that the alleged basis upon which the owner bought the action went beyond the scope of the defendant's duty whether considered in contract or in tort.

In *Bank of Ireland v Faithful & Gould Ltd* [2014] EWHC 2217 (TCC); [2014] P.N.L.R 28, Edwards-Stuart J. considered the proper scope of a valuer's duty in the context of a contribution claim by a project monitor against a valuer. The valuer had been asked to and provided bother a current market value and a gross development value for a substantial commercial development. Both were negligent. However at the time of the valuations, initial finance had already been provided. Furthermore the loss claimed would have been sustained whatever gross development value had been provided as the development failed essentially because the developer (found to be a "rogue" by the Judge) did not complete. In the circumstances the Judge found that any loss flowing from the negligent gross development value was outside the scope of the valuer's duty.

(c) *Remoteness*

[*Add to n.571*] **10–125**

Particular parts of a claim for loss may be found to be too remote as a result of a Claimant's failure to mitigate. Thus in *Webb Resolutions v E. Surv Ltd* [2012] EWHC 3653 (TCC); [2013] P.N.L.R. 253, a lender obtained a warrant for possession of a property and then failed to take any steps to enforce it for a period of four months. It appeared that the file was simply overlooked. The Judge excluded any interest claimed for this four month period.

(i) *Causation*

[Add at end of paragraph] **10–127**

In *Hunt v Optima* [2014] EWCA Civ 714 (for facts, see para.10–023A, above), the Court of Appeal rejected an attempt by some of the Claimant purchasers to establish that they had relied on certificates issued by a surveyor instructed by a developer even when they had entered into contracts before the relevant certificates were issued. The Court found that any attempt to establish liability for negligent misstatement founded on the certificates themselves failed: the Claimants simply could not show that the certificates influenced their minds in deciding to buy. The fact that the surveyor expected that reliance would take place was not enough if it did not, in fact, occur.

In *Bank of Ireland v Faithful & Gould Ltd* [2014] EWHC 2217 (TCC); [2014] P.N.L.R. 28, Edwards-Stuart J. adopted as correct the following passage from Eder J.'s judgment in *Capita Alternative Fund Services v Drivers Jonas* [2011] EWCH 2336 Comm): **10–128**

> "... the Claimants submitted and I accept that they need not show that the Defendants' advice was the only matter relied on in determining to acquire Dockside; it will suffice

if the advice played *'a real and substantial, though not by itself a decisive part, in inducing' the Claimants to act as they did:* see*JEB Fasteners v Mark Bloom [1983] 1 All ER 582* where Stephenson LJ said at p589 ' . . . as long as a misrepresentation plays *a real and substantial part, though not by itself a decisive part, in inducing a plaintiff to act, it is a cause of his loss and he relies on it,* no matter how strong or how many are the other matters which play their part in inducing him to act' [emphasis added]. Whilst Stephenson LJ expressed the test in terms of the effect of a misrepresentation, this was in the context of a claim in respect of the negligent preparation of accounts. Further, the test has been adopted and applied in investment and valuation cases: see, eg, *Cavendish Funding v Henry Spencer [1998] PNLR 122* at para 125, Precis v William M Mercer [2004] EWHC 838 at para 182. Moreover, where a client retains and pays a professional adviser to provide advice a rebuttable presumption will arise that, having sought, paid for and obtained such advice, the client relied upon it: see, eg, *Levicom International Holdings BV v Linklaters [2010] PNLR 29.*" (Original emphasis.)

Having adopted the test, the Judge found that it had not been fulfilled in the slightly unusual circumstances of a contribution claim by a project monitor against a valuer. As set out above, the valuer had been asked to and provided bother a current market value and a gross development value for a substantial commercial development and the Judge found that any loss flowing from the negligent gross development value was outside the scope of the valuer's duty. The Judge accepted that this would not necessarily be the case in relation to the negligent site value. However, on the facts and in the absence of any evidence from the Bank, the Judge was not prepared to hold that the site valuation played any real and substantial part in the decision to provide development finance. Accordingly the contribution claim failed.

(d) *Measure of Damages*

(i) *Negligent Survey or Valuation for a Purchaser who Completes a Purchase*

Collateral benefit

10–158 [*Add at end of paragraph*]

The Court of Appeal allowed an appeal in relation to the principle of giving credit for the tax benefits at [2012] EWCA Civ 1417. The Court unanimously concluded that it was necessary to take into account the fact that the purchase price gave the investors an immediate or almost immediate right to tax relief as tax considerations were integral to the investment and that to ignore the tax element would leave the calculation out of touch with reality. The Court considered that it was entitled to take into account the benefits received by the investors as a result of the statutory regime which entitled investors to claim relief for investments made by the Trust. In assessing the amount of tax relief to be taken into account, the Court considered that credit was only required to be given for that part of the tax relief which would not have been available if an acquisition had been made at a figure which reflected a competent valuation. The consequence was to reduce the damages awarded from £18.05 million to £11.8 million.

(iii) *Negligent Survey or Valuation for Lender*

Evaluating a lender's negligence

[*Add new paragraph to text*] **10–179**

In *Webb Resolutions v E. Surv Ltd* [2012] EWHC 3653 (TCC); [2013] P.N.L.R. 253, Coulson J. pointed out that the cases demonstrated that the starting point, on the authorities, was to compare lending practices, at the time a loan was made with those generally available in the market place. Unless such practices were irrational or illogical, a lender was unlikely to be negligent if it was in line with such practices. As the Judge recognised, this could lead to tensions. It is well known that lending practices are cyclical. As memories of the last property crash fades, lending practices tend to become looser and looser—until the next crash occurs with a consequent tightening. The current approach of the Courts may give too much credit for the "sense" of lenders and take too little account of the extent to which there is a "rush to the bottom" in terms of standards of lending over an economic cycle. The question of the appropriate standard by which to judge lending is probably over-due for consideration at appellate level.

[*Add at end of paragraph*] **10–183**

There have been four recent cases where contributory negligence allegations have been relevant against either centralised or sub-prime lenders. In *Paratus AMC Ltd v Countrywide Surveyors Ltd* [2011] EWHC 3307 (Ch); [2012] P.N.L.R. 12 (for facts see para.10–066, above), the Judge rejected a claim by the Claimant lender against the Defendant valuers in respect of a residential flat. He went on to consider, obiter, issues of contributory negligence and found that had he found primary liability, a deduction of 60 per cent would have been applicable. In reaching this conclusion, he accepted that it was appropriate to consider the standards applicable to a centralised lender who was making loans at high loan to value ratios. However he also found that it was necessary to evaluate matters which were, inevitably, of high importance to such lenders. In the case the lender had a) not taken any apparent account of discrepancies between the borrower's statements as to his debts and that which credit checks showed; and b) had made no enquiries into the borrower's income and ability to service the loan despite its own internal guidance. He found that both the valuer's negligence and that of the lender would have caused the entirety of the loss but that the lender's negligence was comparatively more egregious with the consequence that a greater proportion should be borne by the lender.

In the unusual case of *Platform Funding Ltd v Anderson & Associates Ltd* [2012] EWHC 1853 (for the facts see para.10–027A above), the Judge briefly considered allegations of contributory negligence in relation to sub-prime lending. Having rejected the case on its unusual facts, he found that none of the points made were such that, had liability been found, the underwriting had been exercised without reasonable skill and care. More detailed consideration was given in *Webb Resolutions v E. Surv Ltd* [2012] EWHC 3653 (TCC); [2013] P.N.L.R. 253 where Coulson J. considered practices against the general standard applicable in the market. Thus he rejected a general allegation that a loan to value ratio of just over 85 per cent was too high even though it appeared to the Judge to be inherently risky on the basis that most centralised lenders were applying such a ratio. However in the case of another loan, the Judge found that a 95 per cent loan to value ratio was negligent as even other centralised lenders were not making loans at such a rate. Similarly the Judge found a lender guilty of contributory negligence where a lender treated an application as being self-certifying where it had never been intended to be made on such basis and where details of the applicant's accountant were provided but not followed up. In the circumstances, he assessed the appropriate award of contributory negligence as being 50 per cent.

In *Bank of Ireland v Faithful & Gould Ltd* [2014] EWHC 2217 (TCC); [2014] P.N.L.R. 28 Edwards-Stuart J. considered a contribution claim by a project monitor, who had settled with a lender, against a valuer. As set out above, the claim failed on a combination of causation and scope of duty grounds. In assessing, obiter the amount of contribution that he would have awarded, the Judge held that he would have assessed the liability of the project monitor as being 35 per cent—in other words a contributory negligence finding of 65 per cent, in circumstances where the monitor had not given appropriate advice as to off-site materials. If the Judge had found that the valuer's assessment of site value had been causative, he would have found contributory negligence as between the lender and the valuer of 50 per cent on the basis: (i) that the bank had negligently over-estimated the borrower's equity contribution and, but for the error, would have made no development advance; and (ii) had failed to pick up, as it should have done, some of the valuer's errors. He found, however, that some of the valuer's errors should not have been picked up and there, in any event "gross" errors by the valuer.

10–186 [*Add at the end of the para*]

The approach of Clarke J. in *Nationwide* was followed by Edwards-Stuart J., albeit obiter, when considering how issues of contribution inter-acted with contributory negligence in the case of a contribution claim by a project monitor against a valuer—see further para.10–183 above.

10–186A [*Add new paragraph to text*]

Given the extensive obligations owed by solicitors to lenders, there will often be occasions when both valuers and solicitors are liable to such a lender. In *E-Serv Ltd v Goldsmith Williams* [2014] P.N.L.R. 605, H.H. Judge Stephen Davies QC accepted that a solicitor was in breach of duty in failing to disclose to a lender that a property had recently changed hands at £390,000 which a valuer had valued at £725,000. Had this information been made known to the lender, the lender would have drawn it to the attention of the valuer who would, in turn, have reconsidered his valuation. The Judge found that both the relative blameworthiness and causative potency of the solicitor and valuer were equal and accordingly apportioned liability equally.

CHAPTER 11

SOLICITORS

1. GENERAL

(a) *Duties to Client*

(i) *Contractual Duties*

Formation of the retainer

[*Add to n.18*] **11–004**

In *Edenwest Ltd v CMS Cameron McKenna (A Firm)* [2012] EWHC 1471 (Admin); [2012] P.N.L.R. 27, Hildyard J. held that where a receiver of a company consulted solicitors in connection with his functions, the presumption was that the retainer was with the receiver and not the company: the receiver was an agent of the company in a limited sense, and there might well be a conflict between the interests of the receiver and the company.

The need for writing

[*Add to n.29*] **11–006**

Upheld on appeal, 2012 ONCA 701; (2013) 356 D.L.R. (4th) 54.

Termination of the retainer

[*Add to n.52*] **11–011**

Failure to pay a lawyer's bill, even if larger than the estimate because of unexpected developments, may justify the solicitor terminating the retainer, see *Minkin v Cawdery Kaye Fireman & Taylor (A Firm)* [2012] EWCA Civ 546; [2012] 3 All E.R. 1117. It may be necessary to consider the facts closely as to who determined the retainer, as in *French v Carter Lemon Camerons LLP* [2012] EWCA Civ 1180; [2013] P.N.L.R. 2, where it was held that the client had determined the retainer. Supervening mental incapacity does not terminate a retainer, but only makes it voidable, see *Blankley v Central Manchester and*

Manchester Children's University Hospitals NHS Trust [2014] EWHC 168 (QB); [2014] 1 W.L.R. 2683.

Continuing obligations

11–012 [*Add to n.56*]

Similarly, there will rarely be a general retainer to revisit advice which has given, see *Shepherd Construction Ltd v Pinsent Masons LLP* [2012] EWHC 43 (TCC); [2012] P.N.L.R. 31.

[*Add to n.59*]

In *Maharaj v Johnson* [2015] UKPC 28; [2015] P.N.L.R. 27 the Privy Council followed the line of Court of Appeal authority, and held on the facts of that case that there was no continuing duty as there were no special facts supporting such a duty.

(iii) *Fiduciary Duties*

(7) Confidence

11–028 [*Add to n.151*]

When solicitors are in possession of confidential information, the normal order where they previously acted for the opposing party is to restrain the solicitor from acting, but if they have not acted for the opposing party before, then the normal order is to restrain the solicitors from using the confidential information, see *Stiedl v Enyo Law LLP* [2011] EWHC 2649 (Comm); [2012] P.N.L.R. 4.

Restraint of breach of confidence

11–029 [*Add to n.155*]

In "Judicial disqualification of solicitors with client conflict" [2014] 130 L.Q.R. 498 R. Flannigan argues that the test focuses on negligence by solicitors rather than opportunistic conduct by them, and the test should be that there is no risk of disclosure of relevant confidential information, rather than no real risk. The law is different where solicitors still act for the claimant in other matters, where the disqualification is based on a conflict of interest rather than confidentiality, see *Bolkiah v KPMG*[1999] 2 A.C. 222 at 234G–235A. In Canada and New Zealand solicitors cannot act for both clients, both in related to related and unrelated matters where the immediate interests of the clients are directly adverse in the matters on which the lawyer is acting, see *Canadian National Railway Co v McKercher*2013 SCC 39; [2013] 2 SCR 649, and *Mike Pero Mortgages Ltd v Mike Pero*[2014] NZHC 2798; [2015] 3 NZLR 246.

No confidential information

[*Add to n.157*] **11–030**

In *E-Clear (UK) Plc v Elia* [2012] EWHC 1195 (Ch); [2012] B.P.I.R. 732 the third defendant claimed that the claimant had acted for her son in previous litigation and had confidential information, but the Judge held that the solicitors never had acted for him. In *Maxwell-Smith v S & E Hall Pty Ltd*[2014] NSWCA 146; (2014) NSWLR 481 there was no relevant confidential information, and thus no action lay against the solicitors.

Commonwealth cases

[*Add to n.162*] **11–033**

For a recent application, see *Wallace v Canadian Pacific Railway* 2011 SKCA 108; (2012) 340 D.L.R. (4th) 402.

(iv) *Trust Duties*

Trust and lender claims

[*Replace n.183 with the following*] **11–037**

[1998] Ch. 1, applied in *Nationwide Building Society v Balmer Radmore* [1999] P.N.L.R. 606, and see para.11–037A.

[*Add new paragraph to text*] **11–037A**

A number of recent cases have considered breach of trust in the context of lenders' claims. In the leading case of *Lloyds TSB Bank Plc v Markandan & Uddin (A Firm)* [2012] EWCA Civ 65; [2012] 2 All E.R. 884, solicitors paid away monies without receiving the documents required to register title, but did receive an undertaking by the vendor's purported solicitor to provide such documents. The purported solicitor was in fact a fraudster, and the money was lost. The transaction was on the standard CML terms, which required by cl.10.3.4 that the loan should be held on trust until completion. The Court of Appeal held that "completion" did not mean registration of title, but it did require that the defendant should have received the completed transfer and other documents necessary to obtain and register title, or the vendor's solicitors' undertaking to provide them. As there were no documents provided, and no solicitors' undertaking, the defendants were in breach of trust. The Court stated, obiter, that the release of mortgage funds in exchange for forged documents would be in breach of trust, but innocent solicitors were adequately protected by s.61 of the Trustee Act 1925, which gives a Court a discretion to excuse a trustee who acted reasonably. For a helpful commentary on this case see J. Hall, "Breach of trust by conveyancing solicitors—the strongest of all lender claims?" (2012) 28 P.N. 109. It would appear that the documents necessary to complete transfer which the solicitor should obtain may not include an SDLT certificate, see *D B UK Bank Ltd v Edmunds & Co (A Firm)* [2014] P.N.L.R. 12.

11–037B [*Add new paragraph to text*]

Subsequent cases have considered the circumstances in which relief should be given pursuant to s.61 of the Trustees Act 1925. In *Nationwide Building Society v Davisons Solicitors* [2012] EWCA Civ 1626; [2013] P.N.L.R. 12, the defendants paid away trust money to fraudsters on an undertaking which they believed was from solicitors, and were in breach of trust. However, relief was granted under s.61 as the defendants had checked the existence and office of the solicitors with the Law Society and the SRA. Importantly, at [38], the Court of Appeal held that the solicitor was only required to act reasonably and not comply with best practice in all respects, and the relevant action must be connected with the loss for which relief was sought. In *Santander UK Plc v RA Legal Solicitors (A Firm)* [2014] EWCA Civ 183; [2014] P.N.L.R. 20, the defendant solicitors were in breach of trust in releasing monies against a forged transfer provided by solicitors acting for the purported vendor. They were not relieved of liability pursuant to s.61, as they had failed to follow up unclear Replies to Requisitions. The Court of Appeal held that the solicitors' impugned conduct had to be relevant and materially connected with the loss, but not causative of the loss, and in that case the fraud would have succeeded even if they had acted reasonably. See further S. Charlwood, "Conveyancing solicitors' liability for breach of trust" (2014) 30 P.N. 102. It must be doubted that the earlier case of *Ikbal v Sterling Law* [2013] EWHC 3291 (Ch); [2014] P.N.L.R. 9 was correctly decided.

11–037C [*Add new paragraph to text*]

In *Broker House Insurance Services Ltd v OJS Law* [2010] EWHC 3816 (Ch); [2011] P.N.L.R. 23, solicitors acted for an intended second charge holder, and their instructions were not on the terms of the CML Handbook. They paid away monies without obtaining the first chargeholders' permission to a second charge, but, applying *Bristol West Building Society v Mothew* [1997] 1 Ch. 1, the language of the relevant special condition was not clear enough to make the breach a payment away made without authority. See further, in relation to equitable compensation, *AIB Group (UK) Plc v Mark Reder & Co (A Firm)* [2014] UKSC 58; [2015] P.N.L.R. 10, considered at para.11–242.

Dishonest assistance

11–041 [*Add to n.195*]

, upheld by the New Zealand Court of Appeal sub. nom. *Fletcher v Eden Refuge Trust* [2012] NZCA 124; [2012] 2 NZLR 227, which, following New Zealand Supreme Court authority, applied *Barlow Close International Ltd v Eurotrust Ltd* [2006] 1 W.L.R. 1476 (see n.197 below), and also made clear that following client's instructions was not a defence to dishonest assistance. A claim for dishonest assistance succeeded in *Frank Houlgate Investment v Biggart Baillie*[2014] CSIH 79; [2015] P.N.L.R. 3, as the solicitor made a continuing implied representation that he knew nothing suggesting his client was dishonest in relation to the relevant security, when he did, and he was therefore objectively dishonest.

(b) *Duties to Third Parties*

(i) *General*

Reliance by non-client without duty

[*Add to n.224*] **11–046**

No duty was owed by the solicitors to a lender in *Scott v Valentine* 2012 ONSC 6349; (2013) 99 C.C.L.T. (3d) 159, when the reliance of the lender on the solicitor was unreasonable and the solicitors were not aware of any reliance.

Liability without reliance

[*Add to n.229*] **11–047**

In *Dhillon v Jaffer* 2012 BCCA 156; (2012) 348 D.L.R. (4th) 712, solicitors acted for a wife who unsuccessfully resisted the sale of the matrimonial home to a third party and who relied on a forged power of attorney giving her the right to sell, which she operated. The proceeds of sale were paid to her solicitors, the defendants, who paid them away to her. They owed the husband a duty of care.

No duty

[*Add at end of paragraph*] **11–049**

In *Edenwest Ltd v CMS Cameron McKenna (A Firm)* [2012] EWHC 1471 (Admin); [2012] P.N.L.R. 27, solicitors were instructed by a company's receivers, but owed no duty to the company, not least because the interests of the receiver and the company may be diametrically opposed.

[*Add after first sentence of n.237*]

The same result was reached on similar facts in *Schumann v Veale Wasbrough* [2013] EWHC 3730 (QB); [2014] P.N.L.R. 14.

(ii) *Liability to Beneficiaries without Reliance*

Double recovery

[*Add to n.273*] **11–056**

Cf. *Vagg v McPhee* [2013] NSWCA 29; (2013) 85 NSWLR 154, where no duty of care was owed (inter alia) because the same relief would have been available to the estate.

[*Add to n.278*] **11–057**

Similarly, in *Steven v Hewats* [2013] CSOH 60; [2013] P.N.L.R. 23, a claim by the executors for inheritance tax caused by a defective inter vivos gift was struck out on the basis that the deceased had no cause of action to transmit to the executors.

Application beyond wills and solicitors

11–058 [*Add to n.283*]

In *Steven v Hewats* [2013] CSOH 61; [2013] P.N.L.R. 22 an inter vivos transaction was ineffective, and although corrected before the death of the donor, substantial inheritance tax became payable. A claim by the beneficiary was not struck out.

Other jurisdictions

11–059 [*Add to n.294*]

The duty extends to the means by which the solicitor can ensure that a testator's wishes are carried out, which in Australia includes drawing up an informal will, see *Fisher v Howe*[2013] NSWSC 462; (2013) 85 NSWLR 67.

(iii) *Duty of Care to the Other Side*

Other Commonwealth cases

11–066 [*Add to n.321*]

The same conclusion was reached on a rehearing, [2011] CSOH 160; [2012] P.N.L.R. 2, followed in *NRAM Plc v Bell & Scott LLP* [2014] CSOH 172; [2015] P.N.L.R. 16.

(iv) *Solicitors' Liability on Undertakings*

General

11–070 [*Add to n.337*]

Replace reference to the Senior Courts Act 1981 s.50 with the Solicitors Act 1974 s.50.

Construction of the undertaking

11–073 [*Add at end of paragraph*]

An imprecisely drafted undertaking may be negligent, see *Auckland Standard Committee v W* [2011] 3 N.Z.L.R. 117.

Absolute nature of enforcement

11–074 [*Add to n.374*]

For example, in *Webster v Shueard* [2012] SASC 93; (2012) 113 S.A.S.R. 99 a solicitor gave an undertaking on instructions to a third party to pay monies from the future proceeds of the client's personal injury claim, the client then revoked the instructions, and the solicitor was liable to the third party but with a claim over against the former client.

Impossibility and compensation

[*Add to n.395*] **11–077**

While the award would normally be limited to the present value of the land, it may be the total amount outstanding on the loan in order to uphold the integrity of the institution of the solicitor's undertaking, for instance where the solicitor obtained a loan in a personal capacity and took no steps to fulfil his undertaking, see *ACC Bank Plc v Tobin (practising as John A Tobin & Co Solicitors)* [2012] IEHC 348; [2013] P.N.L.R. 1.

[Add at start of n.396]

In the Irish case of *National Irish Bank v O'Ceallaigh* [2011] IEHC 216; [2012] 1 I.L.R.M 428, it was held that in order for the court to assess appropriate compensation, all relevant facts had to be disclosed in an affidavit.

(v) *Other Liabilities*

Breach of warranty of authority

[*Add to n.421*] **11–080**

and on a rehearing at [2011] CSOH 160; [2012] P.N.L.R. 2. The same result was reached in *Cheshire Mortgage Corp Ltd v Grandison* [2012] CSIH 66; [2013] P.N.L.R. 3, where the Inner House expressly followed *Excel.*

[*Add to n.424*] **11–081**

The law is similar in Ireland, see *Jabaar Ltd v Townlink Construction Ltd* [2011] IEHC 111; [2011] 1 I.R. 767. Quaere whether lack of due diligence must be shown if the solicitors' authority ceases during the proceedings, see *Wilson v Leek General Commissioners* [1994] S.T.C. 147, Knox J. In *Carpathian Resources Ltd v Hendricks* [2012] FCA 496; (2012) 290 A.L.R. 252, no personal costs order was made against solicitors acting for the company in a dispute as to who were the directors of a company, and where those purporting to act for the company were found at trial not to be directors, as it was impossible to predict the outcome of the trial.

[*Add to n.425*]

Similarly, in *Attis v Ontario (Minister of Health)* 2011 ONCA 675; (2012) 343 D.L.R. (4th) 263, a claim for breach of warranty of authority failed because the apparent party had no assets, and thus the claim failed on causation, but in any event the failure to explain costs properly to the client did not invalidate the client's consent to proceedings.

(c) *The Standard of Skill and Care*

(ii) *General Practice as Evidence of Reasonable Skill and Care*

An illustration: taking instructions

11–100 [*In n.481 replace "[1995] N.P.C. 27 QBD." with the following*]

[1997] P.N.L.R. 392.

(d) *Specific Defences to a Claim for Breach of Duty*

(ii) *Abuse of Process*

Other types of abuse of process

11–120 [*Add to n.570*]

For another illustration see *Ridgewood Properties Group Ltd v Kilpatrick Stockton LLP* [2014] EWHC 2502 (Ch); [2014] P.N.L.R. 31. The claimant had entered a contract with a landowner permitting it to develop filling stations owned by the landlord. The claimant had sued the landlord for breach of contract, which claim failed on the basis that planning permissions had lapsed for reasons unconnected with the breach, and the claimant did not pursue an appeal. The claimant's subsequent claim against its solicitors for failing to advise it about its right to terminate the agreement for repudiatory breach was held to be an abuse of process, as it was a collateral attack on the earlier decision of the Court. In contrast, in *Ferrara v Lorenzetti, Wolfe Barristers and Solicitors* 2012 ONCA 852; (2013) 357 D.L.R. (4th) 480 a claim against solicitors was not an abuse of process although the same issue was raised in proceedings against another defendant as there was no possibility of inconsistent results, and the solicitors had repeatedly said they had acted correctly.

(iv) *Acting on Client's Instructions*

Duty to obey client

11–127 [*Add to n.594*]

In *Wellesley Partners LLP v Withers LLP* [2014] EWHC 556 (Ch); [2014] P.N.L.R. 22 solicitors drafted an agreement setting up an LLP giving a bank an option to withdraw half of its contribution within 41 months, rather than after 42 months as instructed, and were held to be negligent.

(e) *Solicitor's Liability for Costs*

11–129 [*In n.608 replace reference to "Jackson v Cambridgeshire CC [2011] P.N.L.R 321." with the following*]

Lloyd v Cambridgeshire County Council [2011] P.N.L.R. 32.

[*Add to n.609*]

A similar jurisdiction exists for tribunals, see *R. (on the application of Okondu and Abdussalam) v Secretary of State for the Home Department* [2014] UKUT 377 (IAC); [2015] I.N.L.R. 99.

[*Add to n.609*]

If the solicitor acting on a CFA fails to obtain ATE insurance in breach of duty, a costs order is only likely to be made against him if it was obvious that the clients would not have proceeded with the litigation without such cover, see *Adris v The Royal Bank of Scotland* [2010] EWHC 941 (QB); [2010] 4 Costs L.R. 598, and *Heron v TNT (UK) Ltd* [2013] EWCA Civ 469; [2013] P.N.L.R. 21. Merely acting on a CFA, where there is no ATE, does not make a solicitor a funder, see *Tinseltime Ltd v Roberts* [2012] EWHC 2628 (TCC); [2013] P.N.L.R. 4.

The inherent jurisdiction

[*Add to n.610*] **11–130**

and for a similar case see *Galganov v Russell (Township)* 2012 ONCA 410; (2012) 350 D.L.R. 679.

Parties and the limits of the jurisdiction

[*Add to n.617*] **11–131**

Nor can a wasted costs order be made in favour of defence counsel under s.19 of the Prosecution of Offences Act 1985, see *R. (on the application of Crown Prosecution Service) v Bolton Crown Court* [2012] EWHC 3570 (Admin); [2013] 1 W.L.R. 1880.

The position of the respondent lawyer and privilege

[*Add to n.636*] **11–134**

And for another example see *Banks v Geddis (Costs)* [2012] NIQB 87; [2013] P.N.L.R. 11, where the error had been admitted.

Procedure

[*Add to n.640*] **11–135**

But the wasted costs application has to be made in the proceedings, which includes in the detailed assessment of costs. In *Sharma v Hunters (Wasted Costs)* [2011] EWHC 2546 (COP); [2012] P.N.L.R. 6 a final judgment and costs order did not determine the proceedings, but what was effectively a settlement (save to enforce the terms of the Tomlin order) of the costs in a Tomlin order did do so, and no wasted costs application could be made thereafter.

11–137

[*Add to n.645*]

While in most circumstances cross-examination of the representative against whom costs are sought will be inappropriate, it may be proportionate and fair in some circumstances, see *Godfrey Morgan v Cobalt* [2011] 6 Cost L.R. 1006, where cross-examination was correctly permitted as the representative no longer acted for the party, privilege had been waived, an oral hearing had been fixed, and there was a conflict on the facts.

[*Add to n.646*]

Thus solicitors were not ordered to show cause in *Kagalovsky v Balmore Invest Ltd* [2015] EWHC 1337 (QB); [2015] P.N.L.R 26, where the allegations concerned participation in the client's fraud, and involved a variety of allegations and volume of material concerning matters which did not occur in the face of the court.

11–138 [*Add to n.653*]

And to identical effect, see *Cheung Shui Han v Luk Ka Ling* [2012] HKLRD 537 HKCA.

11–140 [*Add after first sentence of n.664*]

But such an appeal was allowed to be made (but failed) in *Endowment Fund for the Rehabilitation of Tigray v Rylatt Chubb* [2013] EWCA Civ 1003; [2014] P.N.L.R. 4 as it was on limited grounds and was linked to an appeal of an application that the judge recuse himself.

Causation

11–141 [*Add at end of paragraph*]

A finding that there was no loss was distinguished in *Sharma v Hunters (Wasted Costs)* [2011] EWHC 2546 (COP); [2012] P.N.L.R. 6.

[*Add to n.669*]

In *R. v Fitzgerald* [2012] 3 Costs L.R. 437 the Crown Court held that a wasted costs order was limited to costs actually incurred under the graduated fee scheme. In *Re A (a Child)* [2013] EWCA Civ 43; [2013] 6 Costs L.R. 873 no wasted costs order was made in relation to a series of errors concerning a without-notice application, as no adverse consequences flowed from them.

Hopeless litigation

11–142 [*Add to n.674*]

The law is different in Australia, where the test is whether the solicitor must have a reasonable belief that a claim has reasonable prospects of success, which he did not in *Keddie v Stacks* [2012] NSWCA 254; (2012) 293 A.L.R. 764.

[*Add to n.675*]

In *R. (on the application of Gassama) v Secretary of State for the Home Department* [2012] EWHC 3049 (Admin); [2013] P.N.L.R. 10, the solicitors made an application for judicial review claiming that their client should have indefinite leave to remain in the UK. The claim was stayed pending other litigation which, when decided, was very unfavourable to the claimant, as the Treasury Solicitor pointed out to the solicitors, who withdrew the claim only two days before the hearing, and a wasted costs order was made against them. A wasted costs order was upheld in *Thames Chambers Solicitors v Miah* [2013] EWHC 1245 (QB); [2013] P.N.L.R. 30 where the solicitors acted for a client whom they knew was bankrupt, and they should have realised that the bankrupt's assets were vested in his trustee in bankruptcy.

[*Add to n.679*] **11–143**

In *Re A (a Child)* [2013] EWCA Civ 43; [2013] 6 Costs L.R. 873 no wasted costs order was made against solicitors who pursued an unsustainable application for permission to appeal when the application was driven by the overoptimistic judgment of Counsel.

Misuse of procedure

[*Add to n.692*] **11–146**

In *R. v SVS Solicitors (Wasted Costs)* [2012] EWCA (Crim) 319; [2012] P.N.L.R. 21 a wasted costs order was made and upheld where solicitors had deliberately breached the Criminal Procedure Rules and not put in a defence statement in order to keep the defendant's options open. In *Hu v Su* [2015] EWFC 18; [2015] P.N.L.R. 20 a wasted costs order was made where solicitors failed to observe the Court imposed timetable without an application to the Court to vary it. In *R. (Okondu and Abdussalam) v Secretary of State for the Home Department* [2014] UKUT 377 (IAC); [2015] I.N.L.R. 99 wasted costs orders were made against solicitors for a variety of errors in judicial proceedings, including failing to make adequate enquiries and drafting misleading grounds.

[*Add to n.693*]

In *R. v X (Wasted Costs)* [2013] EWCA Crim 775; [2013] P.N.L.R 31, solicitors failed to give the names and addresses of alibi witnesses, in breach of the Criminal Procedure and Investigations Act 1996 s.6A(2)(a), but no wasted costs order should have been made against them, as they relied on counsel, and the view that there did not have to be such disclosure was widely held. In *FM LLP v JH (Wasted Costs)* [2012] EWHC 408 (Fam); [2012] P.N.L.R. 22, solicitors failed to join the beneficial owners of shares in a company whose interests would be affected by orders made in ancillary relief proceedings, leading to a late adjournment of a preliminary issue. Mostyn J. quashed a wasted costs order made against them, because all the parties to the litigation had assented expressly or tacitly to the hearing of the preliminary issue without the beneficial owners being party to it.

Withdrawal of representation

11–147 [*Add to n.696*]

In contrast, in *Equity Solicitors v Javid* [2009] EWCA Civ 535; [2009] 2 F.L.R. 1011, solicitors who had briefly acted for a party in divorce proceedings on a pro bono basis informed both parties and the Court that they were being replaced by another firm, and they were entitled to rely on the oral assurances by another firm that they would file a formal notice of change of solicitors, and they had not acted negligently. A wasted costs order was upheld in *R v Henrys Solicitors* [2012] EWCA Crim 1480; [2012] P.N.L.R. 32, where the advocate accepted instructions in two cases on the same day in geographically distant courts and there was a real risk of a delay in the first court, which happened.

Other errors

11–149 [*Add to n.701*]

Serving defective pleadings was held to justify a wasted costs order in *Modra v Victoria* [2012] FCA 240; [2012] 291 A.L.R. 427.

(g) *Practice and Procedure*

(i) *Expert Evidence*

Practice abroad

11–152 [*Add to n.714*]

But the Courts of Northern Ireland are more flexible, see *Baird v Hastings & Co (Solicitors)* [2013] N.I.Q.B. 143; [2014] P.N.L.R. 17, echoed by the Northern Ireland Court of Appeal in *Young v Hamilton* [2014] NICA 48; [2014] P.N.L.R. 30 at [39] with the qualification that in that case, concerning conveyancing, it was difficult to see what added value was gained by such evidence.

(ii) *Privilege*

Waiver of privilege

11–153 [*Add to n.723*]

The waiver attached to communications with counsel, and that would include matters in counsel's possession such as his notes or recollection, see *Hellard v Irwin Mitchell* [2012] EWHC 2656 (Ch); [2013] P.N.L.R. 8.

(h) *Authority, Attribution and Vicarious Liability*

Authority from the client

[*Add new paragraph to text*] **11–155**

If an agent has ostensible authority, a solicitor should give advice to the principal where the instructing agent had interests which were potentially in conflict with those of its principal, see *Newcastle International Airport Ltd v Eversheds LLP* [2013] EWCA Civ 1514; [2014] P.N.L.R. 13. It was also held that any such advice would not have been read or properly appreciated, so that no loss was caused.

Liability of partners

[*Add to n.742*] **11–156**

The law in Australia is similar, see *Crouch & Lyndon (A Firm) v IPG Finance Australia Pty Ltd* [2013] QCA 220; [2014] P.N.L.R. 3. In mortgage transactions lenders' monies were paid to the solicitors, but the borrower was fictitious and the monies were extracted by the fraudulent partner. The Queensland Court of Appeal held that solicitors were not generally engaged in mortgage broking, which was being undertaken there and which was illegal for solicitors, and the fraudulent acts were not done in the course of business. However, what was done was not unusual enough to indicate that the partner did not have authority, so he had the apparent authority of the firm to undertake them.

Liability for staff

[*Add to n.746*] **11–158**

Members of staff should be properly supervised, see *Kim v Oh* [2013] NZHC 925; [2013] 2 N.Z.L.R. 825.

2. Liability for Breach of Duty

(b) *Giving Wrong Advice*

On the law

[*Add to n.774*] **11–163**

See also *Hermann v Withers LLP* [2012] EWHC 1492 (Ch); [2012] P.N.L.R. 28, noted at para.11–173 below.

Practical advice

[*Add to n.775*] **11–164**

In *Baker & McKenzie v Grande Holdings Ltd* [2013] HKLRD 63 the Hong Kong Court of Appeal held that the solicitors' advice in proceedings for a Mareva injunction, that a Mr Ho controlled Grande Holdings Ltd, was correct given the instructions from the client to that effect supported by documents.

(c) *Failing to Give Advice*

As to the progress of the cause or matter

11–167 [*Add to n.793*]

In *Gabriel v Little* [2012] EWHC 1193 (Ch); [2013] W.T.L.R. 419, the solicitor had learned that the other side intended to use a loan, which was to be provided by his client and was to be evidenced by a facility letter, mostly to purchase a property, rather than to develop it, and he was negligent in failing to pass this on to the client, and also negligent in failing to make it sufficiently clear in the facility letter that the loan was only to be used for development. The appeal on breach was dismissed by the Court of Appeal, [2013] EWCA Civ 1513.

In respect of matters which he is not asked to investigate or advise upon

11–169 [*Add to n.801 after reference to "Swain Mason v Mills & Reeve (A Firm)"*]

Upheld on appeal at [2012] EWCA Civ 498; [2012] W.T.L.R. 1827.

As to the solicitor's own negligence

11–172 [*Add to n.808*]

Similarly, a professional is rarely required to revisit advice which he or she has given, see *Shepherd Construction Ltd v Pinsent Masons LLP* [2012] EWHC 43 (TCC); [2012] P.N.L.R. 31. There, correct advice given in 1998 became faulty as a result of statutory changes in 2002, but there was no general retainer necessitating a review of earlier advice, even though there were a large number of individual instructions over a period of time.

The duty to warn against particular risks

11–173 [*Add to n.821*]

Similarly, in *Hermann v Withers LLP* [2012] EWHC 1492 (Ch); [2012] P.N.L.R. 28, Newey J. held that the defendant solicitors came to a reasonable view that the construction of an Act of Parliament meant that their clients were entitled to enter and use a communal garden, but negligently failed to explain to them that there was scope for different opinions on the matter.

Explanation of legal documents

11–174 [*Add to n.826*]

The solicitor must inform himself in relation to his client as to his understanding of the transaction and his aims in order to determine what advice needed to be given and the risks involved, see *Robert Bax & Associates v Cavenham Pty Ltd* [2012] QCA 177; [2013] 1 Qd.R. 476.

An exception

[*Add to n.848*] **11–179**

In *Provident Capital Ltd v Papa* [2013] NSWCA 36; (2013); 84 NSWLR 231 a borrower mortgaged property to secure loans made to her, primarily to assist her son's business. Her solicitors should have explained in strong terms the practical consequences of the obligations she was assuming, including obtaining financial advice as to the capacity of the business to service the loan.

The importance of attendance notes and written communication

[*Add to n.855*] **11–182**

However, in *Palios Meegan & Nicholson v Shore* [2010] SASCFC 21; (2010) S.A.S.R. 31, the Full Court of the Supreme Court of South Australia overturned a finding that a solicitor had not advised a client, because the client had signed an acknowledgement that she had received advice, and the solicitor relied on his general practice as to the advice he would have given in the relevant circumstances.

(d) *Misconduct of Litigation*

Pursuing obvious remedy

[*Add to n.875*] **11–187**

In *Rasch Nominees Pty Ltd v Bartholomaeus* [2012] SASC 70; (2012) 114 SASR 448 the clients were in a dilemma as they had contracted to sell property to two different parties, and their solicitor negligently failed to advise them to issue proceedings to resolve the dispute, which would have been much quicker and cheaper to resolve than the proceedings which were eventually issued by one of the competing purchasers, and they also negligently failed to instruct Counsel to advise on what to do.

Pursuing unmeritorious claims or defences

[*Add to n.881*] **11–190**

But there may be point, for instance, in defending a winding up petition to buy more time to satisfy the company's debts, see *AJH Lawyers v Hamo* [2010] VSCA 222; (2010) 29 V.R. 384.

Evidence

[*Add at end of paragraph*] **11–193**

In *Boyle v Thompsons Solicitors* [2012] EWHC 36 (QB); [2012] P.N.L.R. 17, Coulson J. held that it was not negligent for solicitors to fail to seek to bolster the evidence of a medical expert for a number of reasons, including the fact that there was no reason to think that the expert would offer a stronger opinion, and might do the reverse.

Settlement: consulting the client

11–199 [*Add to n.931*]

Sending letters to a client of limited education and understanding of legal concepts was not sufficient, and, even in group litigation with an element of commoditisation, a meeting or telephone call was needed, see *Procter v Raleys Solicitors* [2015] EWCA Civ 400; [2015] P.N.L.R. 24.

Settlement: the merits

11–200 [*Add to n.935*]

In *Gabriel v Little* [2012] EWHC 1193 (Ch); [2013] W.T.L.R. 419 solicitors were not negligent in failing to obtain a binding agreement at a mediation as the clients had not reached one, and it was stated, obiter, that it would normally be part of a solicitor's job in a mediation to explain the nature of the mediation process and the status of any agreement reached. As to whether a solicitor is negligent when the advice is reasonable but the reasoning process is not, see H. Evans, "Negligence and process" (2013) 29 P.N. 212.

(e) *Misconduct of Non-contentious Business*

(i) *Conveyancing*

Proper confirmation

11–203 [*Add to n.948*]

In *Outaouais Synergest Inc v Lang Michener LLP* 2013 ONCA 526; (2013) 116 O.R. (3d) 742 solicitors acting for a purchaser obtained a restrictive covenant which stated that the purchaser would be responsible for municipal charges including costs in relation to a $0.3 million reserve, but failed to enquire further with the municipality, which enquiries would have shown that $240,000 was due. The solicitors were held to be negligent.

Standard of care not absolute

11–205 [*Add to n.956*]

In *Young v Hamilton* [2014] NICA 48; [2014] P.N.L.R. 30, the solicitor received a representation from the vendor's solicitor that there was no claim to an adverse right of way, she inspected the access along a lane which was in fact disputed, and was told that there was no documentary evidence concerning a dispute to a lower part of the lane which did not provide access. The solicitor had no obligation to investigate the matter further.

Communicating with the client

[*Add to n.969*] 11–208

A solicitor should advise that planning enquiries revealed that a nearby school site was to be redeveloped into a larger school, *Orientfield Holdings Ltd (a company registered and incorporated in the British Virgin Islands v Bird & Bird LLP* [2015] EWHC 1963 (Ch); [2015] P.N.L.R. 34.

[*Add to n.974*]

Similarly, in *Baird v Hastings & Co (Solicitors)* [2013] N.I.Q.B. 143; [2014] P.N.L.R. 17 solicitors were held to be negligent in failing to advise the clients of the risks of purchasing a new property with a bridging loan before their house had sold. In *Xenakis v Birkett Long LLP (A Firm)* [2014] EWHC 171 (QB); [2014] P.N.L.R. 16 solicitors were found to be negligent in failing to advise clients that their guarantees of a lease ran from the date of completion of the lease by the landlords and failing to advise about the risks of releasing the documents and procuring the claimants' company to go into occupation before such completion, which caused their guarantee to last nearly a year longer than they had contemplated.

[*Add to n.978*]

And in failing to advise fully on the magnitude of the risks faced in the purchase of an apartment to be built, including the vendor not having any rights to the land on which it was to be built or funding to do so, see *Appleton v Tauranga Law* [2013] NZCA 420; [2013] 3 NZLR 777.

Handing over the purchase money

[*Add to n.993*] 11–210

Where the client purchaser wanted to release a larger than normal deposit to the vendor rather than its solicitors as stakeholders, and the solicitor has given suitable warnings about the risk of loss of the deposit, there was no duty to make a bankruptcy search, as a solicitor generally has no duty to check on the credit status of his client's counterparty, see *Kandola v Mirza Solicitors LLP* [2015] EWHC 460 (Ch); [2015] P.N.L.R. 19

Wider duties

[*Add to n.1006*] 11–213

A purchaser of a public house should be advised about the absence of a covenant of in restraint of competition, see *Luffeorm Ltd v Kitsons LLP* [2015] EWHC B10 (QB); [2015] P.N.L.R. 30.

Mortgages and undue influence

11–216 [*Add to n.1021*]

In *Padden v Bevan Ashford (A Firm)* [2011] EWCA Civ 1616; [2012] 1 W.L.R. 1759 a wife mortgaged her house so that her husband could repay a client he had defrauded, and thus attempt to avoid prosecution. The meeting with the defendant solicitor was short, and they made no charge for it, but the Court of Appeal held that proper advice should have been given. While the solicitor advised that the wife should not proceed with the transaction, he should have advised, amongst other things, that there should be a factual investigation to find out the full nature of the husband's defalcation, which was in fact much greater than the husband had admitted. The matter of causation in particular was sent for a retrial, and the Judge held that the wife would not have entered the transaction if properly advised, which was upheld by the Court of Appeal at [2013] EWCA Civ 824; [2013] P.N.L.R. 34. In *Provident Capital Ltd v Papa* [2013] NSWCA 36; (2012) 84 NSWLR 231 the solicitor negligently failed to advise in strong terms that her home and livelihood were dependent on her son making loan repayment from his business income and recommend in strong terms that she obtain independent financial advice about the capacity of his business to service the loans.

(ii) *The Investment of Money and Claims by Lenders*

11–217 [*Add to n.1023*]

The security property may be shares, and in *Clack v Wrigleys Solicitors LLP* [2013] EWHC 413 (Ch); 92013) 163(7557) N.L.J. 17, the solicitors were negligent in failing to advise the individual who was to lend money not to complete the loan without seeing a copy of the register of members and a share certificate.

CML Handbook

11–218 [*Add to n.1036*]

The Court of Criminal Appeal observed in *R. v Cornelius* [2012] EWCA Crim 500; [2012] P.N.L.R. 23 that the certificate of title must be consistently interpreted without fine distinctions, and if the CML wished to impose liability on conveyancers they must do so in clear terms.

The *Bowerman* duty

11–220 [*Add to n.1051*]

However, in *E.Surv Ltd v Goldsmith Williams Solicitors* [2014] EWHC 1104 (Ch); [2014] P.N.L.R. 25 it was held that the provisions of the Handbook were not exhaustive, and the solicitor had not only to report that the property had been owned by the vendor for less than six months, but also the original purchase price, which was known to the solicitor and was considerably less than the proposed sale price.

(iii) *Wills*

Time

[*Add to n.1120*] **11–235**

In *Feltham v Freer Bouskell* [2013] EWHC 1952 (Ch); [2013] W.T.L.R. 1363; [2014] P.N.L.R. 2 the solicitor reasonably had concerns as to the testator's mental capacity and that the beneficiary may be influencing the testator, but having accepted instructions he should have chased up a medical report from a doctor who had been instructed within ten days or arranged for another doctor to be instructed, and on receipt of the report he should have visited the testator to discuss her instructions rather than choosing to do nothing unless further instructed.

3. Damages

(a) *Breach of Fiduciary Duty and Breach of Trust*

Introduction

[*Add to n.1132*] **11–238**

Remedies include the discretionary remedy of an account, where the claimant does not have to establish that it was the legal or beneficial owner of the funds paid over, see *Barnett v Creggy* [2014] EWHC 3080 (Ch); [2015] P.N.L.R. 13.

The modern law

[*Replace last two sentences with the following*] **11–242**

Subsequent modern cases on breach of trust in lenders claims are considered at para.11–037A–C. See, in the context of the CML conditions: *Lloyds TSB Bank Plc v Markandan & Uddin (A Firm)* [2012] EWCA Civ 65; [2012] 2 All E.R. 884; *Nationwide Building Society v Davisons Solicitors* [2012] EWCA Civ 1626; [2013] P.N.L.R. 12; and *Santander UK Plc v RA Legal Solicitors (A Firm)* [2014] EWCA Civ 183; [2014] P.N.L.R. 20. In *AIB Group (UK) Plc v Mark Reder & Co (A Firm)* [2014] UKSC 58; [2015] P.N.L.R. 10 solicitors on a remortgage were required to pay £1.5 million of the £3.3 million advanced to Barclays Bank under a previous charge, but paid about £300,000 too little. The borrowers defaulted, and the property was later sold for £1.2 million, with the claimant recovering about £900,000. The claimant sued for £2.4 million, being the difference between the amount advanced and the sums recovered. The Supreme Court held that the solicitors were only liable for the loss caused, which was the amount of the further Barclays charge which should have been redeemed of £300,000. The Supreme Court reaffirmed the correctness of *Target Holdings Ltd v Redferns* [1996] 1 A.C. despite subsequent criticism of it. For helpful commentary see S. Charlwood: "*AIB Group plc v Mark Redler & Co Solicitors:* the last word on lenders' breach of trust claims against solicitors?" (2015) 31 P.N. 60; L. Hu,

"Equitable compensation on the road to Damascus?" (2015) 131 L.Q.R. 213, and S. Televantos & L. Maniscalco, "Stay on Target: compensation and causation in breach of trust claims" (2015) 79 Conv. 348.

(b) *Remoteness*

(i) *Causation*

Intervening act of the claimant

11–251 [*Add to text*]

In *Joyce v Darby & Darby* [2014] EWCA Civ 677; [2014] 3 E.G.L.R. 49 the defendant solicitors negligently failed to inform the claimant that property she was buying was affected by a restrictive covenant requiring the consent of neighbours to external alterations. When she undertook such works, the neighbours objected, and the defendant advised her to stop work and reach agreement, or she would be sued. The claimant then carried out further work, and became involved in injunction proceedings, but the costs of them were not recoverable from the defendants.

[*Add to n.1171*]

In *Hudson v Atanskovic* [2014] NSWCA 255; (2015) 311 ALR 290 solicitors drafted a contract which provided that the claimant would be paid by the other contracting party selling the whole of certain land, which was allegedly negligent, but it also included a provision for the claimant to prevent sale of part of that land, which the claimant failed to invoke on such partial sale, and any negligence by the solicitors therefore did not cause the loss of the payment. In contrast, solicitors drafted an illegal lease for the tenant in *Mackinlay v Derry Dew Pty Ltd* [2014] WASCA 24; (2014) 46 WAR 247, and after later negotiations with the landlord had failed, the tenant terminated it is occupancy of the land. That termination was not unreasonable, as the tenant did not have a saleable asset.

(ii) *Foreseeability*

Illustrations

11–257 [*Add to n.1193*]

In *Platform Funding Ltd v Miller Parris Solicitors* (2012) 165(16) S.J.L.B. 39; [2012] 2 P. & C.R. DG7, the obligation was to report any feature of the borrower's title which might reasonably be expected to be material to the value and marketability of the property, the solicitors failed to report a covenant in the lease which materially restricted subletting, and the lender's losses incurred in fighting forfeiture arising from breach of that covenant were reasonably foreseeable. In *Manorgate Ltd v First Scottish Property Services Ltd* [2013] CSOH 108; [2014] P.N.L.R. 1 a property enquiry company produced a certificate for the claimants which negligently failed to reveal that the site which the claimants wished to purchase had been officially designated as being of archaeological significance. Excavations subsequently revealed a mediaeval friary, and the site was mothballed. The claimants' lost trading profits were recoverable, as the defendant knew that the property was zoned for commercial use, but development profits were not, as it was not foreseeable that the claimants might intend to use the site both to trade and to develop.

(iii) *The Scope of the Duty*

Exceptions

[*Add to n.1205*] 11–262

A similar result was reached in *Gabriel v Little* [2012] EWHC 1193 (Ch); [2013] W.T.L.R. 419, where solicitors failed to inform their client that the borrower was going to use loan monies largely to purchase a property, when the client thought that they were to be used to develop it, following *Portman Building Society v Bevan Ashford (A Firm)* [2000] P.N.L.R. 344. However, the Court of Appeal held that the loss was not within the scope of the duty, see [2013] EWCA Civ 1513, which is now being appealed to the Supreme Court. In *Kirton Investments Ltd v VMH LLP* [2011] CSOH 200; [2012] P.N.L.R. 11 solicitors negligently advised developers that they had a legally enforceable right to erect a flue which was necessary for a development, and after a dispute arose that they had a strong case, and as a result the development was delayed. Lord Doherty held that the advice was not merely the provision of information, and the solicitors were held liable for the losses sustained from the downturn of the property market, but he also relied on the mitigation exception, see para.11–259 n.1200 in the main text. Similarly, a claim by developers for losses caused by the fall in the market was not struck out in *Henderson (t/a Henderson Group Development) v Wotherspoon* [2013] CSOH 113; [2013] P.N.L.R. 28. In *Morkott v Watson & Brown Solicitors* [2014] EWHC 3439 (QB); [2015] P.N.L.R. 9 purchasers of property recovered their full losses where they had not been advised that the deposits gifted by the vendor, which was a hallmark of fraud, should have been reported to their lenders, who would not have made the loan. However, in *Credit & Mercantile Plc v Nabarro* [2014] EWHC 2819 (Ch); [2015] P.N.L.R. 14, where the defendant solicitors failed to state that planning permission included part of the site which was not being purchased, the claimant could only recover the diminution in value.

Further cases

[*Add to n.1210*] 11–263

In *Clack v Wrigleys Solicitors LLP* [2013] EWHC 413 (Ch); (2013) 163 N.L.J. 17, solicitors failed to advise an investor not to complete a loan to be secured on shares without seeing the register of members and a share certificate, but for which the loan would not have proceeded. The shares were worthless, but the only recoverable loss was the director's fees which should have been earned.

(c) *Measure of Damages*

(i) *Date of Assessment*

Exceptions

11–267 [*Add to n.1226*]

In *Stewart v Patterson Donnelly Solicitors* [2014] NIQB 103; [2015] P.N.L.R. 7 solicitors failed to secure a timeous final order in divorce proceedings before the claimant's husband went bankrupt, and if they had her lump sum would have been secured on the security of a company. The loss was assessed at the later date of when the security would have been realised.

(ii) *Credit for benefits*

General principle

In *Dhillon v Jaffer* 2042 BCCA 215; (2015) 375 D.L.R. (4th) 288, solicitors negligently paid to a wife proceeds of sale pursuant to a fraudulent power of attorney. As against the money paid away, the husband had to give credit for the recovery he had obtained from a subsequent house which the wife had bought, and for the fact that the wife would have been entitled to half of the sale proceeds in any event, and as a result he made no recovery from the negligent solicitors.

(iii) *Evaluation of a Chance*

Illustrations

11–275 [*Add to n.1244*]

Wright v Lewis Silkin LLP [2015] EWHC 1897 (QB); [2015] P.N.L.R. 32 (on a failure to advise on a jurisdiction clause in an employment contract, causing a delay in subsequent proceedings as jurisdiction was challenged, there was a 20 per cent chance of enforcement before the employer became insolvent).

11–276 [*Add to n.1247*]

And see *Kirton Investments Ltd v VMH LLP* [2011] CSOH 200; [2012] P.N.L.R. 11, where a development was delayed beyond the fall in the market, and the Judge held there was a 40 per cent chance of selling all the town houses, 60 per cent of selling the apartments, and 55 per cent of selling sufficient properties to clear the bank indebtedness before the market turned down. In *Xenakis & Anor v Birkett Long LLP (A Firm)* [2014] EWHC 171 QB; [2014] P.N.L.R. 16 negligence in failing to advise that going into occupation and releasing documents to the landlord before completion caused the claimants to be liable under a guarantee for nearly a year longer than they had contemplated due to the delays in completing the lease, and there was a 50 per cent chance of renegotiating the terms and an 80 per cent chance of getting the lease completed earlier. In *Wellesley Partners LLP v Withers LLP* [2014] EWHC 556 (Ch); [2014] P.N.L.R. 22 solicitors negligently drafted an agreement for an LLP giving a bank the ability to withdraw monies within 41 months rather than after 42 months, as a result of which profits were lost, including a 15 per cent chance of being awarded a sole mandate from a bank in New York and a 45 per cent chance of a half mandate.

The limits of the principle

[*Add to n.1255*] **11–278**

Similarly, in *Feltham v Freer Bouskell* [2013] EWHC 1952 (Ch); [2013] W.T.L.R. 1363 the Court decided, obiter, that what the testatrix would have done is to be judged on the basis of the loss of a chance, although in that case the lost chance was 100 per cent.

(d) *Heads of Damage*

(ii) *Difference in Value of Property*

The normal rule

[*Add to n.1281*] **11–287**

It remains the case that the breach has to be linked to the alleged loss, which a mere list of expenditure did not do in *Wyatt v Crate* [2012] CSOH 197; [2013] P.N.L.R. 16.

(iii) *Loss of Opportunity to Bring Proceedings*

The lower threshold

[*Add to n.1354*] **11–304**

In *Ladner v Wolfson* 2011 BCCA 370; (2012) 343 D.L.R. (4th) 299 it was held that the alleged failure to pursue a claim for a constructive trust failed because there was no basis to pursue such a claim.

The significance of the notional date of trial

[*Add to n.1388*] **11–311**

A similar result was reached, effectively on the grounds of remoteness, in *Witcombe v Talbot Olivier* [2011] WASCA 107; (2011) 280 A.L.R. 177.

(v) *Losses on Loans Secured by Mortgages*

Scope of duty

[*Add to n.1404*] **11–316**

Similarly, in the Irish case of *KBC Bank v BCM Hanby Wallace* [2012] IEHC 120; [2013] P.N.L.R. 7, the solicitors had misled the bank about the availability of the security properties, and were liable for the whole loss, and not just the value of the expected securities. While there was a successful appeal on whether the solicitors had acted dishonestly, there was no challenge to this conclusion on appeal at [2013] IESC 32; [2013] P.N.L.R. 33.

(ix) *Wasted Expenditure*

Later solicitor's costs

11–330 [*Add to n.1450*]

Followed by the Singapore Court of Appeal in *Maryani Sadeli v Arjun Permanand Samtani* [2014] SGCA 55; [2015] SLR 496, which provided an illuminating discussion of the issue.

(x) *Incidental Expenses*

11–331 [*Add to n.1454*]

In *PreMD Inc v Ogilvy Renault LLP* 2013 ONCA 412; (2013) 3 CCLT (4th) 186 solicitors negligently failed to pay maintenance payments on two US patents for the plaintiff developer of medical tools, which recovered damages reasonably incurred in mitigating its loss, including expenses in trying to reinstate the patents and strengthening its remaining patents portfolio.

(e) *Mitigation of Damage*

Examples of failure to mitigate: generous treatment of the claimant

11–337 [*Add to n.1476*]

In *Hermann v Withers LLP* [2012] EWHC 1492 (Ch); [2012] P.N.L.R. 28, there was a dispute as to whether the claimants were entitled to use of communal gardens, and the garden committee offered a 50-year licence for £25,000. The claimants failed to mitigate their loss by refusing this offer, and instead they took proceedings and lost.

4. SHARED RESPONSIBILITY

(a) *Contributory Negligence*

The general rule

11–343 [*Add to n.1496*]

In *Wellesley Partners LLP v Withers LLP* [2014] EWHC 556 (Ch); [2014] P.N.L.R. 22 solicitors negligently drafted an agreement for an LLP giving a bank an option to withdraw half of its contribution within 41 months, rather than after 42 months as instructed, and were held to be negligent. The claimants were not contributorily negligent in failing to notice this. In *Manorgate Ltd v First Scottish Property Services Ltd* [2013] CSOH 108; [2014] P.N.L.R. 1 a property enquiry company produced a certificate for the claimants which negligently failed to reveal that the site which the claimants wished to purchase had been officially designated as being of archaeological significance. The claimants were not contributorily negligent in failing to make their own investigations, in particular because they were keen to secure the transaction.

Illustrations

[*Add to n.1501*] **11–344**

Tran v Kerr 2014 ABCA 350; (2015) 6 Alta. L.R. (6th) 213: the respondent negligently participated in a fraudulent mortgage scheme and failed to raise her concerns or disclose her true role in it. She was 40 per cent contributorily negligent, her solicitor having a greater responsibility as a lawyer.

Claims by lenders

[*Add to n.1507*] **11–345**

In *KBC Bank v BCM Hanby Wallace* [2013] IESC 32; [2013] P.N.L.R. 33 the lender may have been contributorily negligent in failing to verify the assets and income of the borrowers, and possibly failing to overlook the solicitors' errors, but the matters were remitted to the High Court to determine.

Circumstances in which contributory negligence cannot be claimed

[*Add to n.1517*] **11–347**

The issue was not considered on appeal, [2012] EWCA Civ 65; [2012] P.N.L.R. 20.

(b) *Apportionment of Liability*

Apportionment of liability between solicitors and surveyors

[*Add to n.1530*] **11–350**

In *E.Surv Ltd v Goldsmith Williams Solicitors* [2014] EWHC 1104 (Ch); [2014] P.N.L.R. 25 surveyors had overvalued property for a lender, and solicitors had failed to inform the lender that it had been owned by the purchaser for less than six months and bought at a price considerably less than the proposed sale price. The solicitors and surveyors were held to be equally liable.

Other illustrations

[*Add to n.1538*] **11–352**

In *ACC Bank Plc v Johnson & Co (Solicitors)* [2011] IEHC 501; [2012] P.N.L.R. 13, solicitors who had negligently accepted an undertaking and then dispensed lender's monies obtained a 70 per cent contribution against a partner in the firm which had given and broken the undertaking (although under the Irish statute contribution is assessed solely by fault). In *Clydesdale Bank Plc v Workman* [2013] EWHC B38 (Ch); [2014] P.N.L.R. 18 solicitors who repeatedly and negligently failed to procure the registration of a bank's charge over property settled a claim by the bank, and sued for a contribution from solicitors who had dishonestly assisted the owners of the property in disposing of it. Liability was assessed at 35 per cent for the negligent solicitors and 65 per cent for the dishonest assisters.

CHAPTER 12

BARRISTERS

1. GENERAL

(e) *Immunity*

[*Add to n.21*] **12–004**

Nor should a barrister act for a claimant trust when he controlled it and was a discretionary beneficiary of it, see *Sheraz Pt Ltd v Vegas Enterprises Pty Ltd* [2015] WASCA 4; (2015) 319 ALR 709.

(e) *Immunity*

[*Add to n.47*] **12–009**

Immunity applies also to statutory causes of action against the solicitor, see *Nikolaidis v Satouris* [2014] NSWCA 448; (2015) 317 ALR 761.

(g) *Liability for Costs*

Misjudgements on timing

[*Add to n.93*] **12–021**

Similarly, a wasted costs order was upheld in *R. v Henrys Solicitors* [2012] EWCA Crim 1480; [2012] P.N.L.R. 32, where the advocate accepted instructions in two cases on the same day in geographically distant courts and there was a real risk of a delay in the first court, which happened so that she was unable to appear at the second hearing.

2. LIABILITY FOR BREACH OF DUTY

Knowledge of the law

12–024 [*Add to n.102*]

In *Taylor v The Queen* [2009] N.S.W.C.C.A. 180; (2009) N.S.W.L.R. 198, the New South Wales Court of Criminal Appeal observed that the use of electronic aids to legal research was part of the standard that courts were entitled to expect of Counsel.

Is there an error?

12–026 [*Add to text*]

Similarly, in *Schumann v Veale Wasbrough* [2015] EWCA Civ 441; [2015] P.N.L.R. 25 the barrister gave correct advice that the claimant did not have a clinical negligence case, after competent questioning of the expert witnesses.

Failures of advice

12–032 [*Add to text*]

In *Thomas v Albutt* [2015] EWHC 2187 (Ch); [2015] P.N.L.R. 29 a barrister was found to be negligent in failing to advise clients to put in evidence of prejudice in judicial review proceedings to quash planning permission.

Negligence in court

12–040 [*Add to n.252*]

In *Meister v Coyle* 2011 NSCA 119; (2012) 345 D.L.R. (4th) 657, Counsel's strategy of permitting inadmissible re-enactment evidence in a dangerous driving case was acknowledged to be an error of judgment, but the Nova Scotia Court of Appeal upheld the decision that it was not negligent.

3. DAMAGES

Measure of damages.

12–043 [*Add to n.171*]

In *Thomas v Albutt* [2015] EWHC 2187 (Ch); [2015] P.N.L.R. 29 a barrister negligently failed to advise clients to put in evidence of prejudice in judicial review proceedings to quash planning permission, but that would only have improved their prospects of success by 5–10 per cent, which was negligible and below 10 per cent which was considered to be the threshold for a substantial prospect of success, and no damages were awarded. The assessment was based on the additional improvement if such evidence had been put in, and the existing prospects of success were not added to that improved chance.

4. SHARED RESPONSIBILITY

(a) *Apportionment of Liability*

[*Add to n.177*] **12–044**

In *Bray v Dye (No.2)* [2010] VSC 152; (2010) 27 V.R. 324, Judd J. held that there was an equal division of fault between barrister and solicitor for acting for the second plaintiff who had not authorised proceedings. The barrister had introduced the first plaintiff to the solicitor, and both lawyers had failed to make adequate enquiries with the second plaintiff. Quaere whether the barrister would be held liable in this jurisdiction.

CHAPTER 13

MEDICAL PRACTITIONERS

2. GENERAL

(a) *Duties to Patient*

Private patients

13–003 [*Add at end of paragraph*]

In *Dove v Jarvis* [2013] Med L.R. 284, the Court found that the orthopaedic surgeon's assurance to the patient that the knee replacement surgery would be "well done" did not involve the surgeon assuming a higher duty of care than that of an experienced orthopaedic surgeon.

Fiduciary duties

[*Add to n.26*]

13–010 However, see now the decision in *Montgomery v Lanarkshire Health Board* [2015] UKSC 11; [2015] 2 W.L.R. 768, considered further below in 13–059.

(b) *Duties to Third Parties*

13–011 [*Add to n.30*]

See also *Selwood v Durham County Council and others* [2012] EWCA Civ 979, in which the Court of Appeal set aside an order striking out a claim by a social worker, employed by the defendant local authority, who had been attacked by a voluntary patient of two defendant NHS trusts (with whom the local authority worked closely). The defendants had failed to warn the social worker of threats made by the patient that he would harm the social worker if he saw her. Although not a "third party" case, it engages with the issue of when a health professional owes duties in respect of actions threatened by a mentally ill patient.

[*Add to n.31*]

See also *Taylor v A Novo (UK) Ltd* [2013] EWCA Civ 194. Applied in *RS v Criminal Injuries Compensation Authority* [2013] EWCA Civ 1040, which concerned the proper interpretation of para.9(b)(ii) of the Criminal Injuries Compensation Scheme 2008.

[*Add to n.32*]

See also *Liverpool Women's Hospital NHS Foundation Trust v Ronayne* [2015] EWCA Civ 588, where the defendant's appeal was allowed. On the facts of the case, the necessary element of suddenness did not exist and what the claimant husband saw was not horrifying by objective standards. The Court of Appeal applied *Shorter v Surrey and Sussex Healthcare NHS Trust* [2015] EWHC 614 (QB).

[*Add to n.35*] **13–012**

See also the Northern Irish case of *A v A Health and Social Services Trust* [2011] NICA 28, and in respect of this case, see further below at n.242a.

[*Add to n.36*]

This case was considered and applied in another negligence claim against solicitors, *Schumann v Veale Wasbrough* [2013] EWHC 3730 (QB). The claimant's appeal was dismissed by the Court of Appeal in [2015] EWCA Civ 441.

(c) *The Standard of Skill and Care*

The general principle

[*Add to n.40*] **13–013**

See also the appeal, *Penney v East Kent HA* [2000] Lloyd's Rep. Med. 41, where the finding of liability against the health authority was upheld.

[*Add to n.47*] **13–014**

For a useful illustration of the application of the *Bolam* test (with the *Bolitho* modification), see *Ecclestone v Medway NHS Foundation Trust* [2013] EWHC 790 (QB), in respect of different surgical techniques for knee surgery. The judge found that "it would be a very bold and inappropriate step for a court to take to find in effect that the authors of two leading world textbooks on orthopaedic surgery had described a surgical technique which could not be logically supported."

[*Add at end of paragraph*]

In *C v North Cumbria University Hospitals NHS Trust* [2014] EWHC 61 (QB) the Court summarised the principles and considerations applicable in respect of expert evidence when applying the *Bolam* test (see in particularly para.25). The

Court stated inter alia that in assessing whether an act or omission alleged to be negligent is reasonable, the Court must not delegate the task of deciding the issue to the expert. The Court must decide for itself. The Court discussed the meaning of "responsible/competent/respectable" as cited in *Bolitho*. It stated that by far and away the most important consideration is the logic of the expert opinion tendered. The opinion should be tested against the other evidence in the case and against its internal consistency.

(d) *General and Approved Practice*

13–020 [*Add new footnote reference 56a after "unsatisfactory"*]

NOTE 56a. See developments in respect of the Medical Innovation Bill, reintroduced to Parliament in 2014.

(f) *Res Ipsa Loquitur*

Application of the maxim to clinical negligence

13–024 [*Add to n.67*]

For an example of a medical negligence claim which was assessed not to be one of *res ipsa loquitur*, see *Thomas v Curley* [2013] EWCA Civ 117. The Court of Appeal found that the judge at first instance had correctly directed himself to assess the weight of the evidence in respect of why injury was caused during an uncomplicated operation, in an area other than that where the operation took place, and to decide whether negligence had been proved.

(g) *Consent to Treatment*

13–026 [*Remove first sentence of n.73*]

[*Add at end of paragraph*]

The following section in respect of consent must now be read subject to the decision of the Supreme Court in *Montgomery v Lanarkshire Health Board* [2015] UKSC 11; [2015] 2 W.L.R. 768. See also the decision of the Court of Appeal in *Border v Lewisham and Greenwich NHS Trust* [2015] EWCA Civ 8; [2015] Med. L.R. 48. The Court of Appeal found that the only tenable reading of the judgment was that the doctor had inserted a cannula into a patient's arm without her express or implied consent. It was therefore open to the patient to contend on appeal that the finding of a lack of consent should have led the judge to find breach of duty, even though that was not the way she had advanced her case at trial.

(ii) *Voluntary Consent*

[*In last sentence of n.80 remove the words "(A Jehovah's Witness)"*] **13–028**

(iii) *Informed Consent*

[*Add to n.84*] **13–029**

The issue of informed consent has recently been considered by the Court of Appeal in *Meiklejohn v St George's Healthcare NHS Trust* [2014] EWCA Civ 120.

(iv) *Capacity to Consent*

Mentally disordered patients

[*Add to n.96*] **13–034**

See also *Coombs v Dorset NHS Primary Care Trust* [2012] Med. L.R. 438, as affirmed by the Court of Appeal [2013] EWCA Civ 471.

[*Add at end of paragraph*] **13–035**

In *L (Vulnerable Adults with Capacity: Court's Jurisdiction), Re* [2012] EWCA Civ 253, it was confirmed that the Mental Capacity Act 2005 had not removed the High Court's inherent jurisdiction to deal with cases which fell outside the Act, and to protect vulnerable adults. In *Nottinghamshire Healthcare NHS Trust v RC* [2014] EWHC 1317 (COP) the Court found that the administration of a blood transfusion to a Jehovah's Witness who suffered from personality disorders fell within s.63 of the Mental Health Act 1983 and could be lawfully administered without consent in the absence of capacity—but that it would be an abuse of power to do so if the patient had capacity to refuse blood products. The duty to save life was subservient to the right of sovereignty over one's own body (para.26). Reference was also made to the recent case of *Newcastle-Upon-Tyne-Hospitals Foundation Trust v LM* [2014] EWHC 454 (COP).

[*Add to n.105*]

See also *NHS Trust 1 v G* [2014] EWCOP 30, which concerned applications by two NHS trusts in respect of the obstetric case of a mentally ill woman. The Court gave guidance in respect of the circumstances in which applications should be made and as to the procedure to be followed.

Withdrawal of treatment from insensate patients

[*Add at end of paragraph*] **13–036**

The Supreme Court considered the issue of withdrawal of treatment from a critically ill patient lacking capacity in *Aintree University Hospitals NHS Foundation Trust v James* [2013] UKSC 67, including the interpretation of the Mental Capacity Code of Conduct. The focus should be on whether it is in the patient's best interests to give the treatment, rather than on whether it is in his best interests to withhold or withdraw it (para.22). When considering the best interests of a patient at a particular time, decision-makers must look at his welfare in the widest sense (para.39).

[*Add to n.107*]

See also *Re M (Adult Patient) (Minimally Conscious State: Withdrawal of Treatment)* [2012] 1 W.L.R. 1653 in respect of the use of the "balance sheet" approach in determining the best interests of an incapacitated adult. Baker J. found that the balance sheet approach was appropriate in the case of a patient in a minimally conscious (rather than vegetative) state who is clinically stable (para.245). However the application to withdraw artificial nutrition and hydration was dismissed as, in this case, the importance of preserving life was the decisive factor (para.249). This case has been cited in numerous cases since (including *St George's Healthcare NHS Trust v P* [2015] EWCOP 42). See also *An NHS Foundation Trust v M and K* [2013] EWHC 2402 (COP), a decision of Eleanor King J. The judge stated that whilst the presumption in favour of preservation of life is a fundamental principle, "it does not displace the patient's best interests as the paramount consideration for the Court" [para.59]. Further, a central (but not the only) question is whether treatment would be "futile or overly burdensome" or whether it is a case where there is no prospect of recovery [para.61].

(h) *Allied Professions*

13–038 [*Add new footnote reference 113a to end of paragraph*]

NOTE 113a. See for example the application of these principles in the context of the monitoring of foetal well-being during childbirth by midwives, in *Popple v Birmingham Women's NHS Foundation Trust* [2011] EWHC 2320 (QB). The decision at first instance was upheld on appeal: [2013] EWCA Civ 1628. The appeal itself was unusual insofar as it was an appeal only in respect of the judge's findings of fact. See also the case of *Taaffe v East of England Ambulance Services NHS Trust* [2012] EWHC 1335 (QB) for an application in respect of the duties owed by paramedics. In circumstances where paramedics had failed to take a proper history and had failed to appreciate the significance of the patient's signs and symptoms (potentially indicative of acute cardiac syndrome), the *Bolam* defence failed.

(i) *Hospitals and Health Authorities*

13–040 [*Add to n.118*]

Farraj was approved by the Supreme Court in a different context in *Woodland v Swimming Teachers Association* [2013] UKSC 66.

3. Breach of Duty

General

[*Add new footnote reference 123a at end of sub-para.(ii)*] **13–043**

Note 123a. Other duties may be owed by the hospital trust. A full analysis of the issue of duties under art.2 of the Convention is outside the scope of this chapter. In *Rabone v Pennine Care NHS Trust (Inquest and Others Intervening)* [2012] UKSC 2, the Supreme Court found that whilst generally there was no operational duty to protect patients in most cases involving medical negligence, there was an exception in the case of psychiatric patients detained in hospital who were at real and immediate risk of suicide. See also *Coombs v Dorset NHS Primary Care Trust* [2013] EWCA Civ 471 and *R. (on the application of JF) v NHS Sheffield Clinical Commissioning Group* [2014] EWHC 1345 (Admin).

(c) *Wrong Diagnosis*

Failure to detect more serious condition

[*Add to n.137*] **13–049**

See also *Meiklejohn v St George's Healthcare NHS Trust* [2013] EWHC 469, a claim in respect of alleged clinical negligence in the diagnosis of a rare genetic disorder, dyskeratosis congenita. The claim failed: the defendant blood specialist had not failed in her duty by treating him on the basis that he was suffering from a different disorder. The appeal was dismissed in *Meiklejohn v St George's Healthcare NHS Trust* [2014] EWCA Civ 120. The Court of Appeal found that whilst the appeal was advanced as an error of law, it was an appeal on the facts (para.58). The duty to advise and warn about diagnosis, treatment and side-effects was to be assessed in accordance with the practice of a responsible body of doctors. There was no authority for a duty to warn of possible alternative diagnoses not reasonably suspected (para.62).

(e) *Failure of Communication Between Hospitals or Medical Practitioners*

[*Remove the words "were identified by the Court of Appeal" at end of paragraph*] **13–058**

(f) *Failing to Explain Treatment or Warn of Risks*

[*Add after words "proposed medical treatment"*] **13–059**

However, see now the Supreme Court's decision in *Montgomery v Lanarkshire Health Board* [2015] UKSC 11. The Supreme Court held that the analysis of the law by the majority in *Sidaway* was unsatisfactory, insofar as it treated the doctor's duty to advise the patient of the risks of proposed treatment as falling within the scope of the *Bolam* test. It stated that it was unsurprising that courts had found difficulty in the application of *Sidaway*, and that the courts in England and Wales in reality departed from it, a position effectively endorsed in *Chester v Afshar* [2005] 1 A.C. 134. An adult of sound mind was entitled to decide which if any of the available forms of treatment to undergo. The patient's consent had to be obtained before treatment interfering with bodily integrity was undertaken. The doctor was under a duty to take reasonable care to ensure that the patient was aware of any material risks involved in any recommended treatment and of any reasonable alternative or variant treatment. See in particular *Montgomery* at [86]–[88] in respect of the new test for breach of duty. The Court in *Montgomery* approved both *Pearce v United Bristol Healthcare NHS Trust* and the dissenting opinion of Lord Scarman in *Sidaway*. *Montgomery* has since been applied in various cases including *Connolly v Croydon Health Services NHS Trust* [2015] EWHC 1339 (QB) and *Spencer v Hillingdon Hospital NHS Trust* [2015] EWHC 1058 (QB). This recent case law reflects the importance of the patient's personal autonomy and the entitlement of a patient to information and advice. Further, the test of materiality was set out in *Montgomery*: namely, being whether a reasonable person in the patient's position would be likely to attach significance to the risk, or whether the doctor should reasonable be aware that the particular patient would be likely to attach significance to it. Materiality could not be reduced to percentages, as the significance of a given risk was likely to reflect a variety of other facts such as the nature and effect of the risk and any alternatives available. The test is therefore fact-sensitive and sensitive to the characteristics of the patient (see [87] and [89]). This test was applied in *A v East Kent Hospitals University NHS Foundation Trust* [2015] EWHC 1038 (QB); [2015] Med. L.R. 262.

13–060 [*Add to n.164*]

The cases of *Sidaway* and *Birch* were also considered in *Meiklejohn v St George's Healthcare NHS Trust* [2014] EWCA Civ 120.

13–061 [*Add to n.165*]

and the Scottish case of *M's Guardian v Lanarkshire Health Board* [2013] CSIH 3 (IH (Ex Div)). This decision has now been reversed by the Supreme Court in *Montgomery v Lanarkshire Health Board* [2015] UKSC 11.

13–066 [*Add to end of paragraph*]

A medical practitioner is under no duty of care to disclose a father's diagnosis of Huntingdon's disease to a pregnant daughter.[176a]

NOTE 176a. See *ABC v St George's Healthcare NHS Foundation Trust* [2015] EWHC 1394 (QB), in which such a claim was struck out.

4. DAMAGES

(a) *Scope of Duty*

[*Add to n.177*] **13–068**

See also *Less v Hussain* [2012] EWHC 3513 (QB), where the defendant gynaecologist, from whom the claimant mother had sought advice about the safety of pregnancy, argued that, since a stillbirth was caused by hypercoiling of the umbilical cord, which was not a matter about which her advice was sought by the claimant nor a risk or complication which the defendant should have addressed, the subsequent stillbirth and the claimant's consequent psychiatric injury were outside the scope of the defendant's duty. The argument failed: it was held that given that this was advice about conception, loss of the baby during term was a kind of loss in respect of which a duty was owed, and it made no difference that the precise mechanism was not foreseen.

(b) *Factual Causation*

Material contribution

[*Add to n.183*] **13–071**

See also *Nathan Popple v Birmingham Women's NHS Foundation Trust* [2011] EWHC 2320: it was not possible on the scientific evidence to identify the particular point in time, within a certain bracket, at which the claimant had suffered irreversible brain damage during his birth; however, it was held, following *Bailey*, that exposing him to a longer period of damaging hypoxia within that bracket made a material contribution to damage and therefore the limitations of the scientific evidence were not a bar to a finding of causation. The decision was upheld on appeal to the Court of Appeal [2012] EWCA Civ 1628. The test in *Bailey* was also applied in *Leigh v London Ambulance Services NHS Trust* [2014] EWHC 286 (QB).

[*Add to n.184*]

Hotson was also applied in *Hussain v Bradford Teaching Hospital NHS Foundation Trust* [2011] EWHC 2914: the claimant failed to establish causation where a hospital had been negligent in failing to diagnose and treat his Cauda Equina Syndrome. On the expert evidence, on the balance of probabilities the claimant would not have made a good recovery even if the Syndrome had been diagnosed and treated non-negligently, given its rapid onset. The claimant's "fall-back" case that earlier treatment might have resulted in some general improvement to his condition was too speculative and impressionistic to succeed. See also the obiter comments on causation in *Beech v Timney* [2013] EWHC 2345 (QB).

Material increase in risk

13–075 [*Add new footnote reference 195a to end of paragraph*]

NOTE 195a. See also, on the nature of the *Fairchild* exception, *Durham v BAI (Run Off) Ltd* [2012] UKSC 14 and *International Energy Group Ltd v Zurich Insurance Plc UK* [2013] EWCA Civ 39.

Loss of a chance

13–077 [*Add before the final sentence in n.202*]

See also *Hussain v Bradford Teaching Hospital NHS Foundation Trust* (n.184 above); *JD v Mather* [2012] EWHC 3063 (QB); *Oliver v Williams* [2013] EWHC 600 (QB) (in which the appeal has been dismissed by the Court of Appeal); and *Marshall v Hull and East Yorkshire Hospitals NHS Trust* [2014] EWHC 4326 (QB).

Warnings

13–078 [*Add to n.206*]

Indeed, in *M's Guardian v Lanarkshire Health Board* [2013] CSIH 3 the Court of Session (Inner House, Extra Division) expressed the view, albeit obiter, that the modification of causation principles which the House of Lords was prepared to make in *Chester* did not apply generally to all cases in which a medical practitioner has failed in a duty to advise of risks. Rather, it appeared to the Court, *"the situation in which the majority of their Lordships in* Chester v Afshar *considered that liability should exist was one where a warning of risk would have resulted in the patient seeking further advice elsewhere, with resultant uncertainty as to whether the patient would have undergone at a future date an identical procedure in which the same risk might or might not have materialised."* The Court distinguished *Chester* from the instant case, where it was alleged by the claimant that, if she had been advised of a certain risk by a consultant obstetrician, she would have elected a caesarean rather than vaginal delivery. The Court pointed to the fact that *"the birth of a baby cannot simply be put off or postponed, like a planned procedure"*, so that it was not part of the claimant's case that she would have deferred matters and taken further advice, the outcome of which might be uncertain. Moreover, there was an unchallenged finding of fact that, even if properly advised, the claimant would yet have been persuaded to attempt vaginal delivery. As a result, the case was not within the ambit of *Chester v Afshar*. This aspect of the case was not considered by the Supreme Court (see [105]).

Factual causation in wrongful birth and wrongful conception cases

13–080 [*Add at end of paragraph*]

Likewise, where the complaint made relates to advice given by the claimant as to the risks of a pregnancy, the question arises as to whether the parents would nevertheless have been prepared to take those risks and proceed to conception.[209a]

NOTE 209a. In *Less v Hussain* (n.177 above), it was held that a proper explanation of the risks of a pregnancy would not have dissuaded the claimant from becoming pregnant; what would have been required to stop the claimant from taking this step would have been nothing short of advice that she should not try for another child, but such advice was not required to be given by a reasonably competent consultant gynaecologist.

(e) *Remoteness*

[*Add at end of paragraph*] **13–091**

If a claimant is suffering from an existing disability at the time of the negligence, which exacerbates their condition, this should be seen as a reflection of the principle that a tortfeasor had to take his victim as he finds him: *Reaney v University of North Staffordshire NHS Trust* [2014] EWHC 3016 (QB), in particular paras 70–71.

[*Add to n.231*] **13–092**

Also, *Holdich v Lothian Health Board* [2013] CSOH 197.

(f) *Measure of Damages*

(iii) *Damages in Wrongful Birth and Wrongful Conception Claims*

Unwanted healthy child born to a disabled mother

[*Add new footnote reference 242a to end of paragraph*] **13–099**

NOTE 242a. In *Less v Hussain* (n.177 above), Judge Cotter Q.C. declined (albeit obiter) to extend the availability of a "*Rees* award" to a 'wrongful conception' case where the baby was stillborn. Note also that *Rees* was relied upon by the claimant children in *A v A Health and Social Services Trust* [2011] NICA 28, who sought damages to compensate them for the fact that, due to an error on the part of the defendant health authority in carrying out an in vitro fertilisation (IVF) procedure, which led to the sperm used in the process coming from a donor with a different ethnicity from that of the claimants' mother and non-biological father, the claimants had inherited a different skin colour than their parents. The Court of Appeal in Northern Ireland rejected the claim, holding that *"having a different skin colour from the majority of the surrounding population and their parents [could not] sensibly be regarded as damage or disability"*.

CHAPTER 14

REGULATION OF FINANCIAL SERVICES

1. GENERAL

14–001 [*In n.1 replace "Draft Financial Services Bill 2011 therein." with the following*]

Financial Services Act 2012, most of which came fully into force on April 1, 2013.

14–003 [*For "FSA" substitute "FCA"*]

(a) *The FSA*

14–004 [*General note to para.14–004*]

As anticipated in n.8 (and noted in para.14–001, above), since April 1, 2013 (a) the "micro"-prudential regulation of "SIFIs" is now undertaken by the PRA and (b) the FSA has been replaced by the FCA with the narrower remit of regulating conduct of business and markets (and prudentially regulating non-SIFIs). See FSMA, Part 1A (the new regulators), Sch.1ZA (FCA) and Sch.1ZB (PRA), as inserted by the Financial Services Act 2012. The PRA and FCA have the same wide-powers as the FSA, as is consistent with their respective remits.

[*Add to n.9*]

To reflect the amendment of FSMA by the Financial Services Act 2012 to make provision for the new regulatory architecture, Pt X has been replaced by Pt 9A (ss.137A–141A).

[*Add to n.10*]

To reflect the amendment of FSMA by the Financial Services Act 2012 to make provision for the new regulatory architecture, Pt IV has been replaced by Pt 4A (ss.55A–55Z4).

[*Add to n.12*]

Add, in appropriate places: Pt 12A (ss.192A–192N, Power exercisable in relation to parent undertakings), Pt 18A (ss.313A–313D, Suspension and removal of financial instruments from trading)

[*Add to n.13*]

The FCA (see para.14–004, above) is now the "competent authority" and Pt VI has been amended by the Financial Services Act 2012 accordingly.

[*Add to n.14*]

The FCA and PRA also have "objectives": see FSMA, ss.1B–1K (FCA) and ss.2B–2J (PRA), as inserted by the Financial Services Act 2012 and amended (from a date to be appointed) by the Financial Services (Banking Reform) Act 2013, ss.1 and 2.

[*Add to n.17*]

See also *Jeffery v Financial Services Authority* [2012] EWCA Civ 178 (successful appeal from Tribunal decision on point of law relating to time limit under FSMA s.66 (5)(a)); *Financial Conduct Authority v Hobbs* [2013] EWCA Civ 918 (FCA given permission to appeal Tribunal decision); *7722656 Canada Inc (formerly Swift Trade Inc) v Financial Services Authority* [2013] EWCA Civ 1662 (appeal against FSA in market abuse context dismissed); *Abdul Razzaq v Financial Conduct Authority* [2014] EWCA Civ 770 (applicant refused permission to appeal Tribunal decision); *FCA v Macris* [2015] EWCA Civ 490 (on FSMA 2000 s.393: Tribunal ruling against FCA upheld). And see *Bayliss & Co (Financial Services) Ltd, Clive John Rosier v Financial Conduct Authority* [2015] UKUT 265 (TCC) (the Tribunal issued recommendations to the FCA regarding its procedures in relation to the publication of decision notices which had been referred to the tribunal).

[*Add to n.18*]

; (vi) *R. (on the application of C) v Financial Services Authority* [2013] EWCA Civ 677 (*Davies* (above) followed); (vii) (*R. (on the application of Julien Grout) v Financial Conduct Authority* [2015] EWHC 596 (Admin).

Limited immunity

[*Add at end of paragraph*] **14–005**

The FCA and PRA (see para.14–004, above) have corresponding immunity: see Sch.1ZA, para.25 (FCA) and Sch.1ZB, para.33 (PRA).

Other functions

14–006 [*General note to para.14–006*]

Since April 1, 2013, the FCA (see para.14–004, above) has taken over these FSA functions.

[*Add to n.28*]

; (iii) the Recognised Auction Platforms Regulations 2011, SI 2011/2699 (implementing the Emission Allowance Auctioning Regulation (Commission Regulation (EU) 1031/2010)).

(b) *The General Prohibition*

14–007 [*Add to n.37*]

See: (i) *R. v Napoli* [2012] EWCA Crim 1129 (an appeal from a criminal conviction for deposit-taking in breach of s.19); (ii) *R. v Von Badlo (Raj)* [2015] EWCA Crim 1236 (two-year custodial concurrent sentence for breaches of s.21 and s.397 (now Financial Services Act 2012 ss.89–90, where the maximum is seven years). See also Crime and Courts Act 2013 s.45 and Sch.17: deferred prosecution agreement (DPA) available in respect of the offence under s.23.

[*Add to n.38*]

See also *Financial Services Authority v Watkins (t/a Consolidated Land UK)* [2011] EWHC 1976 (declaration that a "land bank" scheme was a collective investment scheme within s.235).

(c) *The Financial Promotion Restriction*

14–009 [*Add to n.46*]

See Crime and Courts Act 2013 s.45 and Sch.17: deferred prosecution agreement (DPA) available in respect of the offence under s.25.

[*Add to n.48*]

Since April 1, 2013, the FCA (see para.14–004, above) makes the financial promotion rules under FSMA s.137R (as inserted by the Financial Services Act 2012).

[*Add at end of n.49*]

Since April 1, 2013, (see para.14–001, above) s.150 has been replaced by s.138D (as inserted by the Financial Services Act 2012), see para.14–071, below.

(d) *Authorised Persons*

[*General note to para.14–011*] **14–011**

Since April 1, 2013, Pt IV has been replaced by Pt 4A (ss.55A–55Z4) by the Financial Services Act 2012. Hence "Pt IV permission" has become "Pt 4A permission" and may be obtained either from the FCA or (in the case of SIFIs: see para.14–004, n.8, above) the PRA.

[*General note to para.14–012*] **14–012**

Since April 1, 2013, Pt IV has been replaced by Pt 4A (ss.55A–55Z4) by the Financial Services Act 2012. Hence "Pt IV permission" has become "Pt 4A permission" and may be obtained either from the FCA or (in the case of SIFIs: see para.14–004, n.8, above) the PRA.

(e) *Approved Persons*

[*General note to para.14–013*] **14–013**

Since April 1, 2013, both the FCA and PRA (see para.14–004, above) operate an "approved person regime" (presently with corresponding "APER" and "FIT" provisions in their respective Handbooks) and FSMA, Pt V has been amended accordingly by the Financial Services Act 2012. Part V has been further extensively amended by the Financial Services (Banking Reform) Act 2013, Pt V (generally coming into force on March 6, 2016: see SI 2015/490), essentially to increase the control over the management of banks and to enable the replacement of APER and FIT with a conduct rulebook applicable to approved persons and others (see the FCA and PRA Consultation Papers, FCA CP14/13 and PRA 14/14: *Strengthening accountability in banking: a new regulatory framework for individuals* (July 2014)).

(g) *Appointed Representatives*

(i) *Status Requirements*

[*Add at end of paragraph*] **14–016**

For a case interpreting an agreement between a principal (an insurance company) and its appointed representatives and the exclusion clauses it contained, see *AXA Sun Life Services Plc v Campbell Martin Ltd* [2011] EWCA Civ 133.

[*Add to n.80 after "arts"*]

24A (added by SI 2012/1906)

(ii) *Liability of Principal under FSMA*

[*General note to para.14–017*] **14–017**

The last two sentences of this paragraph were referred to with approval in *Page v Champion Financial Management Ltd* [2014] EWHC 1778 (QB), [12].

(h) *Members of Professions*

14–018 [*General note to para.14–018*]

Since April 1, 2013, the FSA's functions in relation to the professions are vested in the FCA (see para.14–004, above). Hence FSMA Pt XX has been amended accordingly by the Financial Services Act 2012.

14–019 [*General note to para.14–019*]

Since April 1, 2013, the FSA's functions in relation to the professions are vested in the FCA (see para.14–004, above). Hence FSMA Pt XX has been amended accordingly by the Financial Services Act 2012.

[*Add to n.94*]

See *Fuglers LLP v Solicitors Regulatory Authority* [2014] EWHC 179 (Admin): services provided were essentially "banking" services and not part of solicitor's practice.

(i) *European Aspects*

14–020 [*Add to n.103*]

The Prospectus Directive was amended by Directive 2010/73/EU, implemented by the Prospectus Regulations 2012, SI 2012/1538 (amending, inter alia, FSMA).

[*Add to n.104*]

TOD was amended by Directive 2010/73/EU, implemented by the Prospectus Regulations 2012, SI 2012/1538 (amending, inter alia, FSMA).

[*Add to n.105*]

See also the AIFMD (Alternative Investment Fund Managers Directive 2011/61/EU), implemented on July 22, 2013, primarily by the Alternative Investment Fund Managers Regulations 2013, SI 2013/1773.

[*Add to n.106*]

MAD will be replaced (in July 2016) by Regulation 596/2014 on market abuse and Directive 2014/57 on criminal sanctions for market abuse.

[*Add to n.108*]

See now the Markets in Financial Instruments Directive (MiFID II, Directive 2014/65/EU) and the new Markets in Financial Instruments Regulation (MiFIR, Regulation (EU) 600/2014).

[*Add to n.109*]

See the DGSD (Directive 2014/49 on deposit guarantee schemes (recast), implemented in part by the Deposit Guarantee Scheme Regulations 2015 (SI 2015/486).

2. Application of the FSMA Regulatory Regime

(a) *Regulated Activities*

[*Add at end of paragraph*] **14–023**

Note the new FSMA s.22(1A), added by the Financial Services Act 2012, whereby the Treasury may now specify an activity relating to information about a person's financial standing (such as providing credit references and see SI 2013/1881) or relating to the setting of a specified benchmark (such as LIBOR, and see SI 2013/655 and FSMA 2000, Sch.2, Pt 2B).

The RAO

[*In last sentence replace "four" with "six"*] **14–024**

[*Add at end of paragraph*]

The Financial Services and Markets Act 2000 (Regulated Activities) (Amendment) Order 2012, SI 2012/1906, added a new specified activity: art.24A (bidding in greenhouse gas emissions auctions). This implements the EU Emission Allowance Auctioning Regulation (Regulation (EU) 1031/2010) so that the United Kingdom has legislation for the FSA to authorise certain categories of people to make them eligible to bid in auctions of emissions allowances on their own account or on behalf of clients.

As a result of amendments made by the Financial Services Act 2012, there are two more new categories of "regulated activity". *First*, providing information in relation to specified benchmarks or administering such benchmarks is a "regulated activity" (see FSMA, s.22(1A)(b)—which enables any specified "benchmark" (as defined in subs.(6)) to be covered; LIBOR and other financial benchmarks have been specified: see RAO Chap.15E and Sch.5, added on April 2, 2013 by SI 2013/655) and amended by SI 2015/369. *Second*, consumer credit (and hire) activities, originally regulated by the OFT under the Consumer Credit Act 1974, are expected to become "regulated activities" under FSMA on April 1, 2014 (and see FSMA 2000, s.22(1A)(a) (enabling credit reference agencies to be covered) and the amendments to FSMA Sch.2 (see the substituted para.23 and new paras 23B, 24A–24D) as well as RAO, arts 36A–36G (credit broking), arts 36H–36J ("P2P" lending), arts 39D, 39H–39L (debt adjusting), arts 39E, 39H–39L (debt counselling), arts 39F, 39H–39L (debt collecting), arts 39G, 39H–39L (debt administration), arts 60B–60M, 60R (consumer lending), arts 60N–60Q, 60R (consumer hire)).

[*In n.129 replace "72F" with "72H"*]

[*In n.130 replace "72F" with "72H"*]

[*In n.132 replace "9AB" with "9AC"*]

[*Add at end of n.137*]

But note that the FSA "clarified" the effect of *Da Costa* in its Handbook (now the FCA Handbook), PERG 2.7.2B adding that the judgment "should be considered in the light of the case to which it relates".

[*Add at end of n.142*]

Note the extensive amendments to Ch.X as a result of the implementation of the AIFMD (Alternative Investment Fund Managers Directive 2011/61/EU) by the Alternative Investment Fund Managers Regulations 2013, SI 2013/1773 (see above, n.105).

[*Replace text after "arts" in n.153 with the following*]

5, 9B, 10, 25D, 51, 52, 63N

(c) *Investment*

14–028 [*Add at end of paragraph*]

The Financial Services and Markets Act 2000 (Regulated Activities) (Amendment) Order 2012, SI 2012/1906, added a new specified investment: 82A (greenhouse gas emissions allowances). This implements the EU Emission Allowance Auctioning Regulation (Regulation (EU) 1031/2010), see para.14–025, above.

In anticipation of the transfer of consumer credit (and hire) regulation from the OFT to the FCA on April 1, 2014, the Financial Services Act 2012 enabled rights under *any* credit contract (not only one secured on land, as was the previous position under the old Sch.2, para.23) (and certain hire contracts) to be "specified investments", and hence enabled the regulation of (consumer) credit (and hire) activities under FSMA (see FSMA, Sch.2, para.23 (as replaced by the Financial Services Act 2012, s.7(3)) and new para.23B (hire) (as inserted by the Financial Services Act 2012, s.7(4)), in force January 24, 2013 (see SI 2013/113)). Consequently new "specified investments" and "controlled investments" have been added to the RAO and FPO respectively, by the Financial Services and Markets Act 2000 (Regulated Activities) (Amendment No.2) Order 2013, SI 2013/1881, see RAO art.88D (credit agreements), art.88E (hire agreements) and FPO, Sch.1, para.26D (credit agreements), Sch.1, para.26E (hire agreements).

14–029 [*Add to n.193*]

See also the "land banking" cases where the property was land: *Financial Services Authority v Watkins (t/a Consolidated Land UK)* [2011] EWHC 1976;

Financial Services Authority v Asset L.I.Inc (t/a Asset Land Investment Inc) [2014] EWCA Civ 435; *Financial Conduct Authority v Capital Alternatives Ltd* [2014] EWHC 144 (Ch).

(d) *Nature of the Services*

[*Add at end of n.197*] **14–030**

Note that the FSA Handbook has now been replaced by the FCA and PRA Handbooks (see para.14–034 et seq., below).

(e) *Status of Provider of Financial Services*

[*Add at end of n.199*] **14–031**

However note that exceptionally an authorised person who undertakes "credit-related" regulated activities outside his permission does commit an offence: FSMA, s.23(1A).

3. Duties and Liabilities Under FSMA

[*General note to para.14–033*] **14–033**

On April 1, 2013, the FSA was replaced by the new regulators, the FCA and PRA (see para.14–004, above) which have similar rule-making etc. powers under FSMA, as amended by the Financial Services Act 2012.

4. Regulatory Rules and the FSA Handbook

(a) *General*

[*General note to paras 14–034 to 14–061*] **14–034**

Note that the new regulators (the FCA and PRA, see para.14–004) have each issued their own Handbook, which (from April 1, 2013) replaced the FSA Handbook. The rule-making power of the new regulators is now in FSMA, Pt 9A (ss.137A–141A), replacing the old Pt 10. The Financial Services Act 2012 (Transitional Provisions) (Rules and Miscellaneous Provisions) Order 2013, SI 2013/161 enabled the FCA and PRA (by means of a process of 'designation', see esp. arts 2 and 3) to adopt FSA 'instruments' such as rules so that they are to be treated as if they had been made by the new regulators. Hence, by this process of 'designation' a significant portion of the new Handbooks replicate the provisions in the old FSA Handbook, as is appropriate to the new regulators' functions. Essentially, the FCA Handbook replicates the old FSA Handbook (with an almost identical format) whilst the PRA Handbook replicates those parts of the old FSA Handbook that are relevant to its (prudential) regulatory functions.

However, the PRA has embarked on a process of converting its "Handbook" in to a "Rulebook".

Hence the text of Pt 4 of this chapter should now be read bearing in mind that it essentially applies to the new FCA Handbook (noting that the PRA Handbook contains more limited but similar provisions and is in the process of being converted into a "PRA Rulebook") made under the new rule-making power.

(b) *FSA Handbook*

(i) *Sourcebooks*

14–036 [*Add before "The contents page . . . "*]

The specialist sourcebook relating to credit unions has now been replaced by The Credit Unions New Sourcebook (CREDS for short). It came into force on January 8, 2012.

The Electronic Money Sourcebook is no longer in force, April 29, 2012 being the last day the material was in force.

The Credit Rating Agencies Guide is no longer in force, December 8, 2011 being the last day the material was in force.

(d) *Statements of Principle and Code of Practice for Approved Persons (APER)*

14–044 [*General note to paras 14–044 to 14–061*]

When in force, (expected date for this purpose, March 6, 2016), the Financial Services (Banking Reform) Act 2013, Pt V will amend FSMA, Pt V so as to (inter alia) enable the regulators to make "rules" rather than "Statements of Principles" and the corresponding "Code of Practice" for approved persons.

(e) *Conduct of Business Sourcebook (COBS)*

14–045 [*Add to n.268*]

The case citation should read *Rubenstein v HSBC Bank* [2011] EWHC 2304. On appeal, *Rubenstein* was reversed on an unrelated point ([2012] EWCA Civ 1184): see paras 15–078 to 15–078A, below.

(iv) *Categorisation of Clients*

14–049 [*Add to n.293*]

On the interpretation of COBS 3.5.9R, see *Bank Leumi (UK) Ltd v Wachner* [2011] EWHC 656 (Comm).

(vi) *Discharge of Services*

[*Add to n.314*] **14–054**

On the interpretation of COBS 9, see *Redmayne Bentley Stockbrokers v Isaacs* [2010] EWHC 1504, *Zaki v Credit Suisse (UK) Ltd* [2011] EWHC 2422 (Comm) (considered on another point: [2012] EWCA Civ 583) and *Basma Al Sulaiman v Credit Suisse Securities (Europe) Limited* [2013] EWHC 400 (Comm).

[*Add to n.321*] **14–055**

On the interpretation of COBS 10.2, see *City Index Ltd (t/a FinSpreads) v Balducci* [2011] EWHC 2562 (Ch).

(f) *The "Clients Assets" Sourcebook (CASS)*

[*Add at end of paragraph*] **14–061**

See *Joint Liquidators of Direct Sharedeal Ltd, Petitioners* [2013] CSOH 45; 2013 G.W.D. 12–257: the court could imply into CASS 7 a judicial power to give directions to liquidators on application of CASS 7 to insolvent's client assets.

[*In n.348 replace "[2010] EWCA Civ 917." with the following*]

[2012] UKSC 6.

5. FSMA IMPOSED REGULATORY LIABILITIES

(a) *Liabilities Related to Lack of Authorisation*

(i) *Liability for Contravention of the General Prohibition*

[*Add to n.351*] **14–064**

See (i) *R. v Napoli* [2012] EWCA Crim 1129 (an appeal from a criminal conviction for deposit-taking in breach of s.19); (ii) *R. v Von Badlo (Raj)* [2015] EWCA Crim 1236 (two-year custodial concurrent sentence for breaches of s.21 and s.397 (now Financial Services Act 2012 ss.89–90, where the maximum is seven years). See also Crime and Courts Act 2013 s.45 and Sch.17: deferred prosecution agreement (DPA) available in respect of the offence under s.23.

[*Add to n.353*]

See *Bull v Gain Capital Holdings Inc* [2014] EWHC 539 (Comm).

(i) *Liability for Contravention of the Financial Promotion Restriction*

14–065 [*Add to n.355*]

See Crime and Courts Act 2013 s.45 and Sch.17: deferred prosecution agreement (DPA) available in respect of the offence under s.25.

(b) *Liabilities Imposed on Authorised Persons*

14–066 [*Add to n.360*]

Note that FSMA s.150 has been replaced by FSMA s.138D, see para.14–071, below. See also *Camerata Property Inc v Credit Suisse Securities (Europe) Ltd* [2012] EWHC 7 (Comm).

[*Add to n.362*]

; *Gestmin SGPS SA v Credit Suisse (UK) Ltd* [2013] EWHC 3560 (Comm).

(i) *"Private Person"*

14–067 [*In n.372 move the second sentence to n.375*]

[*Add to n.373*]

See also *Nextia Properties Ltd v Royal Bank of Scotland* [2013] EWHC 3167 (strike out as claimant clearly not a private person) and *Gestmin SGPS SA v Credit Suisse (UK) Ltd* [2013] EWHC 3560 (Comm).

(ii) *Liability for Acting outside Permission*

14–068 [*General note to para.14–068*]

Note that since April 1, 2013, Pt IV has been replaced by Pt 4A (ss.55A–55Z4) by the Financial Services Act 2012. Hence "Pt IV permission" has become "Pt 4A permission" and may be obtained either from the FCA or (in the case of SIFIs: see para.14–004, n.8, above) the PRA.

[*Add to n.375*]

See *City Index Ltd (t/a FinSpreads) v Balducci* [2011] EWHC 2562 (Ch): on the facts, no breach of s.20.

See also *Camerata Property Inc v Credit Suisse Securities (Europe) Ltd* [2012] EWHC 7 (Comm). See also *Grant Estates Ltd (In Liquidation) v The Royal Bank of Scotland* [2012] CSOH 133 at [45]–[62], a Scottish decision of the Outer House, Court of Session.

(iii) *Liability for Employment of Certain Persons*

[*General note to para.14–069*] **14–069**

Since April 1, 2013, both the FCA and PRA (see para.14–004, above) may impose "prohibition orders" and both operate an "approved person regime". Hence FSMA, s.56 and Part V have been amended accordingly by the Financial Services Act 2012.

(iv) *Authorised Persons' Liability for Contravention of FSA Rules*

[*General note to paras 14–070 to 14–072*] **14–070**

Note that FSMA s.150 has been replaced by FSMA s.138D which is to very similar effect but for one important distinction between breaches of PRA rules on the one hand, and breaches of FCA rules on the other. For a breach of a PRA rule to be civilly actionable, the PRA rule must so specify (s.138D(1)), whereas a breach of an FCA rule will be actionable under s.138D unless the FCA specifies that it is not so actionable (s.138D(2),(3)).

[*Add at end of paragraph*]

The s.138D right of action also does not apply to the following rules: (a) rules under s.137O (threshold condition code) and (b) rules under s.192J (provision of information by parent undertakings).

[*In n.383 after the reference to "Wilson" add the following*]

; (v) *Rubenstein v HSBC Bank* [2011] EWHC 2304 (see paras 15–78 to 15–78A (reversed on appeal on an unrelated point ([2012] EWCA Civ 1184))); (vi) *Zaki v Credit Suisse (UK) Ltd* [2011] EWHC 2422 (Comm) (unsuccessful); (vii) *Camerata Property Inc v Credit Suisse Securities (Europe) Ltd* [2012] EWHC 7 (Comm) (unsuccessful claim: claimant not "private person"); (viii) *Nextia Properties Ltd v Royal Bank of Scotland* [2013] EWHC 3167 (strike out as not private person); (ix) *Green v Royal Bank of Scotland Plc* [2013] EWCA Civ 1197 (s.150 claim time-barred); (x) *Saville v Central Capital Ltd* [2014] EWCA Civ 337 and *Figurasin v Central Capital Ltd* [2014] EWCA Civ 504 (both successful PPI claims for breach of ICOB/ICOBS).

[*Add to n.383*]

; (iv) *City Index Ltd (t/a FinSpreads) v Balducci* [2011] EWHC 2562 (Ch); (v) *Gestmin SGPS SA v Credit Suisse (UK) Ltd* [2013] EWHC 3560 (Comm) (claimant not "private person").

[*Add to n.393*] **14–071**

; *Camerata Property Inc v Credit Suisse Securities (Europe) Ltd* [2012] EWHC 7 (Comm) and *Nextia Properties Ltd v Royal Bank of Scotland* [2013] EWHC

3167 and *Gestmin SGPS SA v Credit Suisse (UK) Ltd* [2013] EWHC 3560 (Comm).

14–072 [*Add to n.400*]

See, to the same effect, *Basma Al Sulaiman v Credit Suisse Securities (Europe) Limited* [2013] EWHC 400 (Comm), Cooke J.: the common law 'adds little or nothing' to a s.150 (as it then was) claim.

[*Add to n.401*]

See also *Gestmin SGPS SA v Credit Suisse (UK) Ltd* [2013] EWHC 3560 (Comm).

[*Add to text after reference to n.401*]

But note *Green v Royal Bank of Scotland Plc* [2013] EWCA Civ 1197 where it was held that (the s.150 claim being time-barred) the common law duty would not be *extended* so as be to co-extensive with the s.150 duty.

[*Add to n.403*]

; (ix) *Rubenstein v HSBC Bank* [2011] EWHC 2304 (see paras 15–78 to 15–78A (reversed on appeal on an unrelated point ([2012] EWCA Civ 1184))); (x) *Green v Royal Bank of Scotland Plc* [2013] EWCA Civ 1197; (xi) *Gestmin SGPS SA v Credit Suisse (UK) Ltd* [2013] EWHC 3560 (Comm).

[*Add to n.405*]

See *Thakker v Northern Rock (Asset Management) Plc* [2014] EWHC 2107 (QB): s.151(2) applied so that alleged breaches of MCOB in a mortgage transaction did not made the right to possession unenforceable (as the contravention of an MCOB rule did not make the transaction void or unenforceable).

6. FSMA REMEDIES

(a) *Remedies Available to Regulators*

14–078 [*General note to paras 14–078 to 14–092*]

Since April 1, 2013, both the FCA and PRA (see para.14–004, above) may apply for these remedies (in specified circumstances, reflecting their remits) and FSMA, ss.380 and 382 have been amended accordingly by the Financial Services Act 2012 (with the FCA, only, having the power to apply for these remedies in relation to market abuse).

14–079 [*Replace last two sentences of paragraph with the following*]

See now *FSA v Sinaloa Gold Plc* [2013] UKSC 11, where, on appeal, it was held that the "dispensation principle" did apply in relation to third parties.

(i) *Grounds for Application to Court*

[*Add to n.440*] **14–080**

The Financial Services Act 2012 added a reference to "a qualifying EU provision" specified by Treasury Order, the relevant Order being the Financial Services and Markets Act 2000 (Qualifying EU Provisions) Order 2013, SI 2013/413).

Requirements imposed by or under FSMA

[*Add at end of paragraph*] **14–081**

Note n.440 (as amended above): now requirements imposed by "a qualifying EU provision" as specified by Treasury Order (see the Financial Services and Markets Act 2000 (Qualifying EU Provisions) Order 2013, SI 2013/413 which contains an extensive list of EU provisions) are also covered.

For "FSA rules" read now "FCA and PRA rules" (see Pt 4, above).

Requirements imposed by or under any other Act

[*Add at end of paragraph*] **14–082**

Since April 1, 2013, both the FCA and PRA (see para.14–004, above) have powers under FSMA to prosecute for certain breaches.

[*Add to n.451*]

The Money Laundering Regulations have further been amended by SIs 2009/209; 2010/86; 2010/22; 2011/99; 2011/781; 2011/2699; 2011/2833; 2012/1906; 2012/2298; 2013/472; 2013/1881

(iii) *Orders Available*

Injunction

[*Add to n.463*] **14–086**

FCA v Da Vinci Invest Ltd [2015] EWHC 2401 (Ch) (FCA claim for injunction under s.381 and penalty under s.129 for breach of s.118(5)).

(iv) *The FSA's Extra-judicial Power to Require Restitution*

[*Add at end of paragraph*] **14–091**

Since April 1, 2013, both the FCA and PRA (see para.14–004, above) have the power to require restitution under s.384 and that provisions has been amended accordingly by the Financial Services Act 2012 (with the FCA, only, having the power to act in relation to market abuse).

(v) *The FSA Enforcement Guidance*

14–092 [*Add at end of paragraph*]

The FCA (only) has issued such guidance (and it forms part of its Handbook, see para.14–034 et seq., above).

(b) *Remedies Available to Private Litigants*

(i) *Recovery of Money or Property Paid under Agreements Made by or through Unauthorised Person*

Contravention of the general prohibition (non-banking)

14–094 [*General note to para.14–094*]

In the case of so-called "credit-related activity" (i.e. consumer credit lending and credit broking) agreements made by *authorised* persons in contravention of their Pt 4A permission are unenforceable and voidable: see FSMA, s.26A, added by the Financial Services Act 2012, s.37 and Sch.9, para.5.

[*Add to n.491*]

See also *Andrew Brown v Innovatorone Plc* [2012] EWHC 1321 and *Bull v Gain Capital Holdings Inc* [2014] EWHC 539.

Court's discretion

14–095 [*General note to para.14–095*]

In the case of "credit-related agreements" (see above, general note to para. 14–094), it is the FCA (rather than the court) that has the discretion to uphold the agreements: see FSMA, s.28A, added by the Financial Services Act 2012, s.37 and Sch.9, para.8.

7. THE OMBUDSMAN SCHEME

14–100 [*General note to paras 14–100 to 14–121*]

Since April 1, 2013, the FSA's functions in relation to the Ombudsman Scheme are vested in the FCA (see para.14–004, above). Hence FSMA Pt XVI and Sch. 17 have been amended accordingly by the Financial Services Act 2012. The rules are therefore now in the FCA Handbook (the DISP Module), see para.14–034 et seq., above.

Moreover, the "consumer credit jurisdiction" ceased to exist on April 1, 2014 and was subsumed into the "compulsory jurisdiction", when consumer credit regulation was transferred to the FCA by virtue of the Financial Services Act 2012.

The FOS is "an ADR entity" for the purposes of the ADR Directive,[a] with the FCA as the "competent authority" ensuring that the FOS qualifies as such and meets the quality requirements of that Directive.

NOTE a: Directive 2013/11 on alternative dispute resolution for consumer disputes, implemented by the Alternative Dispute Resolution for Consumer Disputes (Competent Authorities and Information) Regulations 2015 (SI 2015/542).

(a) *Introduction*

Scope of jurisdictions

[*Replace last sentence with the following*] **14–102**

The respondent has eight weeks to respond to a complaint by issuing a "final response". (For the "final response", see below. See further DISP 2.8.)

[*Add to end of n.536*] **14–103**

This case was approved in *Clark v In Focus Asset Management & Tax Solutions Ltd* [2014] EWCA Civ 118. Hence a complainant cannot pursue civil proceedings for further compensation, having accepted a FOS determination.

(b) *Compulsory, Consumer Credit and Voluntary Jurisdiction*

(ii) *The Consumer Credit Jurisdiction*

[*General note to para.14–105*] **14–105**

Omit paragraph as the "consumer credit jurisdiction" ceased to exist on April 1, 2014 and was subsumed into the "compulsory jurisdiction" when consumer credit regulation was transferred to the FCA by virtue of the Financial Services Act 2012.

(e) *The Investigation*

[*Add to n.574*] **14–113**

For other unsuccessful challenges to FOS, see also *R. (on the application of Green) v Financial Ombudsman Service Ltd* [2012] EWHC 1253 (Admin); *R. (on the application of Bankole) v Financial Ombudsman Service* [2012] EWHC 3555 (Admin); *R. (on the application of Calland) v Financial Ombudsman Service Ltd* [2013] EWHC 1327 (Admin); *R. (on the application of London Capital Group) v Financial Ombudsman Service Ltd* [2013] EWHC 2425 (Admin)); *R. (on the application of Fisher) v Financial Ombudsman Service* unreported; *Westscott Financial Services Ltd v Financial Ombudsman Service* [2014] EWHC 3972 (Admin); *R. (on the application of Bluefin Insurance Ltd) v Financial Ombudsman Service Ltd* [2014] EWHC 3413 (Admin); *R. (on the application of Chancery (UK) LLP v Financial Ombudsman Service* [2015] EWHC 407 (Admin).

For leave to appeal to challenge FOS, see: *R. (on the application of London Capital Group Ltd) v Financial Ombudsman Service Ltd* [2013] EWHC 218 (Admin).

[*Add to n.576 before "R. v Personal Investment Authority Ombudsman"*]

R. v Insurance Ombudsman Bureau Ex p. Aegon Life Assurance Ltd [1995] L.R.L.R. 101; [1994] C.L.C. 88; and

(f) *The Award*

14–115 [*Add to n.586*]

This case was approved in *Clark v In Focus Asset Management & Tax Solutions Ltd* [2014] EWCA Civ 118.

(h) *Consumer Redress Schemes*

[*Add new heading (h) and paragraph to text*]

Consumer Redress Schemes

14–121A See FSMA 2000 ss.404–404G, inserted (in place of the old, much more limited, s.404) by the Financial Services Act 2000, as amended by the Financial Services Act 2012 (conferring the FSA's power under those sections on the FCA). These provisions enable the FCA to make rules (after consultation with the FOS, see para.14–100 et seq, above) in certain circumstances (in particular where there has been "widespread or regular failure") requiring authorised persons to establish and operate a "consumer redress scheme" (as described in the section) for providing redress to "consumers" (as defined in s.404E). See now the CONRED Module of the FCA Handbook (see para.14–034, above) and previously, the FSA Policy Statement CP12/9: "Consumer redress scheme in respect of unsuitable advice to invest in Arch cru funds" (CP12/9), December 2012 (preceded by the FSA consultation paper: Redress scheme for Arch cru investors, CP12/9, April 2012). Note that in *R. (on the application of British Bankers Association) v Financial Services Authority* [2011] EWHC 999 (Admin) Ouseley J. held that the power to initiate a consumer redress scheme (under the previous s.404) did not limit the powers of the (then) FSA to proceed by other means in seeking redress for consumers (in that case the issue of a package of measures (detailed in its Policy Statement 10/12: "The assessment and redress of Payment Protection Insurance Complaints") which involved the determination of complaints by the FOS). At issue in that case were (inter alia) breaches of rules that were non-actionable under s.150(2) (now s.138D(2)) (namely, the "Principles for Business" in the "PRIN" module of the FSA Handbook) but which might give rise to redress under FOS (which may give redress even if none is available at common law: see FSMA s.228). Whilst Ouseley J. opined that measures "impermissibly targeting Principles, and evading safeguards" provided by the s.404

scheme might be challenged, in the case before him this was not the case and the FSA could proceed by alternative (to s.404) means.

8. FINANCIAL SERVICES COMPENSATION SCHEME

[*General note to paras 14–122 to 14–137*] **14–122**

Since April 1, 2013, the FSA's functions in relation to the FSCS are vested in the FCA (see para.14–004, above). Hence FSMA Pt XV has been amended accordingly by the Financial Services Act 2012. The rules are therefore now in the FCA Handbook (the COMP Module).

(c) *Structure*

[*Add new paragraph to text*] **14–125**

See above, where it is noted that the rules are in the COMP Module of the FCA Handbook, see para.14–034 et seq., above)

(d) *Qualifying Conditions for Compensation*

[*In n.612 replace "FSA" with "FCA" (twice)*] **14–126**

(v) *Assignment of Rights*

[*In n.629 after "COMP 3.2.1(3), 7.2.1" add the following*] **14–131**

: see *Financial Services Compensation Scheme v Larnell Insurance* [2005] EWCA Civ 1408.

(e) *Compensation*

(iv) *Challenging the FSCS*

[*Add to first sentence in n.653*] **14–137**

and *Emptage v Financial Services Compensation Scheme Ltd* [2013] EWCA Civ 729 (award by FSCS quashed on basis that it had misdirected itself and acted irrationally.)

CHAPTER 15

FINANCIAL PRACTITIONERS

1. GENERAL

(a) *Scope*

15–002 [*Add to n.2*]

The overhaul (see now the Financial Services Act 2012) did not affect the issues in this chapter (although, most notably, on April 1, 2013, FSMA s.150 was replaced by FSMA s.138D, see para.14–071, above).

(d) *The Misrepresentation Act 1967*

15–014 [*Add to n.8*]

For a successful s.2 claim in the investment context, see *Taberna Europe CDO II Plc v Selskabet (Formerly Roskilde Bank A/S) (In Bankruptcy)* [2015] EWHC 871 (Comm).

2. DUTIES AND LIABILITIES

(e) *Contractual Duties*

(iii) *Incorporation of Regulatory Duties in Contract*

The duty and the standard

15–022 [*Add to n.38*]

; *Rubenstein* was reversed on appeal [2012] EWCA Civ 1184), but on other grounds.

[*Add to n.39*]

, as amended by the Consumer Rights Act 2015 Sch.1 para.38(c). See the interest rate hedging products (IRHPs) mis-selling cases: *Crestsign Ltd v National Westminstr Bank Plc* [2014] EWHC 3043 (Ch); *Hockin v Marsden* [2014] EWHC 763 (Ch); *Kays Hotels Ltd (t/a Claydon Country House Hotel) v Barclays Bank Plc* [2014] EWHC 1927 (Comm).

(iv) *Duty of Care and Skill*

Utility

[*Add to n.44*] **15–023**

See per Cooke J. in *Basma Al Sulaiman v Credit Suisse Securities (Europe) Limited* [2013] EWHC 400 (Comm): the common law "adds little or nothing" to a s.150 (as it then was) claim.

[*In n.45 after "EWHC 211 Comm" add the following*]

; *Camerata Property Inc v Credit Suisse Securities (Europe) Ltd* [2012] EWHC 7 (Comm); *Nextia Properties Ltd v Royal Bank of Scotland* [2013] EWHC 3167 (QB); *Gestmin SGPS SA v Credit Suisse (UK) Ltd* [2013] EWHC 3560 (Comm).

[*Add to n.45*]

On April 1, 2013, FSMA s.150 was replaced by FSMA s.138D, see para.14–071, above.

[*Add to n.47*]

Nextia Properties Ltd v Royal Bank of Scotland [2013] EWHC 3167 (QB); *Gestmin SGPS SA v Credit Suisse (UK) Ltd* [2013] EWHC 3560 (Comm).

(f) *Tort-based Duties*

(iii) *Negligence*

[*Add new paragraph to text*] **15–034A**

In the Scottish case of *Grant Estates Ltd (In Liquidation) v The Royal Bank of Scotland*,[71a] a decision of the Outer House, Court of Session, Lord Hodge derived five propositions from the authorities:

> "(1) It is not sufficient to set up a duty of care to assert the existence of an 'advisory relationship'. There is a clear distinction between giving advice and assuming legal responsibility for that advice. A salesperson of a financial product may give investment advice or express opinions without becoming an investment adviser and undertaking duties of care as such. Whether the giving of advice gives rise to legal obligations in tort or delict to exercise reasonable care or to advise on certain matters depends on the terms

of the legal relationship between the parties: *Standard Chartered Bank*, Hamblen J. at paras 505ff, 544.

(2) The absence of any written advisory agreement is a significant pointer against the existence of an advisory obligation: *Springwell* (first instance), Gloster J. at para.440; *Wilson* v *MF Global*, Eady J. at para.174.

(3) Parties can enter into a contract which defines the basis of their trading or banking relationship and allocates risk in a way which negates any possibility of a general or specific advisory duty coming into existence: *Springwell* (1st instance), Gloster J. at paras 475 and 478. The outcome can be expressed in different ways but with the same meaning. The contractual terms can define the parties' relationship in a way that no assumption of responsibility can be inferred. The relationship so defined is not equivalent to that of professional adviser and advisee which would make it just and reasonable to impose a duty of care: *IFE Fund SA*, Toulson J. at paras 70–71.

(4) The contractual delineation of responsibility and allocation of risk may preclude a party from founding on the actual reality which eventuates if he has contracted to accept a particular state of affairs as true. Thus if A and B agree that B will not advise A and A will not rely on any statement by B as advice, the contract will bar A from asserting the giving of that advice and his reliance on it. See, for example, the non-reliance statements in *Standard Chartered Bank* which prevented Ceylon Petroleum Corporation from asserting that advice had been given and relied on (para.544). See also *Peekay Intermark Ltd*, Moore-Bick L.J. at para.56; and *Springwell* (CA), Aikens L.J. at para.156f . . .

(5) The approach in (4) above extends to a retrospective agreement in relation to past events. A and B may agree that their relationship will be on the basis of a certain state of affairs in the past which they know not to be the case, such as that B had not made any representations, and A will thereafter be obliged to act on the basis of that acknowledgement. See *Peekay*, Moore-Bick L.J. at para.57; *Springwell* (CA), Aikens L.J. at paras 141–171."

NOTE 71a. [2012] CSOH 133.

15–036 [*Replace n.73 with the following*]

The claim failed at first instance on the basis that the loss was too remote, a finding that was reversed on appeal ([2012] EWCA Civ 1184). The defendant bank did not seek to appeal the finding that it owed an advisory duty to the claimant: see paras 15–078 to 15–078A, below (as amended).

15–041 [*Add to n.89*]

On April 1, 2013, FSMA s.150 was replaced by FSMA s.138D, see para.14–071, above.

3. BREACH OF DUTY

(a) *General*

15–051 [*Add at end of paragraph*]

Note that on April 1, 2013, the FSA Handbook was replaced by the FCA and PRA Handbooks (see para.14–034 et seq., above).

(b) *Misleading Promotion*

(ii) *Financial Promotion Documents*

[*Add at end of paragraph*] **15–053**

On April 1, 2013, FSMA s.150 was replaced by FSMA s.138D, see para.14–071, above. On April 1, 2013, FSMA s.397 was replaced by the Financial Services Act 2012, Part 7.

[*Add to n.129*]

See also *Andrew Brown v Innovatorone Plc* [2012] EWHC 1321 (Comm) (documents promoting a collective investment scheme).

(iii) *Customer Classification*

[*Add to n.132*] **15–054**

; *Gestmin SGPS SA v Credit Suisse (UK) Ltd* [2013] EWHC 3560 (Comm).

[*Add to n.134*]

Rubenstein was reversed on appeal [2012] EWCA Civ 1184 (see paras 15–078 to 15–078A, below), but not on this point.

(iv) *Advising and Selling*

[*Add at end of paragraph*] **15–055**

Note that on April 1, 2013, the FSA Handbook was replaced by the FCA and PRA Handbooks, see para.14–034 et seq., above.

[*Add to n.152*] **15–059**

Rubenstein was reversed on appeal [2012] EWCA Civ 1184 (see paras 15–074 to 15–074A, below), but not on this point. See also *Zaki v Credit Suisse (UK) Ltd* [2011] EWHC 2422 (Comm) (but no reliance on advice given and hence loss not caused by breach).

[*Add to n.153*]

See also *City Index Ltd (t/a FinSpreads) v Balducci* [2011] EWHC 2562 (Ch) (execution-only agreement); *Nextia Properties Ltd v Royal Bank of Scotland* [2013] EWHC 3167 (QB) (execution-only agreement); *Gestmin SGPS SA v Credit Suisse (UK) Ltd* [2013] EWHC 3560 (Comm). And note the IRHP mis-selling cases: *Crestsign Ltd v National Westminstr Bank Plc* [2014] EWHC 3043 (Ch); *Hockin v Marsden* [2014] EWHC 763 (Ch); *Kays Hotels Ltd (t/a Claydon Country House Hotel) v Barclays Bank Plc* [2014] EWHC 1927 (Comm).

(v) *Dealing and Managing*

15–066 [*In n.168 after "[2011] EWHC 656 (Comm)" add the following*]

and *City Index Ltd (t/a FinSpreads) v Balducci* [2011] EWHC 2562 (Ch).

4. DEFENCES AND RELIEF

(a) *General*

15–067 [*Add to n.170*]

On April 1, 2013, the FSA Handbook was replaced by the FCA Handbook, see para.14–034 et seq., above.

(c) *Restriction of Liability by Contract*

Unfair Contract Terms Act 1977

15–070 [*Add at end of paragraph*]

Note the Consumer Rights Act 2015, Pt 2, which rationalises the law as to unfair terms in consumer contracts. It amends UCTA so as confine it to non-consumers (with consumers being covered by the new Consumer Rights Act 2015).

[*Add to n.180*]

And note *Crestsign Ltd v National Westminster Bank Plc* [2014] EWHC 3043 (Ch) ("basis" clause accepted as limiting the scope of the duty undertaken).

[*Add to n.182*]

On April 1, 2013, FSMA s.150 was replaced by FSMA s.138D, see para.14–071, above.

15–071 [*Add at end of paragraph*]

Note the Consumer Rights Act 2015, Pt 2, which rationalises the law as to unfair terms in consumer contracts. It amends s.3 so as confine it to non-consumers (with consumers being covered by the new Consumer Rights Act 2015).

[*Add to n.186*]

See also *Standard Chartered Bank v Ceylon Petroleum Corp* [2011] EWHC 1785 (Comm) (approved on other grounds: [2012] EWCA Civ 1049): "entire agreement" clause satisfied requirements of reasonableness.

[*Add to n.189*]

See also *Standard Chartered Bank v Ceylon Petroleum Corp* [2011] EWHC 1785 (Comm) (approved on other grounds: [2012] EWCA Civ 1049).

[*Add new paragraph to text*] **15–071A**

Unfair Terms in Consumer Contract Regulations 1999.

These regulations (SI 1999/2083), which apply if the customer is a "consumer" (essentially a natural person not acting in the course of business: see reg.3(1)), render terms (including terms excluding liability) that are held to be "unfair" not binding on the consumer (see further *Chitty on Contracts* (31th edn), Ch.15). In *Spreadex Ltd v Cochrane* [2012] EWHC 1290 (Comm) the claimant relied on a clause that deemed the customer to have authorised all trading under his account name. Donaldson QC (sitting as a High Court Judge) refused an application for summary judgment and (as well as holding that the clause had not become a term of the individual dealing contracts at issue) held that (if it was a term) the term was "unfair".

But note the Consumer Rights Act 2015, Pt 2, which rationalises the law as to unfair terms in consumer contracts and replaces these Regulations with almost identical provisions.

5. Remedies Including Damages

(c) *Remedies Available to Private Litigants*

(iii) *Damages or Compensation*

Remoteness

[*In n.195 after "[1997] A.C. 191" add the following*] **15–078**

applied in *Camerata Property Inc v Credit Suisse Securities (Europe) Ltd* [2012] EWHC 7 (Comm); note that this case was distinguished on the basis of the findings of fact as to remoteness in *Rubenstein v HSBC Bank Plc* (per Rix L.J. at [110]–[112]).

[*Delete text from "A stark illustration . . . " to end of paragraph (including n.196 to n.198), and replace with the following*]

The issue of remoteness received detailed consideration by Rix L.J. in *Rubenstein v* HSBC.[196a] At first instance,[196b] the judge had found that the defendant bank's representative had been negligent and in breach of his statutory duty to the claimant; despite the claimant stating that he did not want to be exposed to any degree of market risk, the claimant was advised to invest in an enhanced variable rate fund (EVRF), an investment that exposed the claimant to market risks.[196c] The judge also found that the claimant had relied on that advice and had suffered loss as a consequence of his investment in the EVRF.[196d] However, the judge went on to hold that the loss suffered by the claimant was too remote to be recoverable from the defendant bank, in that the loss arose from the unforeseeable collapse of Lehman Brothers and the consequences of that collapse on AIG, the entity behind the EVRF.[196e] The decision was reversed on appeal. Rix L.J. held that, because the claimant made clear that he did not want to be exposed to market risks, and because the EVRF did expose the claimant to such risks, the loss suffered by the claimant arising from his exposure to that market risk was loss that fell within the bank's scope of duty.[196f]

NOTE 196a. [2012] EWCA Civ 1184.
NOTE 196b. [2011] EWHC 2304 (QB).
NOTE 196c. ibid. [94]–[97].
NOTE 196d. ibid. [98]–[103].
NOTE 196e. ibid. [104]–[117].
NOTE 196f. [2012] EWCA Civ 1184 at [118].

15–078A While the Court of Appeal's decision ultimately turned on the finding that the claimant had made clear that he did not want to be exposed to any degree of market risk, Rix L.J.'s judgment is significant in three further respects. First, Rix L.J.'s judgment contains a helpful discussion of how the authorities on remoteness should be applied in the context of financial markets.[196g] Rix L.J. made clear that the mere fact that a specific event contributing to a loss may have been unforeseeable at the time that the advice was given does not mean that the loss itself necessarily will be regarded as too remote, when judged against the historic booms and busts of financial markets.[196h] Echoing the reasoning applied in *Hughes v Lord Advocate*,[196i] Rix L.J. stated that "where the obligation of a defendant is not merely to avoid injuring his claimant [sic] but to protect him from the very kind of misfortune which has come about, it is not helpful to make fine distinctions between foreseeable events which are unusual, most unusual, or of negligible account."[196j] Second, Rix L.J. stated that questions as to scope of duty in the context of s.150 claims are to be answered by reference to the statute itself, and "the position in negligence and contract will fall in behind the statutorily discerned purpose."[197] Third, in rejecting the argument that the bank was not liable for the loss on the basis that the loss was sustained two years outside the period the claimant indicated he wished his investment last for, Rix L.J. considered the extent to which an adviser will be held liable for the consequences of negligent advice. He suggested that while, in a contractual setting, the question of remoteness is to be determined by reference to the reasonable contemplation of the parties, in the context of statutory protection for the consumer, there may be an onus on the adviser to make clear any limitations that exist on the advice given.[198]

NOTE 196g. ibid. at [94]–[112].
NOTE 196h. "although the Lehman Brothers collapse was both a symptom and a contributory cause of market turmoil, the underlying causes of that turmoil went infinitely beyond Lehman Brothers' difficulties. It stretched to a failure of confidence in marketable securities in which there had previously been greater confidence. And what is new about that?": see Rix L.J. at [117].

NOTE 196i. [1963] AC 837 (a case cited by Rix L.J. in [2012] EWCA Civ 1184 at [97]).
NOTE 196j. ibid. at [124].
NOTE 197. ibid. at [114]. See also [45]–[46] and [114]–[115] generally.
NOTE 198. ibid. at [120]–[125].

Causation illustrations

[*Add at end of paragraph*] **15–079**

See also *Zaki v Credit Suisse (UK) Ltd* [2011] EWHC 2422 (Comm): no reliance on advice given in breach of COBS 9.2 and hence loss not caused by breach.

Measure of damages

[*Add to n.217*] **15–085**

See also *Gestmin SGPS SA v Credit Suisse (UK) Ltd* [2013] EWHC 3560 (Comm): had claimant succeeded on liability, as he also failed to prove a claim for damages for loss of profits from any alternative use of money, claimant would have been confined to a claim for interest under s.35A of the Senior Courts Act 1981.

Benefits received

[*Add to n.224*] **15–089**

Needler was also cited with approval by Rix L.J. on the appeal in *Rubenstein* ([2012] EWCA Civ 1184 at [134]–[135]).

[*Add at end of paragraph*] **15–092**

The Judge's decision and reasoning on this point was upheld on appeal ([2012] EWCA Civ 1184, per Rix L.J. at [133]–136]).

6. SHARED RESPONSIBILITY

(a) *Contributory Negligence*

[*Add to n.234*] **15–094**

; *Rubenstein* was reversed on appeal ([2012] EWCA Civ 1184), but on an unrelated point: see paras 15–078 to 15–078A, above.

7. THE PROCESS OF RESOLVING CLAIMS

[*Add to n.240*] **15–096**

See para.14–121A.

CHAPTER 16

INSURANCE BROKERS

1. GENERAL

16–003 [*Add at end of paragraph*]

In some cases the intermediary will act as the agent of the insured for some purposes, and as the agent of the insurer for other purposes. See for example *Hua Tyan Development Ltd v Zurich Insurance Co Ltd (The "Ho Feng 7")* [2012] HKCFI 1185; [2013] 1 Lloyd's Rep. I.R. 39.

ICOB & ICOBS

16–007 [*Replace first sentence with the following*]

Between January 2005 and March 2013 the Financial Services Authority ("FSA") was responsible for regulating insurance brokers, who were required to be authorised by the FSA and were obliged to comply with the applicable rules in the FSA's handbook. Since April 1, 2013 the FSA's responsibilities have been assumed by the Financial Conduct Authority ("FCA"), and insurance brokers are required to comply with the applicable rules in the FCA's Handbook.".

[*Replace last sentence with the following*]

Pursuant to s.138D of the Act, a breach of the rules by an authorised broker may be actionable at the suit of a private person who suffers loss as a result of the breach, subject to the defences and other incidents applying to actions for breach of statutory duty. See, for example, *Saville v Central Capital Ltd* [2014] EWCA Civ 337 in which the effect of the ICOB rules was discussed. In that case the Court of Appeal stated that the test to be applied to the issue of causation in an action for breach of statutory duty was to ask whether, if the duty had not been breached, the damage would have occurred.

16–008A [*Add new paragraph to text*]

Consumer Insurance. The obligations upon an insurance broker arranging contracts of consumer insurance after April 1, 2013 have changed as a result of the coming into force on that day of the key provisions of the Consumer Insurance (Disclosure and Representations) Act 2012. The Act applies to "consumer insurance contracts" which are defined as contracts of insurance between (a) an individual who enters into the contract wholly or mainly for purposes unrelated to the individual's trade, business or profession, and (b) a person who carries on the business of insurance and who becomes a party to the contract by way of that business.

[*Add new paragraph to text*] **16–008B**

Section 2 of the Act makes provision about disclosure and representations by a consumer to an insurer before a consumer insurance contract is entered into or varied. More particularly, s.2(2) provides that it is the duty of the consumer to take reasonable care not to make a misrepresentation to the insurer, and s.2(4) provides that such duty replaces any duty relating to disclosure or representations by a consumer to an insurer which existed in the same circumstances before the Act applied. By s.11, ss.18–20 of the Marine Insurance Act 1906 are disapplied in relation to consumer insurance contracts.

[*Add new paragraph to text*] **16–008C**

It follows that a broker procuring a consumer insurance contract no longer owes his client a duty to take reasonable care to disclose any material facts of which he (the broker) is aware. Nor does the broker owe a duty to advise his client of the duty to disclose all material circumstances (since there is no longer any such duty). The broker will be obliged to consider whether or not the contract being procured is a consumer insurance contract within the meaning of the 2012 Act. If the contract *is* a consumer insurance contract, then the broker's duty will be limited to advising his client of the obligation imposed by the Act, namely a duty to take reasonable care not to make a misrepresentation to the insurer. Indeed, if a broker himself discloses, or advises his client to disclose, material circumstances which there is no obligation to disclose, then the broker may be exposed to a liability to the consumer client if the result of such disclosure is that the client is either unable to obtain insurance at all, or only on terms which are less favourable to the client than would have been available had the unnecessary disclosure not been made.

[*Add new paragraph to text*] **16–008D**

Subsection 3(1) of the Act provides that whether or not a consumer has taken reasonable care not to make a misrepresentation is to be determined in the light of all the relevant circumstances. Subsection 3(2) lists examples of matters which need to be taken into account in making a determination under subs.3(1). One of those matters is "whether or not an agent was acting for the consumer." Schedule 2 to the Act sets out rules for determining, for the purposes of the Act only, whether an agent through whom a consumer insurance contract is effected is acting as the agent of the consumer or of the insurer. Ordinarily an insurance broker will be acting as the agent of the consumer, and therefore the fact that he was acting for the consumer will be taken into account when determining whether or not the consumer has taken reasonable care not to make a misrepresentation to the insurer. The role of the broker is likely to be of particular significance if, for example, an insurer asks the consumer whether the consumer is aware of any material facts beyond those set out elsewhere on the proposal form. If the consumer is being advised by an insurance broker, then the consumer might reasonably be expected to ask his agent (the broker) for assistance in answering the question, and the broker would then be obliged to give the consumer advice as to the matters which are material to disclose. The broker would be obliged to exercise due skill and care in giving such advice. However, it is unclear what the consequence would be if the broker gave incorrect advice to the consumer with the result that the consumer made a misrepresentation—on one view the consumer would have taken reasonable care not to make the misrepresentation (by seeking advice from the broker) with the result that the insurer would have no relief under the terms of the Act because there would have been no qualifying misrepresentation as set out in s.4 of the Act. Thus the consumer (and ultimately the broker) might be protected from the consequences of the broker's negligence.

[*Add to n.18*]

The background to the introduction of the ICOB Rules was set out by the Court of Appeal in *Harrison v Black Horse Ltd* [2011] EWCA Civ 1128.

(a) *Duties to Client*

(ii) *Duties Independent of Contract*

16–011 [*Add to n.31*]

More recently in *Equitas Ltd v Walsham Bros & Co Ltd* [2013] EWHC 3264(Comm); [2014] P.N.L.R. 8, Males J. held that Lloyd's brokers owed co-existing duties in contract and tort to reinsurers in relation to the administration of reinsurance policies.

(b) *Duties to Third Parties*

(i) *Duties to Insurers*

16–017 [*Add at beginning of paragraph*]

Save in relation to consumer insurance contracts (as to which see para.16–017A below),

16–017A [*Add new paragraph to text*]

Consumer Insurance

Section 19 of the Marine Insurance Act 1906 was amended by the Consumer Insurance (Disclosure and Representations) Act 2012, with effect from April 6, 2013 (see the Consumer Insurance (Disclosure and Representations) Act 2012

(Commencement) Order 2013). The effect of the amendment is to provide that s.19 does not apply in relation to "consumer insurance contracts." A consumer insurance contract is defined as a contract of insurance between (a) an individual who enters into the contract wholly or mainly for purposes unrelated to the individual's trade, business or profession, and (b) a person who carries on the business of insurance and who becomes a party to the contract by way of that business. Therefore a broker seeking to procure a consumer insurance contract (as defined) no longer owes an obligation to insurers to disclose all material facts."

(c) *Sub-brokers*

[*Add at the end of the paragraph*] **16–033**

By contrast, in *Involnert Management Inc v Aprilgrange Ltd* [2015] EWHC 2225 (Comm) Leggatt J. held that an English sub-broker who had placed insurance in the London market on behalf of a Greek company at the request of a Greek producing broker did not owe a duty of care to the insured, on the basis that the sub-broker had not assumed responsibility to the insured. There was no evidence that the insured was relying on the expertise of the sub-broker, and the insured communicated only with the producing broker.

(d) *The Standard of Skill and Care*

[*Add at the end of the paragraph*] **16–039**

In *Involnert Management Inc v Aprilgrange Ltd* [2015] EWHCC 2225 (Comm) Leggatt J. observed (at [294]) that the general duties of insurance brokers have been considered by the courts in many cases and, to a substantial extent, have become a matter of law. He stated (at [297]) that, as a result, it should not be automatically assumed that in every case where an allegation of negligence is made against an insurance broker expert evidence is reasonably required to resolve the proceedings.

2. Liability for Breach of Duty

(a) *Failing Adequately to Assess the Client's Needs*

[*Add to n.119*] **16–044**

See also *Eurokey Recycling v Giles Insurance Brokers* [2014] EWHC 2989 (Comm) (Blair J.) at para.86. In *Involnert Management Inc v Aprilgrange Ltd* [2015] EWHC 2225 (Comm) Leggatt J. observed (at [296]) that "what matters a broker has a duty to explain to the client, or is entitled to assume or accept without question, is likely to depend on the level of knowledge and sophistication of the client or of the individual(s) giving instructions on the client's behalf, as reasonably perceived by the broker."

16–048 [*Add at end of paragraph*]

Similarly, in *Eurokey Recycling v Giles Insurance Brokers* [2014] EWHC 2989 (Comm) (Blair J.) the broker was found not liable, despite the insured's business interruption insurance being inadequate, because the broker arranged cover based on the figures provided by the insured, and the broker had no reason to suppose that those figures were inadequate.

16–050 [*Add at end of paragraph*]

Similarly, if a client who appears to be well-informed about his business provides a broker with information, the broker is not expected to verify that information unless he has reason to believe that it is not accurate: *Eurokey Recycling v Giles Insurance Brokers* [2014] EWHC 2989 (Comm) (Blair J.) at para.86.

16–063 [*Add new footnote reference 170a at end of paragraph*]

NOTE 170a. See also *Hua Tyan Development Ltd v Zurich Insurance Co Ltd (The "Ho Feng 7")* [2012] HKCFI 1185; [2013] 1 Lloyd's Rep. I.R. 39 in which the Hong Kong Court of First Instance held that (had a deadweight tonnage condition been incorporated into the insured's policy of cargo insurance) then the broker would have been in breach of duty in failing to ensure that the policy met the insured's requirement that the policy was effective for the cargo which was being shipped."

(d) *Failing to Effect Insurance which meets the Client's Requirements*

16–063A [*Add new paragraph to text*]

The fact that an insured knows what insurance it is purchasing does not mean that the policy is in fact suitable for its demands and needs. Thus in *Saville v Central Capital* [2014] EWCA Civ 337 the insureds had purchased PPI cover with a five year term. The trial judge rejected their claim on the basis that they knew what they were getting. That decision was reversed by the Court of Appeal which held that the mere fact that the insureds knew exactly what they were getting did not mean that the policy was suitable for their demands and needs, which depended on their individual financial circumstances. Floyd L.J. observed that if the insured's knowledge were an adequate basis for a finding that the policy was suitable, then the responsibility for assessing whether the policy was suitable would be shifted from the broker (where it belonged) to the customer (where it did not).

16–068 [*Replace second sentence with the following*]

The broker is not expected to value the insured property or interest himself. However, he should advise his client what the sum insured should represent (e.g. the value of the property insured, or alternatively its replacement cost, as appropriate). Where there is any complexity in determining the appropriate sum insured (as with, for example, business interruption insurance), then the broker should advise his client how the sum insured should be calculated (see e.g. *Arbory Group Ltd v West Craven Insurance Services (A Firm)* [2007] P.N.L.R. 23 (HHJ Grenfell) in which the broker failed to explain to his client how a gross profit sum insured should be calculated). A broker is not itself obliged to calculate the business interruption sum insured or to choose the indemnity period, which are matters for the client, but it must provide sufficient explanation to the client to enable it to do so. This will include an explanation of the method of calculating the sum insured, which is likely to require an explanation of terms such as "estimated gross profits" and "maximum indemnity period" (*Eurokey Recycling v Giles Insurance Brokers* [2014] EWHC 2989 (Comm) (Blair J.) at para.86). The broker should also draw his client's attention to the consequence of underinsurance, particularly where the policy is subject to average with the result that (in the event of a loss) the insured will not be entitled to a full indemnity for its loss even if that loss is less than the amount of the sum insured. The adequacy of the sums insured should be checked on each renewal, particularly if the policy is written on a reinstatement basis (as the costs of reinstatement are likely to increase each year).

[*Add to n.185*] **16–069**

See also *Café de Lecq Ltd v R.A. Rossborough (Insurance Brokers) Ltd* [2012] JRC053 (Royal Court of Jersey) in which the broker was found to be in breach of duty in failing to advise his client that the sum insured for buildings' cover should represent the cost of reinstating the buildings in the event of their destruction.

[*Add new paragraph to text*] **16–070A**

Not only should the sums insured be adequate, the duration of cover should also be adequate for the insured's requirements. This is particularly significant in relation to the indemnity period in policies of business interruption insurance. If the indemnity period is too short, then the insured may not be entitled to an indemnity for all its on-going financial losses in the event of a peril. Therefore the broker should consider with the insured how long its business might be interrupted in the event of a loss, and thus what indemnity period would be suitable. If the broker fails to do so, then it will be in breach of duty: *Café de Lecq Ltd v R.A. Rossborough (Insurance Brokers) Ltd* [2012] JRC053 (Royal Court of Jersey).

(g) *Liability Arising out of Material Non-disclosure*

[*Add to n.230*] **16–081**

See also *Involnert Management Inc v Aprilgrange Ltd* [2015] EWHC 2225 (Comm) at [318] per Leggatt J.

[*Add new paragraph to text*] **16–084A**

In *Involnert Management Inc v Aprilgrange Ltd* [2015] EWHC 2225 (Comm) Leggatt J. stated (at [311]) that, normally at least, it is no part of a broker's duty to protect the assured from the adverse consequences of failing to disclose information which the insured does not need to disclose (for example, because the disclosure of information is waived).

16–085 [*Add at end of paragraph*]

In *Involnert Management Inc v Aprilgrange Ltd* [2015] EWHC 2225 (Comm) Leggatt J. stated (at [321]) that the broker "should seek to elicit from the client matters which ought to be disclosed, bearing in mind that the client may not realise without assistance that a particular matter is or is arguably material."

16–086A [*Add new paragraph to text*]

If the broker elicits information from its client, then the broker is entitled to proceed on the assumption that the information is accurate. If a client who appears to be well-informed about his business provides a broker with information, the broker is not expected to verify that information unless he has reason to believe that it is not accurate: *Eurokey Recycling v Giles Insurance Brokers* [2014] EWHC 2989 (Comm) (Blair J.) at para.86.

(h) *Liability Arising out of a Misrepresentation to the Insurer*

[*Add to n.254*]

16–091 In *Involnert Management Inc v Aprilgrange Ltd* [2015] EWHC 2225 (Comm) Leggatt J. stated (at [308]) that a reasonably competent broker ought to ensure that a proposal form is fully completed and all questions on the proposal are answered by the insured.

[*Add at end of paragraph*]

If a broker, without the knowledge or agreement of the insured, adds information to a proposal form after the form has been signed by the insured, then the broker will be in breach of duty: *Involnert Management Inc v Aprilgrange Ltd* [2015] EWHCC 2225 (Comm) Leggatt J. (at [313]).

(i) *Failing to Advise on the Existence or Terms of Cover*

16–095 [*Add to n.263*]

See also *Hua Tyan Development Ltd v Zurich Insurance Co Ltd (The "Ho Feng 7")* [2012] HKCFI 1185; [2013] 1 Lloyd's Rep. IR 39 in which the Hong Kong Court of First Instance held that (had a deadweight tonnage condition been incorporated into the insured's policy of cargo insurance) then the broker would have been in breach of duty in failing to advise the insured of the requirement of that condition.

[*Add to n.264*]

See also *Café de Lecq Ltd v R.A. Rossborough (Insurance Brokers) Ltd* [2012] JRC053 in which the Royal Court of Jersey held that the broker was negligent in failing to draw to the insured's attention the terms of a deep fat fryer warranty in the policy, and the consequences of non-compliance with that warranty.

(k) *Failings after the Risk has been Placed*

[Add new paragraph to text] **16–106A**

Lloyd's Brokers. A Lloyd's broker will often have a continuing relationship with syndicates on whose behalf it collects and remits funds, maintains accounts and administers the syndicates' reinsurance policies. In such a situation the broker's obligation to remit funds is a continuing obligation: *Equitas Ltd v Walsham Bros & Co Ltd* [2013] EWHC 3264 (Comm); [2014] P.N.L.R. 8.

[*Add at end of paragraph*] **16–109**

By contrast, the decision in *HIH Casualty* was distinguished in *Eurokey Recycling v Giles Insurance Brokers* [2014] EWHC 2989 (Comm) (Blair J.). In that case the broker was sent draft accounts which indicated that the business interruption cover it had arranged was inadequate. The accounts were sent to the broker for onward transmission to a premium credit provider. The Judge held that, in the absence of anything to alert the broker to the fact that the information in the accounts could have a material and potentially deleterious effect on insurance cover, he was under no obligation to read them.

[*Add at end of paragraph*] **16–110**

However, what (if any) duty the broker owes to the insured will depend on the scope of the broker92s instructions. Thus in *Involnert Management Inc v Aprilgrange Ltd* [2015] EWHC 2225 (Comm) Leggatt J. rejected an allegation that the broker was negligent in failing to advise the insured of a policy requirement to file a sworn proof of loss within 90 days. The insured had not asked the broker to advise on the requirements for making a claim under the policy, and indeed was being assisted by other advisers. Leggatt J. stated (at [324]): "I do not believe there is any rule of law which obliges a broker who has not been asked to assist the assured in dealing with a potential claim to volunteer advice on claim procedures."

3. DAMAGES

(a) *Causation*

(ii) *The Claimant Would Not Have Received an Insurance Payment in Any Event*

Insurance not available

[*Add at end of paragraph*] **16–134**

More recently, in *Eurokey Recycling v Giles Insurance Brokers* [2014] EWHC 2989 (Comm) Blair J. rejected the broker's argument that it was unlikely that the business interruption cover which the insured alleged it ought to have had would have been unavailable. He also rejected the broker's argument that damages ought to be assessed on a loss of a chance basis, because he was satisfied that alternative cover could and would have been obtained if it had been sought.

The insured loss would not have occurred

16–141 [*Replace first sentence of n.363 with the following*]

The insured's appeal was dismissed, and Rix L.J. commented that Steel J.'s reasoning (as to why the insured's loss directly caused by the fire was not recoverable from the broker) had much to commend it: [2011] EWCA Civ 1152 at 34.

[*Delete last sentence of n.363*]

(b) *Assessment of Damages*

16–146 [*Add to note 373*]

In *Involnert Management Inc v Aprilgrange Ltd* [2015] EWHC 2225 (Comm) Leggatt J. held that the broker had acted negligently, with the result that the insurer was entitled to avoid the policy. If the broker had not acted negligently, then the insured would have had a valid policy to insure its yacht for €8 million. However, he also held that, if the policy had not been avoided, then the amount recoverable by the insured under the policy would have been limited to €2 million as a result of the insured's failure to comply with a policy requirement to file a sworn proof of loss within a 90 day time limit (which failure was not as a result of any breach of duty by the broker). Thus the claimant was only able to recover damages in the sum of €2 million, rather than €8 million.

(c) *Contributory Negligence*

16–164 [*Add new footnote references 438a and 438b at end of paragraph*]

NOTE 438a. See also *Eurokey Recycling v Giles Insurance Brokers* [2014] EWHC 2989 (Comm) in which Blair J. stated that, had he found in favour of the insured, then he would have assessed contributory negligence on the insured's part at 50 per cent.

NOTE 438b. See also *Café de Lecq Ltd v R.A. Rossborough (Insurance Brokers) Ltd* [2012] JRC053 in which the Royal Court of Jersey rejected the broker's submission that the insured was contributorily negligent in failing to read the policy documents more carefully than it did, and in failing to give more careful consideration to the appropriate sums insured for buildings and business interruption cover.

CHAPTER 17

ACCOUNTANTS AND AUDITORS

2. DUTIES

(a) *The Statutory Context*

(i) *Companies Legislation: the Company Audit*

The preparation of accounts

[*Add after the second paragraph*] **17–012**

In November 2012 the Financial Reporting Council (FRC) issued FRS 100 (Application of financial reporting requirements), FRS 101 (Reduced disclosure framework) and FRS 102 (The financial reporting standard applicable in the UK and Republic of Ireland). These will define the new UK GAAP regime. The standards will apply to accounting periods beginning on or after 1 January 2015 but it will be possible to opt in sooner. The broad intention is to give entities greater flexibility as to which reporting standard to adopt. Because of the inevitable time lag before claims arise, these changes are unlikely to affect claims against auditors for some time. In June 2014 the FRC published a paper confirming that the need to give a "true and fair" view remains a requirement under the new standards. In July 2015 the FRC issued amendments to FRS 100.

Sections 392–398 of the Companies Act 2006 will be deleted by s.19 and Sch.6 Pt 6 to the Deregulation Act 2015 from a date to be appointed.

Resignation of auditors

Companies Act 2006 s.519 will be amended by the Deregulation Act 2015 s.18 from a date to be appointed. This will alter, and largely simplify, the procedure for notification of the reasons for an auditor's ceasing to hold office. **17–016**

The role of the FRC in operating a disciplinary scheme for accountants was put under the spotlight in *R. (on the application of Baker Tilly UK Audit LLP) v Financial Reporting Council* [2015] EWHC 1398 (Admin), Singh J.

[*Add to n.37*]

On October 8, 2013, Martin Moore QC wrote a further Opinion (in answer to an opposing view put forward by George Bompas QC) confirming that there was no tension between the duty under the 2006 Act to give a true and fair view and the duty under IAS1 to "present fairly". He also pointed out that the requirement of prudence did not require excessive caution where there was no uncertainty (see FRS18 paras 37 and 38). The Opinion is on the FRC website.

17–013 [*Add to n.55*]

The Companies Act 2006 (Strategic Report and Directors' Report) Regulations 2013 (SI 2013/1970) has inserted sections into the 2006 Act requiring certain companies to provide a strategic report. Where this applies, it would seem that the auditor is required to state in his audit report whether the information given in the relevant strategic report is consistent with those accounts.

(b) *Duties to Client*

(iii) *Fiduciary Duties*

Confidentiality

17–025 [*Add at end of paragraph*]

The duty of confidentiality under the general law will usually overlap, but not necessarily be synonymous, with a duty under the relevant professional code of conduct: *R. (Margaret May) v Chartered Institute of Management Accountants* [2013] EWHC 1574 (Admin), Stadlen J.

However, although an accountant owes a duty of confidentiality to his client, communications between them do not attract legal professional privilege, even if they relate to tax advice: *R. (Prudential plc) v Special Commissioner of Income Tax* [2013] UKSC 1; [2013] 2 AC 185.

(c) *Duties to Third Parties*

(i) *Overview*

The different tests

17–027 [*Add at end of paragraph*]

In *Swynson Ltd v Lowick Rose LLP* [2014] EWHC 2085 (Ch); [2014] P.N.L.R. 27, C1 was a company which was ultimately owned by C2. C2 was a wealthy businessman who would lend money at high rates of interest to businesses which interested him. C1 made a loan of £15 million to Evo in reliance on a due diligence report by its accountant, D. Evo's financial position then worsened and C2 made two further loans, which Rose J. accepted were in reasonable mitigation. There was then a partial refinancing under which the debt was acquired by C2 from C1. Negligence and causation were conceded but D argued (i) that the refinancing had extinguished C1's loss and (ii) that no separate duty of care was owed to C2. Rose J. concluded that the refinancing was *res inter alios acta* which did not affect D's liability to C. However, (although, in the circumstances, this made no difference to the result) she also held that the accountant instructed by C1 owed no separate duty of care to C2, its ultimate beneficial owner. The judge found that D knew that C2 ultimately owned C1 and was ultimately the person whose assets were at stake. It was therefore foreseeable that C2 would suffer loss if D was negligent. However that was insufficient to create a duty of care to C2.

Although the term is not mentioned in the judgment, this case may be seen as an application of the reflective loss principle (see para.17–075 of the main text), at least in respect of the loss suffered by C2 prior to the refinancing.

Swynson went to appeal ([2015] EWCA Civ 629; [2015] P.N.L.R. 28) on the question of *res inter alios acta*. The majority of the Court of Appeal (Davis L.J. dissenting) dismissed the appeal on the ground that the repayment was an act of benevolence by C2 and that it would be a triumph of form over substance if it had to be brought into account.

(iii) *Factors which may be Relevant*

Factor (3): The relationship between the advisee and any relevant third party

[*Add at end of paragraph*] 17–033

In *Arrowhead Capital Finance Ltd v KPMG LLP* [2012] EWHC 1801 (Comm); [2012] P.N.L.R. 30, KPMG gave advice about VAT to its client. Arrowhead was not the client but was an investment fund which indirectly lent money to the client. Stephen Males QC struck out the claim on the basis that KPMG did not assume any responsibility towards Arrowhead. KPMG realised that the client was seeking investment and was informing potential investors of the VAT advice given by KPMG, but this was not sufficient. Any potential investor would have realised that KPMG's duties were likely to be contained in a letter of engagement, and would not extend to the assumption of an unlimited responsibility towards third parties. The judge reached the same conclusion on the alternative three-fold test (see para.17–027 of the main text), saying that it would not be fair, just and reasonable to impose a duty.

In *Makar v PricewaterhouseCoopers LLP* [2011] EWHC 3835 (Comm), a former director sued the company's auditor for breaches of duty which she claimed had led to her dismissal. In striking out the claim, Teare J. followed *Siddell* and *Coulthard* and held that the pleading failed to disclose any exceptional circumstances or any special relationship which would give rise to a duty of care in favour of the director.

(iv) *Categories of Advisee*

Directors

[*Add at end of paragraph*] 17–042

Coulthard was applied in *Makar*: see para.17–033, above.

(d) *The Standard of Skill and Care*

(i) *General*

[*Add at end of paragraph*] 17–050

In *Mehjoo v Harben Barker* [2014] P.N.L.R. 24; [2014] EWCA Civ 358, C was born in Iran but had been resident, though not domiciled, in the UK for many years. He sold his business at a substantial gain, on which he was assessed to Capital Gains Tax. He then sued his accountant D for failing to advise him that he was potentially a "non-dom", that he might be able to avoid CGT and that he should seek specialist tax advice on how to do so. If so advised, it was argued that he could and would have used a bearer warrant scheme ("BWS") which (until this loophole was closed) enabled non-doms to avoid tax on the disposal of assets by moving them offshore. There was a letter of retainer under which D undertook to assist C in fulfilling his annual obligations to pay tax. This included "general tax-planning advice on the best use of reliefs". Silber J. held that the letter of retainer was insufficient to impose liability in this case. However there was also evidence that on a number of occasions D had gone beyond the terms of the retainer and had proffered unsolicited routine advice on the tax consequences of transactions. The judge held that D had thereby assumed a more extensive duty which required it to volunteer advice as alleged, even though not asked to do so.

Silber J.'s judgment was reversed on appeal. Patten L.J. gave the leading judgment. He said that, although the evidence demonstrated that D had indeed assumed a responsibility which went beyond the terms of the letter of retainer, it was limited to giving tax advice of a routine nature and did not extend to the much more sophisticated form of tax planning exemplified by the BWS. This case underlines the importance of correctly analysing the nature of the service for which the accountant has assumed responsibility. It is not sufficient merely to call it "tax advice", since that covers a wide spectrum from simple mitigation of tax to complex tax-avoidance schemes which require the underlying transaction to be reformulated. D had in fact suggested in general terms that C might want to seek specialist tax advice in relation to the transaction and C had not followed up this suggestion. C's complaint was that D had not specifically linked this advice to the possible exploitation of C's status as a non-dom. However, Patten L.J. observed that, as a generalist adviser, D did not actually know, and could not reasonably have been expected to know, that a non-dom could potentially avoid CGT by entering into a scheme such as the BWS which involved moving the asset offshore; hence D owed no duty to advise as alleged. Lewison L.J., agreeing with Patten L.J., echoed the words of Oliver J. in *Midland Bank v Hett Stubbs & Kemp* [1979] Ch 384 at 402 that there is no such thing as a general retainer.

In *Altus Group (UK) Ltd v Baker Tilly Tax and Advisory Services LLP* [2015] EWHC 12 (Ch) (discussed at 17–075 below), it was held at [82] that a higher standard of care is expected of a firm which puts itself forward as providing a top-level specialist service.

Sources of evidence

17–051 [*Add at end of paragraph (2)*]

In *Pantelli Associates Ltd v Corporate City Developments Number Two Ltd* [2011] P.N.L.R. 12, Coulson J. purported to lay down a general principle that it was always necessary to adduce expert evidence from an expert in the relevant discipline, even at the pleadings stage (discussed in the main work at para.9–147). The decision has not met with universal approval. In *Mehjoo v Harben Barker* (discussed at para.17–050, above), Silber J. at [90] and [97] accepted expert evidence from a solicitor who worked for a firm of accountants, even though the expert was not himself an accountant. (The decision was reversed on appeal on other grounds: see above.)

In *Caribbean Steel Co Ltd v. Price Waterhouse* [2013] P.N.L.R. 27; [2013] UKPC 18, the trial judge in Jamaica had found an auditor negligent in his valuation of shares. The claimant had relied on evidence from an expert who had never prepared a company valuation and never conducted a company audit. The Court of Appeal allowed the auditor's appeal on the basis that it was wrong to treat the issue of negligence as being one of common sense which did not require any expertise in share valuation. The Privy Council upheld the Court of Appeal.

(ii) *Auditing*

The detection of fraud

[*Add at end of paragraph*] **17–053**

The FRC's Auditing Practices Board has produced a discussion paper on professional scepticism, which traces the roots of the concept in Greek philosophy and in scientific empiricism. The paper suggests that the appropriate mindset for an auditor is as follows:

> "What would the shareholders (and other stakeholders) expect the auditor to ask, what matters would they expect them to challenge and what evidence would they need to satisfy those challenges? . . . [W]hilst the sceptical mindset is a constant, the degree of action taken by a sceptical auditor (by way of inquiry, challenge and testing) is responsive both to the expectations of shareholders (and other stakeholders) and to what emerges as the audit proceeds."

It concludes that in an appropriately sceptical audit:

> "The auditor's risk assessment process should involve a critical appraisal of management's assertions, actively looking for risks of material misstatement. These may arise due to fraud or error and may reflect weaknesses in the design or the operation of management's system for controlling and reporting the entity's financial position and performance (such that relevant matters are not identified, or are not adequately controlled or reported, or that the design has not been implemented and operated effectively)."

(e) *Limitation of Liability*

Non-audit engagements

[*Add to n.316*] **17–056**

See *Arrowhead Capital Finance Ltd v KPMG LLP* [2012] P.N.L.R. 30, [2012] EWHC 1801 (Comm) (discussed above at para.17–033).

In *Barclays Bank Plc v Grant Thornton UK LLP* [2015] EWHC 320 (Comm), the claimant bank alleged that its loan to V Ltd had been made in reliance on the defendant's audit report on V Ltd's accounts. V Ltd was a one-man company with a sole director who was also the sole shareholder. The accounts were non-statutory accounts which were not intended to be filed at Companies House.

Cooke J. accepted that there was arguably sufficient proximity between the auditor and the bank to found a claim in tort. The issue was whether the claim was barred by a *Bannerman* disclaimer in the audit report, which said that the report was made solely to V Ltd's director and that the auditor accepted no responsibility to anyone other than "the company and the company's director as a body". The auditor accepted, for the purpose of the application to strike out, that the disclaimer had to satisfy the test of reasonableness in the Unfair Contract Terms Act 1977. The bank argued that the disclaimer parted company with reality, in that the sole purpose of producing the accounts was to satisfy the bank. However, the judge struck out the claim on the ground that the disclaimer was clear on its face and should have been read and understood by the bank.

(f) *Specific Defence to a Claim for Breach of Duty*

17–057 [*Add at end of paragraph*]

In *Bilta UK Ltd v Nazir (No.2)* [2015] UKSC 23; [2015] 2 W.L.R. 1169, the Supreme Court took the unusual, if not unprecedented, step of declaring that *Stone & Rolls* should be treated as a case on its own facts which was not to be followed. Lords Neuberger, Clarke and Carnwath said at [30] that it should be put on one side and marked "not to be looked at again", whilst Lords Toulson and Hodge said at [154] that it was a case which had no majority ratio. Ironically, the same criticism could be made of *Bilta*, insofar as some of the judgments went further than that of Lord Neuberger.

The facts of *Bilta* were briefly that B and C were the sole directors of B Co and that B was the sole shareholder. It was alleged that B and C conspired with the defendants to divert money away from B Co in order to evade VAT. B Co was wound up and (acting by its liquidator) it sued the defendants, who raised the defence of illegality. The seven-man court was unanimous in holding that this defence failed. The ratio is to be found in the judgment of Lord Neuberger (with whom Lords Clarke and Carnwath agreed). He summed up the rule of attribution as follows at [7]:

> "Where a company has been the victim of wrongdoing by its directors, or of which its directors had notice, then the wrongdoing, or knowledge, of the directors cannot be attributed to the company as a defence to a claim brought against the directors by the company's liquidator, in the name of the company and/or on behalf of its creditors, for the loss suffered by the company as a result of the wrongdoing, even where the directors were the only directors and shareholders of the company, and even though the wrongdoing or knowledge of the directors may be attributed to the company in many other types of proceedings."

He added at [9] that

> "whether or not it is appropriate to attribute an action by, or a state of mind of, a company director or agent to the company or the agent's principal in relation to a particular claim against the company or the principal must depend on the nature and factual context of the claim in question."

Lords Toulson and Hodge agreed with Lord Neuberger but went further. They said that illegality was a doctrine of public policy which depended on the context.

At [123]–[127] they stated that the law protects creditors by imposing on the directors a duty to the company to have regard to the creditors when the company is insolvent.

Lord Mance gave a speech broadly agreeing with Lords Neuberger, Toulson and Hodge.

Lord Sumption reached the same result, but by a different route. He sought to uphold and explain *Stone & Rolls* and to give a different explanation of the principle of illegality, but Lords Toulson, Hodge and Mance disagreed with him, whilst Lords Neuberger, Clarke and Carnwath found it unnecessary to decide between the competing arguments.

(ii) *Limitation*

[*Add at end of paragraph*] **17–058**

The claim in *Arrowhead* (referred to at para.17–033) was also struck out on the additional ground of limitation. The court accepted that loss was not necessarily suffered at the moment when the claimant lent money to the company in the belief that the company was operating a scheme that would enable it to recover VAT; however loss was suffered at the latest when the Revenue rejected the company's claim to VAT. This was because it was clear from the outset that the company's ability to make full repayment would depend on the its ability to recover VAT.

3. Liability for Breach of Duty

(a) *Auditing*

(iii) *Evidence*

Sufficient appropriate evidence

[*Add to n.371*] **17–063**

ISA 700 was revised in June 2013. In broad terms, the effect of the changes to ISA 700 and ISA 705, 607 and 720A is firstly to enhance auditor communications by requiring communication of relevant information to the audit committee, and secondly to require the auditor's report to state any concerns about the board's statement that the annual report and accounts taken as a whole are fair, balanced and understandable. Because of the inevitable time lag before claims arise, it is unlikely that these changes will be relevant to auditors' negligence for some time.

(iv) *Reporting*

[*Add at end of paragraph*] **17–065**

The FRC has prepared a compendium of illustrative auditor's reports on unlisted UK private sector financial statements for the period ended on or after December 15, 2010. This is in the form of a bulletin, which has the status of being persuasive, not prescriptive. The bulletin can be found on the FRC's website at *http://www.frc.org.uk/getattachment/fc7312df-3256-46d4-ade4-4f72405e640b/Bulletin-2010-2-Compendium-of-Illustrative-Auditor-s-Reports-on-United-Kingdom-Private-Sector-Financial-Statements-for-periods-ended-on-or-after-15-December-2010.aspx.*

[*Add to n.409 and n.412*]

See para.17–063, above.

(b) *Other Breaches of Duty*

Preparation of tax returns

17–067 [*Add to n.424*]

See also *Smith v Revenue & Customs Commissioners* [2011] UKUT 270 (TCC); [2011] S.T.C. 1724, where Arnold J. held that the First-Tier Tax Tribunal had been entitled to make a finding under ss.29 and 36 of the Taxes Management Act 1970 that an accountant had been guilty of negligent conduct in his application of accounting standards, with the result that insufficient tax had been paid.

Advice

17–068 [*Add at end of paragraph*]

See *Mehjoo v Harben Barker* (discussed at para.17–050, above).

In *Altus Group (UK) Ltd v Baker Tilly Tax and Advisory Services LLP* [2015] EWHC 12 (Ch) (discussed at 17–075 below), it was held at [79] that, if in the course of dealing with a client's tax return the accountant becomes or ought to become aware of a change in the law, it is his duty to notify that change to his client.

[*Add to n.426*]

In *Integral Memory Plc v Haines Watts* [2012] EWHC 342 (Ch), Richard Sheldon QC held that an accountant's duty to advise on a change in the tax law was not a continuing duty; hence a claim brought more than six years after the date when advice allegedly should have been given was statute-barred.

4. DAMAGES

(a) *Remoteness*

(i) *Causation*

General

17–069 [*Add at end of paragraph*]

In *Peter Lingham & Co v Lonnkvist* [2000] Lloyd's Rep. PN 885 the majority of the CA, applying *Galoo* and *SAAMCO*, held that an accountant who failed in his capacity as finance broker to provide accurate answers to a potential lender's request for information was not liable for losses arising out of the subsequent failure of the business which the client acquired. The effective cause of the loss was the client's decision to purchase the business, but the defendant had no responsibility to advise the client on the wisdom of the purchase.

Damages are generally assessed at the date of breach: see the discussion at para.11–266 of the main work. In *Murfin v Ford Campbell* [2011] P.N.L.R. 28; [2011] EWHC 1475 (Ch), the claimant sued for loss arising out of allegedly negligent advice which had resulted in his giving warranties on a share sale agreement. Although the seller was found to be in breach of warranty, it later became apparent that no sum was due to the buyer. H.H. Judge Pelling QC granted summary judgment to the defendant on the basis that, on the unusual facts of the case, loss should be assessed at the date of trial. If, contrary to his primary view, loss was to be assessed at the date of breach, the court was nevertheless permitted to have regard to later facts.

[*Add to n.434*]

In *Assetco Plc v Grant Thornton UK LLP* [2013] EWHC 1215 (Comm), Blair J., in refusing pre-action disclosure, placed particular reliance on the claimant's failure to comply with the Pre-Action Protocol.

(b) *Measure of damages*

In *Altus Group (UK) Ltd v Baker Tilly Tax and Advisory Services LLP* [2015] EWHC 12 (Ch) the defendant firm of accountants, which had advised the claimant LLP on tax mitigation, was held to have been negligent in failing to advise on changes in the legislation which had fiscal consequences. The LLP claimed that, if properly advised, it would have undergone a restructuring in order to save tax. The defendant argued that tax avoidance is a social evil and hence it was contrary to public policy to apply the "loss of chance" principle to the possibility that the restructuring might have been effective as a matter of law in saving tax. H.H. Judge Keyser QC, sitting in the Chancery Division, held at [61]–[63] that the question how a tribunal or court would have decided proceedings is usually treated as a loss of chance question. It does not matter that the proceedings turn on a question of law, although in some cases it might be appropriate to decide the question of law. Nor does it make any difference that the point of law concerns tax law. **17–075**

(c) *Heads of Damage*

(vi) *Tax Advice and Returns*

[*Add to n.492*] [*In n.492 delete the second sentence (Re Grimm v Newman) and substitute the following*:] **17–082**

In *Grimm v Newman* [2002] EWCA Civ 1621; [2003] 1 All E.R. 67, an accountant advised that the taxpayer could make a gift of foreign emoluments to his fiancée without incurring liability to UK tax, provided that it was a gift on marriage. The Revenue subsequently claimed tax. The taxpayer paid the tax without dispute and then sued his accountant. The Court of Appeal held that, where an issue arose as to whether the advice was negligent, it was necessary for the court to decide whether the advice was correct, even if the Revenue was not present to argue the contrary. The court held that the advice was correct and hence there was no negligence. Carnwath L.J. dissented on the ground that a reasonable accountant should have appreciated, and warned the client, that the transaction exposed him to a risk of challenge; however the majority disagreed on the basis that that issue had not been pleaded. The court also held that the claimant had failed to establish that any other scheme would have worked and had therefore suffered no loss, even if there had been negligence.

CHAPTER 18

ACTUARIES

1. INTRODUCTION

[*Replace first three sentences with the following*] **18–002**

Formerly there were two professional bodies which regulated the conduct of actuaries in the United Kingdom: the Institute of Actuaries (in England) and the Faculty of Actuaries (in Scotland). These two bodies issued Actuarial Professional Standards and (in a subsequent period) Professional Conduct Standards. However on August 1, 2010 the two bodies were merged into a single body, the Institute and Faculty of Actuaries.

2. DUTIES

(a) *The Statutory Context*

(i) *Pensions*

Occupational pension schemes

[*Add at end of paragraph*] **18–005**

The distinction between "defined benefit" and "money purchase" schemes was discussed by Lord Walker in *Bridge Trustees Ltd v Yates* [2011] 1 W.L.R. 1912; [2011] UKSC 42.

The Pensions Act 1995

[*Add to n.13*] **18–007A**

The Actuarial Profession has produced a guide on whistle-blowing. This can be found on its website at *http://www.actuaries.org.uk.*

(b) *Duties to Client*

(i) *Contractual Duties*

18–013 [*Add to n.39*]

The Institute and Faculty of Actuaries have published a consultation paper on conflicts of interest and have made changes to APS P1. Version 2.0 is effective from July 1, 2013. Because of the inevitable time lag arising in claims for negligence, these are unlikely to be relevant for some years.

(iii) *Fiduciary Obligations*

Loyalty

18–018 [*Add at end of paragraph*]

See para.18–013 in relation to conflicts of interest.

(d) *The Standard of Skill and Care*

18–030 [*Add to n.65*]

Campbell v Edwards and *Jones v Sherwood* were applied by Lewison J. in *Cornwell v Newhaven Port & Properties* [2005] Pens. L.R. 329; [2005] EWHC 1469 (Ch). He held that, where the scheme actuary certified a deficiency in a pension scheme by following the prescribed methodology, the parties were bound by the determination. However he added at [23] that he did not rule out the possibility of an action for breach of statutory duty if the actuary performed these functions negligently.

Limitation

18–037A In *Ballinger v Mercer Ltd* [2014] EWCA Civ 996; [2014] 1 W.L.R. 3597, the present trustees of an occupational pension scheme sued the scheme's actuary in respect of its actuarial valuation reports. The trustees alleged that the reports had negligently overvalued the assets, that this had caused the previous trustees to seek insufficient contributions from the employer company, which had subsequently gone into liquidation, and that the shortfall in contributions had caused the scheme to go into deficit. The actuary raised a limitation defence, which the trustees countered by relying on s.14A of the Limitation Act 1980 (see para 5–078 of the main work). The case came before the Court of Appeal on the trustees' application to amend its particulars of claim outside the primary limitation period. One proposed amendment was to add an allegation that the same errors had occurred in relation to a subsequent valuation; another was to add a new error. The court held that the burden of proof was on the claimant seeking to amend to show that there was no arguable limitation defence in respect of each amendment. On the facts, the trustees were unable to discharge this burden. The court then had to consider whether the amendments arose out of the same or substantially the same facts as the claim already pleaded. The court held that the amendment to allege the same errors in relation to the subsequent valuation did not arise out of the same or substantially the same facts as the allegation in relation to the earlier valuations. A later valuation report was not simply a matter of adjusting and updating a previous report but was an independent and free-standing exercise which should be based on different data and different assumptions. As for the proposed amendment to allege a different error in relation to the reports which were already the subject of complaint, this would give rise to new factual enquiries and was therefore also disallowed.

Chapter 19

MEMBERS' AND MANAGING AGENTS AT LLOYD'S

1. General

(a) *Lloyd's of London*

19–001 [*Add to n.2*]

FSMA has now been amended by the Financial Services Act 2012 and Lloyd's is now regulated by the Financial Conduct Authority ("FCA") and the Prudential Regulation Authority ("PRA"). The complementary roles of the FCA and PRA with regard to Lloyd's are set out in the Memorandum of Understanding between the FCA and PRA which provides that the PRA has "*responsibility for promoting the safety and soundness or the Society of Lloyd's and its members taken together including the central fund. The PRA is also the prudential regulator of managing agents*". So far as the FCA is concerned it provides: "*The FCA regulates the conduct of the Society of Lloyd's, managing agents, and on a prudential conduct basis, the members' agents and advisors, and Lloyd's brokers*".

[*Add to n.3*]

In June 2013 the FCA and Society of Lloyd's agreed the "FCA-Lloyd's Co-operation Arrangements". This sets out the basis upon which the FCA and Lloyd's will co-operate and share information. It states in its preamble: "*As part of its oversight of the market, the FCA will seek to benefit from Lloyd's systems and controls in respect of the monitoring of managing agents, syndicates and individuals. To the extent that Lloyd's controls are regarded as effective by the FCA, then the FCA's view of risk posed by managing agents and syndicates is reduced accordingly. However, nothing in these arrangements can fetter its discretion with respect to carrying out its statutory duties and functions*".

In December 2013, the PRA and Society of Lloyd's entered into a Co-operation Agreement. This document sets out how the PRA and Lloyd's envisage working together to ensure the "*effective supervision of managing agents, including, but not limited to, how they will co-ordinate in those areas where managing agents are potentially within the scope of both the PRA and the Society's powers*".

[*Replace "Pt IV permission" in the last sentence with the following*] **19–004**

Pt 4A permission

(b) *The Regulatory Regime*

[*Add to n.11*] **19–005**

As amended by the Financial Services Act 2012.

[*Replace second sentence of n.12 with the following*]

FSMA provides that a regulator may exercise its powers by giving directions to either the Society or the Council (FSMA s.318).

[*Replace third sentence with the following*] **19–006**

At the time of writing, 38 such byelaws are in force.

[*Replace all references to "FSA" with the following*] **19–007**

FCA

[*Replace (a) with the following*] **19–008**

The applicable ICOBS rules, which can be found on the FCA's website (www.fshandbook.info).

[*Replace first sentence with the following*] **19–010**

The Performance Framework covers the following areas: *Claims Management, Risk Management, Underwriting Management, Effective Operational Processes, Governance, Management of Investment Risk and Protecting Lloyd's Reputation and Brand.*

(c) *Duties to Client*

(iv) *Duties Imposed by the FCA*

[*Replace first sentence with the following*] **19–025**

As previously noted, members' and managing agents are required to be authorised by the FCA and PRA, and are required to comply with the regulatory regime established under the Act.

[*Add to n.45*]

Note that FSMA s.150 has been replaced by FSMA s.138D which is to very similar effect save that for a breach of a PRA rule to be civilly actionable the

PRA rule must so specify whereas a breach of a FCA rule will be actionable unless the FCA specifies that it is not so actionable.

3. LIABILITY FOR BREACH OF DUTY

19–032 [*Replace (iv) with the following*]

Breach of one of more of the PRA or FCA's rules.

[*Replace n.61 with the following*]

This may give rise to liability pursuant to s138D FSMA.

Chapter 20

INFORMATION TECHNOLOGY PROFESSIONALS

1. General

(b) *Can Software be Characterised as Goods*

[*Add at end of paragraph*] **20–005**

Further support of the view of Akenhead J. can be found within the recent judgment of Mr Justice Mann in the case of *Fern Computer Consultancy Ltd v Intergraph Cadworx & Analysis Solutions Inc.*[17a] In that case the claimant was applying to the court for permission to serve the defendant outside the jurisdiction. Mann J. held that the claimant could not establish any of the jurisdictional gateways presently relied upon, but left open the question of whether other gateways might be available upon any renewed application. It was not therefore strictly necessary to his decision to determine whether the claimant could pass the threshold of a real prospect of success on the merits, but Mann J. made an obiter ruling on this issue in any event. One of the questions arising, when deciding whether the claimant had a real prospect of success on its claim under the Commercial Agents (Council Directive) Regulations 1993, was whether the claimant was selling "goods", so as to bring itself within the operation of the relevant Regulations.

The claimant sold software which was supplied on physical media (CDs or CD-ROMs) along with a physical ESL (Electronic Software Lock—a dongle which fits into a USB port). The evidence also suggested that some manuals might be included, although any necessary documentation was in any event included on the CD-ROM. If an upgrade was provided, this was provided on a new CD-ROM but the ESL was not physically renewed—it was updated via transmitted software codes. If the ESL was lost or damaged it could be replaced, but only at the cost of the entire software package. The claimant's case was that on the authorities it was at least arguable, if not correct, that software was capable of being, and should be treated as being, "goods" for the purposes of the relevant

Regulations. Alternatively the claimant argued that the physical (tangible) parts of the package provided to end-users (the CDs, documentation and ESL) amounted to goods in any event and there was thus a sale of goods in any event.

The defendant's case was that the supply in question was one of software, which is not "goods", emphasising that what was sold was described as "software products", with no suggestion that that description was to include any hardware (or goods). It was submitted that the CD-ROM was packaging for the main thing sold (software).

At paras 71 to 84 of his judgment, Mann J. reviewed the relevant authorities, including all of those set out above in this chapter, and stated (at para.84), in relation to the approach of Akenhead J. in *The Mayor and Burgesses of the London Borough of Southwark v IBM UK Ltd*, that:

> "I do not need to decide whether that analysis is correct, but in my view there is a lot to be said for it and I would, if necessary, have been minded to agree with it."

At para.86 Mann J. concluded that:

> "The effect of all this authority, and of the principles underlying the argument in those cases, is that where software is supplied on CDs there is a real prospect of success in arguing that that is the supply of goods. Where that supply is accompanied by a physical dongle and documentation then the argument is even stronger. While there is an argument that what is really being supplied is software, which is not goods, that argument is not so strong as to make the contrary argument unsustainable. Indeed, if I had to decide it I would probably decide that it is wrong, but I do not have to go that far. I bear in mind that the Regulations do not contain a definition of goods corresponding to the Sale of Goods Act, and that the analysis of the expression is not constrained by reference to the word 'chattels', so it becomes easier to argue that such a supply is the supply of goods."

The case accordingly provides yet further, albeit obiter, support for the proposition that software supplied on a physical medium can constitute "goods" as a matter of law.

NOTE 17a. [2014] EWHC 2908 (Ch).

(c) *Supply of Goods or the Supply of Services*

20–006 [*Add new footnote reference 18a at end of first sentence (ending "... by the contractor, or its end product?")*]

NOTE 18a. For a recent decision in which the Court had to grapple with the question of whether a contract was for the supply of goods or services, see the Court of Appeal decision in *Trebor Bassett Holdings Ltd & Another v ADT Fire & Security Plc* [2012] EWCA Civ 1158: the Court had to determine whether a contract for the design and supply of a fire suppression system could properly be considered a contract for the supply of goods. The Court of Appeal held that the proper characterisation of the contract was that the Defendant had agreed to supply primarily design skills and reasonable care in exercising them, not goods. The goods which had been supplied were of good quality. The shortcomings in the system were matters of design (i.e. in particular the positioning of a crucial fire detection sensor), not the inherent quality of the goods which were also supplied.

CHAPTER 21

PATENT ATTORNEYS AND TRADE MARK ATTORNEYS

1. GENERAL

21–001 [*Add to n.3*]

Birss J. agreed with this analogy and cited para.21–001 of *Jackson & Powell* (7th edn) at para.24 of his judgment in *Baillie v Bromhead & Co* [2014] EWHC 2149 (Ch); [2015] F.S.R. 16.

(a) *The Function of a Patent Attorney*

Court proceedings

21–003 [*Replace para.21–003 with the following*]

Patent attorneys may conduct proceedings relating to patents before the Comptroller.[9] The Chartered Institute of Patent Attorneys is a relevant approved regulator under the Legal Services Act[10] and is therefore able to authorise patent attorneys to conduct litigation and appear as advocates in a wide range of proceedings. The rules governing the rights to conduct litigation and of audience are contained in the Rights to Conduct Litigation and Rights of Audience and Other Reserved Legal Activities Certification Rules 2012.[11] The rules provide that a patent attorney may apply to the Patent Regulation Board to be granted any of the following certificates: an Intellectual Property Litigation Certificate, a Higher Courts Litigation Certificate and a Higher Courts Advocacy Certificate.[12] A holder of a Higher Courts Advocacy Certificate has a right of audience before the High Court, the Court of Appeal and the Supreme Court in proceedings which may be conducted by an attorney holding a Higher Courts Litigation Certificate. European patent agents may appear before the European Patent Office. Patent attorneys may instruct counsel directly.[13]

[*Replace n.9 with the following*]

Copyright, Designs and Patents Act 1988, s.274(1). The Comptroller General of Patents, Designs and Trade Marks controls the Patents Office, see Patents and Designs Act 1907, s.62. Any person may appear in person or as a representative before the Comptroller, see the Patents Act 1977, s.102.

[*Replace n.10 with the following*]

Part 1 of Sch.4 to the Legal Services Act 2007. The Chartered Institute was appointed as an authorised body under the now repealed Courts and Legal Services Act 1990.

[*Replace n.11 with the following*]

The scheme came into force on January 1, 2013 and was issued by the Intellectual Property Regulation Board. The CIPA Higher Courts Qualification Regulations 2007 ceased to be effective on December 31, 2012.

[*Replace n.12 with the following*]

The rights are described in r.2.2 of the Rights to Conduct Litigation and Rights of Audience and Other Reserved Legal Activities Certification Rules 2012.

[*Replace n.13 with the following*]

In Pt IV, para.401(a) of the Code of Conduct of the Bar of England and Wales, a barrister in independent practice may only supply services if appointed or instructed by a Court or if instructed by a professional client, a licensed access or a public access client. In the definitions of Pt X, para.1001, "professional client" includes a patent agent and trade mark attorney.

[*Replace n.15 with the following*]

Intentionally blank

[*Replace n.16 with the following*]

Intentionally blank

[*Replace n.17 with the following*]

Intentionally blank

Alternatives to litigation

[*Replace para.21–005 with the following*]

A disappointed client may complain to the Legal Ombudsman in respect of poor service. The Legal Ombudsman may order a patent attorney to pay compensation up to the sum of £50,000 and limit fees to a specified amount.[24] The Legal Ombudsman will not consider whether the conduct complained of amounted to professional negligence. Ordinarily a complainant must refer a complaint to the Legal Ombudsman within six months of the patent attorney's written response and either within six years of the act or omission complained of or within three years from when the complainant should reasonably have known there was a cause for complaint without taking advice from a third party.[25]

(b) *The Function of a Trade Mark Attorney*

21–006 [*Replace para.21–006 with the following*]

It is the function of a trade mark attorney to advise on trade mark law, including protection and infringement of trade marks, and to act for clients to obtain registration of a trade mark. His work includes clerical tasks such as filing forms at the Trade Mark Registry and paying renewal fees, but also matters requiring technical and legal skill such as selecting new marks and advice on infringement. The rights of trade mark attorneys to conduct litigation and rights of audience are contained in the Rights to Conduct Litigation and Rights of Audience and Other Reserved Legal Activities Certification Rules 2012.[27] Trade mark attorneys may instruct counsel directly.[28]

[*Replace n.27 with the following*]

See para.21–003, above. The ITMA Trade Mark Litigator and Trade Mark Advocate Certificate Regulations 2009 ceased to be effective on December 31, 2012.

[*Replace n.28 with the following*]

The Institute of Trade Mark Attorneys is an approved regulator for the purposes of the Legal Services Act 2007.

[*Replace n.29 with the following*]

Intentionally blank

[*Replace n.30 with the following*]

Intentionally blank

(c) *Duties to Clients*

21–009 [*Add at end of paragraph*]

In *Baillie v Bromhead & Co*[37a] Birss J. considered whether the defendant patent attorney owed a duty of care to an investment company which was an investor and shareholder in two technology companies which were claimants to the claim. It was not in dispute that the defendants owed a duty of care in contract and in tort both to the claimant developers and to the claimant technology companies. There was no contractual relationship between the investment company and the defendant patent attorney and no direct communication between them. Birss J. held that the defendant patent attorney knew that a "To whom it may concern" letter he had prepared would be shown to putative investors and therefore that he owed a duty of care to any investor who did in fact rely on that advice. The judge went on to find that none of the investors had, in fact, relied on the defendant patent attorney's advice.[37b]

NOTE 37a. [2014] EWHC 2149 (Ch).
NOTE 37b. At paras 326–329. In reaching his decision Birss J. relied on the factors set out by Neill L.J. in *McNaughton v Hicks Anderson* [1991] 2 QB 113 at 125F–127B.

(g) *Liability for Costs*

[*Replace n.46 with the following*] **21–014**

The Senior Courts Act 1981, s.51(6) permits a court to make a wasted costs order against a "legal or other representative". The Civil Procedure Rules Pt.46.8 refers to "legal representative", which is defined in r.2.3 as including "a person who, for the purposes of the Legal Services Act, is an authorised person in relation to an activity which constitutes the conduct of litigation (within the meaning of that Act), on which see para.21–003, above.

(h) *Privilege*

[*Replace n.48 with the following*] **21–015**

Copyright, Designs and Patents Act 1988 s.280 and the Legal Services Act 2007 s.190. See also *Atrium Medical Corp v DSB Investment Holding SA* [2011] EWCA 74 for the application of these provisions in the context of a patent attorney litigator. By the Patents Act 1977 s.103, legal professional privilege will extend to communications between a solicitor and his client relating to pending or contemplated proceedings before the Comptroller or courts under certain conventions. Thus this privilege will extend to communications between a patent attorney and his client.

2. LIABILITY FOR BREACH OF DUTY

General

[*Replace para.21–016 with the following*] **21–016**

Given the paucity of reported cases, there are few illustrations of the type of circumstances in which patent attorneys or trade mark attorneys may be found to be negligent. One particular area in which patent attorneys and trade mark attorneys are obviously vulnerable is in relation to missing deadlines for the registration of documents. An illustration is afforded by *Kerr v Laurence Shaw & Associates.*[51] In that case the claimant asked patent agents to delay a patent application in North America until the last moment, which was over a year away, but they failed to do so. Proudman J. held that the defendants were negligent in failing to implement a system of reminders or remind the claimant of the deadline.

[*Replace n.51 with the following*]

[2010] EWHC 585 (Ch); [2010] P.N.L.R. 24.

[*Replace n.52 with the following*]

Intentionally blank

[*Replace n.53 with the following*]

Intentionally blank

Ignorance of the law

21–017 [*Add to n.54*]

Birss J. accepted in *Baillie v Bromhead & Co* [2014] EWHC 2149 (Ch) at paras 25–26 that per *Lee v Walker "a patent attorney must have adequate knowledge of the law and practice relating to the activities that he undertakes."*

Taking proper instructions

21–018 [*Add at end of paragraph*]

A facet of taking proper instructions is obtaining the relevant documents from the client and, if necessary, the client's previous professional advisers. The extent of that duty was considered in *Baillie v Bromhead & Co.*[62a] The claimant inventors had produced a "masterbatch" of material which glowed in the dark and intended to use the material to make a torch called the GloTorch. The first firm of patent attorneys retained by the inventors advised them that they could not patent the material but that they ought to apply for patents based on specific applications of the material. On the basis of that advice a patent application focused on a torch coated in the inventors' material was filed. However, the inventors considered that the application was too narrowly drafted and a further application was filed the following day. The claimant inventors subsequently terminated their retainer with the first firm of patent attorneys and instructed the defendant firm to claim priority from the second patent application made by the first firm. The claimant inventors did not inform the defendant patent attorney about the first patent application and there was nothing in the materials provided to the defendant to suggest that the first application existed. The judge found that the defendant patent attorney had only been instructed to file an application to claim priority from the second application and that although many patent attorneys might have requested the claimants' file from his previous advisers the defendant patent attorney was not negligent in not doing so.

NOTE 62A. [2014] EWHC 2149 (Ch) at paras 201–204.

[*Add to n.60*]

Birss J. accepted in *Baillie v Bromhead & Co* [2014] EWHC 2149 (Ch) at paras 25–26 that per *Andrew Master Homes v Cruikshank and Fairweather* a patent attorney is *"obliged to take full and proper instructions from their clients."*

Giving proper advice, including commercial advice

[*Add to n.64*] **21–019**

Birss J. accepted in *Baillie v Bromhead & Co* [2014] EWHC 2149 (Ch) at paras 25–26 that per *Halifax Building Society v Urquart-Dykes and Lord* a patent attorney *"must inform their client of any matter in respect of which they need to take instructions in order to give proper advice."* Birss J. also accepted that a patent attorney must tailor his advice according to the client and relied on *Phelps v Stewart* [2007] P.N.L.R. 32, a case about a solicitor, in support of that proposition.

[*Add at end of paragraph*]

Jacob J.'s explanation was considered by Birss J. in *Baillie v Bromhead & Co.*[65a] In that case the claimant developers had created glow in the dark plastics which had a long night-time glow but which also had a bright attractive day-time colour. The claimant technology companies, which had been established by the inventors to exploit the material they had created, purchased a US patent which the defendant patent attorney had advised them they were at risk of infringing. Birss J. explained the decision in *Halifax* as follows:

> *"The normal duties of a patent attorney are focussed on patents and patent prosecution. The normal advice is about validity, infringement and what steps to take in the process of patent prosecution. Patent attorneys do not normally advise their clients what commercial steps to take. That is not the same point made in* Halifax. *The fact that an attorney may be required to warn a client of possible commercial consequences of a step rather than its purely legal consequences does not mean that they have to advise their client what to do and take responsibility for the commercial risk."*

Birss J. held that the defendant patent attorney's advice on the US patent was not confined to patent matters but amounted to commercial advice to buy the patent. Accordingly, had the patent been worthless, as the claimants alleged, then the defendant would have been liable for negligent advice and all of the losses flowing from the purchase transaction. However, the judge also held that the patent was not worthless and therefore the defendant's advice had been reasonable.[65b]

The defendant patent attorney also advised the claimants on the prosecution and validity of the PCT he filed on their behalf. The judge found that the defendant's key advice that the claimants' core inventive concept was patentable was not negligent. Commercial decisions made by the claimants on the basis of that advice were decisions taken by the claimants and were a matter for the claimants.[65c]

Note 65a. [2014] EWHC 2149 (Ch) at 317.
Note 65b. The judge also found that a number of the claimants' criticisms of the defendant patent attorney were well-founded and that he had given inexplicable and negligent advice. However, the judge held that this negligent advice had not caused any loss. Per Birss J. at 333.
Note 65c. [2014] EWHC 2149 (Ch) at paras 248–299.

2. DAMAGES

Causation and loss of a chance

21–021 [*Add at end of paragraph*]

In *Baillie v Bromhead & Co*[73a] the court held that although the defendant patent attorney had given inexplicable and negligent advice the loss suffered by the claimants had not been caused by that advice.

NOTE 73a. [2014] EWHC 2149 (Ch) at 333.

The scope of protection

21–022 [*Replace n.74 with the following*]

[2005] EWHC 2481. Smith J.'s construction of s.68 of the Patents Act 1977 was doubted by the Court of Appeal in *Schutz (UK) Ltd v Werit UK Ltd* [2011] EWCA Civ 1337. However, the Supreme Court stated that the Court of Appeal's reasoning should not necessarily be regarded as correct [2013] 2 All E.R. 177.